# Professional
# Visual C++
# ISAPI Programming

## Michael Tracy

Wrox Press Ltd.®

# Professional Visual C++ ISAPI Programming

Published by Wrox Press Ltd. 30 Lincoln Road, Olton, Birmingham, B27 6PA
Printed in Canada
Library of Congress Catalog no. 96-61409

ISBN 1-874416-66-4

## Trademark Acknowledgements

Wrox has endeavored to provide trademark information about all the companies and products mentioned in this book by the appropriate use of capitals. However, Wrox cannot guarantee the accuracy of this information.

## Credits

**Author**
Michael Tracy

**Technical Editors**
Julian Dobson
Jon Hill

**Technical Reviewers**
Matt Winter
Zor Gorelov
Mark Simkin
David Hunter

**Development Editor**
John Franklin

**Design/Layout**
Neil Gallagher
Andrew Guillaume

**Proof Readers**
Pam Brand
Simon Gilks

**Index**
Simon Gilks
Dominic Shakeshaft

**Cover Design**
Third Wave

For more information on Third Wave, contact Ross Alderson on 44-121 236 6616
Cover photo supplied by Tony Stone

# Table of Contents

# Introducing ISAPI

Welcome to **Professional Visual C++ ISAPI Programming**. This book is, surprisingly, about writing programs that use the Internet Server Advanced Programming Interface (ISAPI), to perform tasks that the Internet Server was never intended to do. Maybe that's stating the case a little strongly, but the whole point of ISAPI is to give you, as a programmer, the means of extending the functionality of your web site.

## Who this Book is For

In general, this book was written for programmers. To use the book effectively, you should have an understanding of Windows programming concepts, a firm grasp of the C++ programming language, and some exposure to Visual C++.

The audience for this book is considered to be those moderate to advanced Visual C++ programmers who have worked previously on Visual C++ applications for Windows. If you've worked your way through Ivor Horton's *Beginning Visual C++ 4* or Mike Blaszczak's *Revolutionary MFC 4* (also from Wrox Press) then this book is a great next step.

> All the code for this book (and many other Wrox titles) is available for free download from http://www.wrox.com/, or you can send off for a disk. See the offer at the back of the book for details.

## What You'll Learn from this Book

This book is designed to be a comprehensive tutorial and guide to ISAPI programming. If you've had some previous network programming experience, using CGI for example, that's going to be helpful; we draw parallels where they exist. However, don't worry if you're completely new to the subject. A little knowledge is never a bad thing, but we don't assume any prior experience, and all the examples are built and explained from scratch.

You should learn several things from this book, quite apart from the obvious goals of being able to write ISAPI extensions and filters. The main piece of knowledge that you should learn is how to write multithreaded applications, and in particular, how to synchronize access to resources. You should also learn a fair bit about OBDC, both in the form of the MFC database classes, and the ODBC API directly. Lastly, you will gain knowledge of Sockets programming and using SMTP to send mail.

# What You'll Need to Use this Book

The ISAPI filters and extensions developed in this book are written in Visual C++ 4.2, and many of them use the Microsoft Foundation Classes (MFC) to implement the technology behind the components. This means that you'll need a copy of Visual C++ 4.1 or greater (at the time of writing, Visual C++ 4.2 was the latest version available).

Of course, to run Visual C++, you'll need a computer running Windows 95 or Windows NT. All of the code for this book was developed using a 486/66 and a Pentium/133. To get the best use out of the development environment and the operating system, it's recommended that you have at least 16 megabytes of memory and at least a VGA monitor. Note that these are the requirements for using Visual C++ itself, *not* for the extensions developed here.

The extensions and filters that make use of databases also use the Visual FoxPro OBDC driver as this is thread-safe. You don't strictly need this driver, but if you intend to work with the database provided on the Wrox Press web site then you should use it.

To test the extensions and filters, you will need access to Microsoft's Internet Information Server (IIS), version 1.0 or higher—so you will need a machine running Windows NT as well. Windows NT 4.0 (both server and workstation editions) come with IIS 2.0 as standard, and you can download IIS from Microsoft if you have Windows NT 3.51. Although not strictly necessary, it is a good idea to have a browser as well, so that you can call the extensions and observe the returned results.

> *We have also provided code for an ISAPI Debugger (Appendix A) which allows you to test extensions without the need for IIS. However, it can't provide all the functionality of IIS, and shouldn't be relied upon as the only test environment before going live with your extensions.*

> **You can download IIS 1.0 from**
> `http://www.microsoft.com/Infoserv/iisinfo.htm`
> **and the Visual FoxPro OBDC driver from**
> `http://www.microsoft.com/kb/softlib/mslfiles/VFPODBC5.EXE`

# Conventions

We use a number of different styles of text and layout in the book to help differentiate between different kinds of information. Here are some examples of the styles we use and an explanation of what they mean.

> *Extra details, for your information, come in boxes like this.*

> **Important information that you should take careful note of appears in the text like this.**

▲ **Important Words** are in a bold type font.

▲ Words that appear on the screen, such as menu options, are a similar font to the one used on screen, e.g. the File menu.

▲  Keys that you press on the keyboard, like *Ctrl* and *Enter*, are in italics.

▲  All filenames are in this style: **StdAfx.cpp**.

▲  Function names look like this: **GetLength()**

```
// Code listings look like this if it's code you need to add yourself
// Or this if you've seen the code before or it's something added by one
// of the wizards.
```

# Tell Us What You Think

We've worked hard on this book to make it useful to you. We've tried to understand what you're willing to exchange your hard-earned money for, and we've tried to make the book exceed expectations. But we're only human, and sometimes we make mistakes. We greatly appreciate error reports on our text or constructive comment on content, all of which help us make a better book.

# Customer Support

If you do find a mistake, please have a look at the errata page for this book on our web site first. The full URL for the errata page is:

**http://www.wrox.com/Scripts/Errata.idc?Code=664**

If you can't find an answer there, tell us about the problem and we'll answer promptly! There are several ways to contact us about errors: you could send us a letter to either:

Wrox Press Inc.,
2710 West Touhy,
Chicago,
IL 60645

or:

Wrox Press Ltd.,
30 Lincoln Road,
Olton,
Birmingham,
B27 6PA

A quicker method is to send e-mail to **support@wrox.com**. If you could place the book code (**664**) as the subject, this will help us make sure the right person sees your query for a faster response.

Lastly, you can fill in the form on our web site:

**http://www.wrox.com/Contact.htm**

## General Comments

Apart from mistakes, we'd also like to know what you think about this book in general. Tell us what we did wrong and what we did right. This isn't just marketing flannel—we really do all huddle around the e-mail to find out what you think. If you don't believe it, send us a note. We'll answer and we'll take whatever you say on board for future editions. The easiest way to get in touch is to use e-mail:

**feedback@wrox.com**
**CompuServe 100063,2152**

You can also find more details about Wrox Press on our web site. Here you'll find the code from our latest books, sneak previews of forthcoming titles and information about the authors and editors. You can order Wrox titles directly from the site or find out where your local bookstore carrying Wrox titles is located. Look at the advert in the back of this book for more information. The address of our site is:

**http://www.wrox.com**

# What is ISAPI?

The Internet Server Application Programming Interface (ISAPI) is an open API developed by Process Software and Microsoft, in order to deal with the shortcomings of CGI (Common Gateway Interface). While the Microsoft Internet Information Server (MSIIS) was the first server to support this API model, ISAPI programming is by no means limited to the MSIIS, or even to servers running the Windows95/NT operating systems. This book, however, will only focus on ISAPI programs that run on web servers running under Windows NT 3.51 or higher, and most examples will require at least Microsoft Visual C++ 4.2.

# ISAPI, CGI, and WinCGI

To the end user surfing your site, there's no difference between an ISAPI program (typically referred to as an extension) and a CGI or WinCGI program. To the programmer, the main difference is in the interface between the server and the program.

Under CGI, when a request is received for a program, the information about that request is passed as environment variables, and the response is returned to the web server via standard output. Thus, CGI programs require that the language you write them in is able to read and write from standard input and output; this precludes many popular Windows programming languages from being easily used for CGI programming.

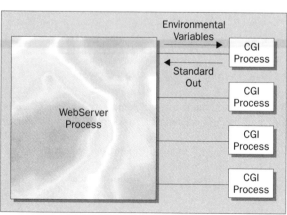

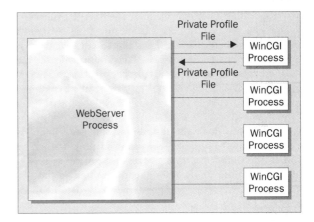

In order to use Windows-based programs for CGI, you must use WinCGI. When the web server uses the WinCGI interface, the data is passed back and forth by means of a private profile file. While CGI and WinCGI were how most Windows web applications used to be written, each has a layer that separates the web server from the web application. This extra layer is rather cumbersome when it comes to performance, which leads us into the new alternative: ISAPI.

In order to eliminate the extra interface layer, ISAPI allows the web server to communicate with your ISAPI application through an Extension Control Block (ECB) structure. While the name may seem a little intimidating at first, the ECB is simply a pointer to relevant code and data that your ISAPI application might want to access. The reason the ISAPI program requires only a pointer to pass information is that all ISAPI DLLs run *inside* the process space of the web server itself. For each ISAPI request, the web server simply creates a unique ECB structure, and passes a pointer to it across to your ISAPI functions. In this way, the ISAPI extension can quickly find the information it needs—simply by using the reference to the ECB that the server created for it. The exact mechanism for how this works will be covered in detail in the next chapter.

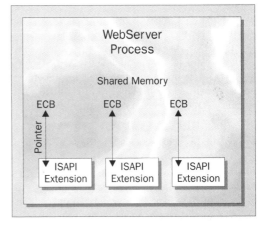

Another difference between CGI and ISAPI is the variety of languages at your disposal to write with. While CGI programs can be written in any language which can write to standard output, ISAPI programs can only be written in languages that can produce regular DLLs.

> **Visual Basic 4.0 produces OLE DLLs which can't be directly used as ISAPI extensions, but can be used through an ISAPI to OLE interface.**

The biggest difference between ISAPI and CGI is that ISAPI programs run within the address space of the web server itself (i.e. they are in-process), as opposed to the separate process demanded from a CGI program.

# ISAPI Extensions

Under traditional CGI programming, for every request received, a separate process is created, executed, and then terminated—all, usually, in less than a second. The constant creation and termination of processes can lead to excessive time and memory usage. ISAPI extensions, on the other hand, are created and run as DLLs rather than executables. The ISAPI extension runs as a thread in the same process/memory space as the web server itself. As a result, the code segment is only loaded once, no matter how many instances are active at a given time. Since the ISAPI extension runs as a web server thread, it has direct access to the web server's address space. Thus, information is quickly and easily transferred from the web server to your application and back again. The overhead of creating an additional thread to handle the ISAPI request is trivial compared to the overhead of creating a separate process and passing it the data that it needs.

Of course, you don't get all these advantages without paying a little price. The drawback is that all ISAPI extensions must be thread-safe, and the programmer must be very conscious of memory usage. Since your ISAPI application has direct access to the web server's address space, any wandering pointers could overwrite crucial server information. As seen in the diagram of the ISAPI web server, the ISAPI extensions have access via pointers to any data in the web server. This has the benefit of making it very easy for two ISAPI extensions to communicate with each other (as indicated by the overlapping ISAPI extensions in the diagram). Unfortunately, it also makes it easy for one extension to damage data in another extension or even to bring the entire server to a halt.

In addition to the caveats mentioned above, the ISAPI programmer must also be vigilant in the freeing up of memory. Since the ISAPI DLL runs as part of the web server, it shares the same heap. Under a CGI executable, if you forget to free up some memory, the operating system takes care of it for you when the CGI program terminates. Under ISAPI, if you create a variable using 'free store' memory (for example, using the **new** operator) and don't free up the storage, the memory will be held until the web server process itself is ended. This could result in an ISAPI extension that appears to work normally but is actually using up memory each time it's called. Eventually, the extension will bring down the server.

# ISAPI Filters

Another difference between CGI and ISAPI is that there are two distinct types of ISAPI programs: extensions and filters. ISAPI extensions are, except as noted above, the same as CGI programs: they take input from the client browser and supply some output. However, the ISAPI specification includes a class of programs which have no CGI equivalents; these are referred to as ISAPI filters. The ISAPI filter is a DLL that is loaded at the time the web server is started and is called every time the web server gets a request or 'hit'. This allows you to customize the flow of data in and out of your web server. While you'll probably not spend much time writing ISAPI filters, a few well-written ones can make your site much easier to manage and give it a 'cutting edge' look. As shown in the accompanying diagram, filters get called for every type of web server request: HTML, GIF, JPEG, ISAPI, CGI, everything. The ability to intercept web requests and alter them both before and after the web server has processed them is a very powerful tool. As you can imagine, it's imperative that these filters be highly tested and optimized for speed, since even minor inefficiencies can be greatly magnified on a high-traffic site. We'll cover ISAPI filters in detail in the second half of this book.

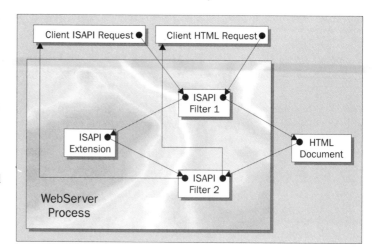

# Threads

If you haven't been exposed to multithreaded programming before, you may be wondering how all these ISAPI extensions and filters can run inside a single process. The answer is that while only one process is running, multiple threads are running inside that process. While we will be discussing multithreaded programming issues throughout this book, we first need to start with a brief introduction to what threads and processes are.

A thread is nothing more than a sequence of code being executed inside a process. Before we look any deeper at the thread, we must look at the context in which a thread runs. There are no 'free threads' running around your system. Each thread must be associated with a process. Thus, in order to know what a thread is, you must first know what a process is. The chances are that you have created quite a few processes in your programming career, so you might be a little surprised by the definition of a Win32 process, which is that it's simply an allocation of memory. The process doesn't execute a single line of code. In order to execute code, the process must own a thread. Thus, every process must have at least one thread to be of any use. Before we go into any more of the details of threads, let's take a minute to cover some properties of Win32 processes, so that we can see how they will affect our ISAPI programming in a multithreaded environment.

# Address Space

Every Win32 process created receives its own private, linear address space that is 4 gigabytes in size. By *private*, I mean that no other process can access it, and by *linear*, I mean that the address space starts at 0x00000000 and runs without breaking to 0xFFFFFFFF. You will notice that this address space is the maximum space that can be addressed by a 32-bit number (it's no coincidence that NT is a 32-bit operating system). Throughout this book, we will refer to this 4 gigabytes of memory as the process's address space, or alternatively as the process space.

Since your computer probably doesn't have 4 gigabytes of RAM, and you don't get any Out Of Memory messages when you run three or four applications simultaneously (even though this appears to require 12–16 gigabytes of RAM), you might be questioning the validity of this section. The explanation is that the memory is, of course, virtual. Windows NT manages this virtual memory for you by loading and unloading appropriate code and data into physical RAM when necessary. The most important thing to know is that it is impossible for a Win32 process to access memory that is not in its address space. By imposing this restriction, Win32 prevents one process from inadvertently overwriting or altering data in another process.

> *Of course, there are techniques for sharing memory between processes. The most common is to use memory mapped 'files'. This technique maps the same virtual memory into two separate address spaces. Thus, while one process can write data to another process, it's only because the relevant address is inside the first process's 4 gigabyte address space as well as the address space of the second process. Techniques for sharing data across processes will not be covered in this book as they have little use in standard ISAPI programming.*

When a new process is created, NT allocates its address space, loads in the appropriate code, creates a thread, and the thread begins execution. Once this has happened, the thread itself can create additional threads that run inside the same process space. We will cover thread creation later in the book, but for now just think of creating a thread as calling a function that will run simultaneously with the code that called the function. (It's good to think of threads in this way, as that is exactly what they do.) To visualize this, look at the following pseudo-code:

```
main()
{
   int x;

   printf("Primary Thread Started\n");
   CreateThread(MyThread);

   for (x=0; x<1000; x++);

   printf("Primary Thread Finished\n");
}
...
DWORD MyThread(pvoid* parameter)
{
   int y;
   printf("Second Thread Started\n")
   for(y=0; y<10; y++);
   printf("Second Thread Finished\n");
   return 0;
}
```

The output would read:

```
Primary Thread Started
Second Thread Started
Second Thread Finished
Primary Thread Finished
```

The two threads would be executing code 'simultaneously'. The reader with only one CPU in their machine may be wondering how two threads could possibly be executing simultaneously on the single machine. The answer is that with only one CPU, the threads are not really running simultaneously. Windows NT, which schedules execution time for each thread, allocates a certain amount of CPU time for each thread to run in. NT allows the thread to run for its specified amount of time and then suspends its execution so that other threads can run. The amount of time allocated for a given thread to run (called either a time slice or quantum) is small, and so the threads appear to be running at the same time, even though they are not. Of course, on machines with multiple CPUs, the code does indeed run simultaneously.

## Sharing Data

In ISAPI programming, data exchange between the web server and the ISAPI extension takes place instantaneously, because the ISAPI extension has direct access to the memory of the web server. This access to the memory of the owning process is by no means exclusive to ISAPI programming. In every multithreaded program, every thread running inside the process has access to the same 4 gigabytes of memory. While this makes it extremely easy to share data, it also makes it extremely easy to misuse data. For example, consider the following pseudo-code:

```
int x;

DWORD Thread1(void* WhoCares)
{
   for (x=0; x<100; x++);
   return 0;
}
```

```
. . .
DWORD Thread2(void* WhoCares)
{
    for(x=50; x>0; x--);
    return 0;
}
```

If both threads are running at the same time, one will be incrementing the value of **x** and the other will be decrementing it. This will lead to very unpredictable results at best, and a permanent loop at worst. (The results are unpredictable because NT, not the user, controls which threads are run, when they are run, and how long they are run for.)

Fortunately, just as processes have private memory to protect their data from other processes, threads have a type of private memory as well. Each time a thread is created, it's given its own stack. The stack is allocated from the process's address space, and by default is one megabyte in size. Although wandering pointers of other threads can still overwrite data in a thread's stack, each thread having its own stack does offer enough data protection for properly written programs. Thus, if the above code were rewritten as:

```
DWORD Thread1(void* WhoCares)
{
    int x;

    for (x=0; x<100; x++);
    return 0;
}
. . .
DWORD Thread2(void* WhoCares)
{
    int x;

    for(x=50; x>0; x--);
    return 0;
}
```

there would be no problem for either thread, as both **x** variables were created on the stack of their respective threads.

> *There is another type of private thread storage that is indeed private. This type is referred to as Thread Local Storage (TLS), but will not be covered in this book.*

An important rider to this is that when a thread terminates, the only memory that is freed is that which was on the thread's stack. Thus the thread:

```
DWORD MemoryHogThread(void* WhoCares)
{
    CHAR* pszBigString = new CHAR[4096];
    return 0;
}
```

will allocate 4K of memory each time it is run, and the memory can never be freed. This is because the pointer to the memory was created on the stack, but the actual memory was allocated from the heap (shared memory). The pointer is erased when the thread's stack is removed, but the 4K taken from the heap is never freed up.

We will find out a lot more about threads during the course of this book, and the reader should pay particular attention to the sections on programming thread-safe applications. It's very easy to develop an ISAPI extension that seems to work fine in the single user development environment, but fails completely when more than one user is requesting the extension.

# IIS Thread Model

In this book, the most important process, as far as we're concerned, is the web server itself, and the most important threads are the ones that run our ISAPI extensions. While not every web server's thread model will be identical, and Microsoft's is sure to change over time, it's still instructive to know a little bit about how a typical ISAPI web server works before doing any ISAPI programming.

When the IIS starts up, it is allocated a pool of threads to handle regular HTTP requests for things such as HTML pages, GIF images, WAV files, etc. The problem with ISAPI extensions is that they may take a long time to complete. Thus, if many ISAPI requests come in simultaneously, all the available threads in the pool might get used up by the ISAPI requests. This would mean that the web server would not be able to handle any new requests until some of the ISAPI extensions finished. To eliminate this problem, ISAPI requests are not handled from the normal pool of existing threads. Instead, IIS creates a new thread for each ISAPI request, and terminates when the process has finished.

# Programming ISAPI

In this book, we will be using Microsoft's Visual C++ to create our ISAPI filters and extensions. In Visual C++ 4.1, Microsoft released an ISAPI wizard and some supporting ISAPI classes to help speed up development. While these tools do allow us to produce working extensions and filters quickly and easily, they don't give us everything we need. For ISAPI extensions, we will extend the MFC classes and create some classes of our own to give us the required flexibility.

In the section on ISAPI filters, we will depart from MFC altogether, because the overhead of using it is too great.

# What ISAPI is Not

With all the fuss about ActiveX, we should take a minute to reflect on ISAPI's humble role in the grand scheme of things. First of all, remember that ISAPI is not proprietary to Microsoft. Many other vendors support the ISAPI standard, and there is even an effort to make an ISAPI server for UNIX. Also, while Microsoft did, at one time, distribute the ISAPI SDK inside the ActiveX SDK, the two should not be confused. ISAPI is simply a specification for how data will be delivered to your DLL. ActiveX, on the other hand, is a rapidly expanding umbrella which covers everything that has to do with objects being developed on Microsoft operating systems. Many ActiveX controls will be run on the client-side in a fashion similar to Java applets, or will provide access from a scripting language such as VBScript or JavaScript. One can even include ActiveX controls in ISAPI extensions or filters. While the technology is still a little too new to be covered in this book, one could envisage using ActiveX controls and ISAPI to provide such things as real-time audio feeds, or to assist in web conferencing.

# Synopsis

Before we get underway with our investigation of all things ISAPI, let's take a quick look ahead to exactly what we'll be covering in the rest of this book. Hopefully, it'll give you an idea of where you're headed and what you'll learn along the way.

## Chapter 2: ISAPI Extensions

Because it's the first chapter, it deals with the fundamentals: exactly what constitutes an ISAPI extension, the specification and interface, and the variables and information available to you, the programmer.

Following that, we present a quick and simple ISAPI extension example, before examining what MFC provides to make our lives easier. We'll use MFC for all our subsequent example extensions.

## Chapter 3: Navigational Redirection

In this chapter, we'll develop our first 'real-life' ISAPI extension: an HTML control that lets a user select a topic or destination from a drop-down box before clicking a button to confirm that choice. In doing so, we'll need to learn a little about the HTTP protocol, and some more about the specifics of implementing extensions using MFC.

At the end of the chapter, we discuss the options available for debugging ISAPI extensions, and present a solution for anyone without access to a machine running Windows NT Server: the Wrox ISAPI Debugger.

## Chapter 4: Accessing Databases

As well as the popular subject of database handling over the Internet (particularly client browsers talking to database servers), this chapter also introduces the issues of ISAPI thread safety and thread synchronization.

The example extension developed uses Microsoft's free-for-download Visual Foxpro ODBC driver, to allow clients to read from and write to a server database.

## Chapter 5: Using Cookies

Cookies are a hot topic right now because they're the first means we've had to allow a server to record state information about a client. We begin this chapter by discussing the limitations of MFC ISAPI programming and creating some classes of our own. Then, we develop a 'custom page' extension which allows browsers that support it to use the **HTTP-COOKIE** mechanism to store a 'hot list' on the server.

## Chapter 6: E-mailing Form Data

Our final chapter on extensions covers the implementation, in ISAPI, of something often seen in the world of CGI and UNIX: a program which pipes data from an HTML form to the **sendmail** command.

Because NT has no such command, our extension will have to communicate directly with an SMTP server, and therefore we'll be learning enough about SMTP to know exactly what's going on. By necessity, the chapter also talks about sockets programming inside an ISAPI extension and some more about thread synchronization.

# Chapter 7: ISAPI Filters

Part two of the book starts here with this introduction to ISAPI filters, which form a layer between a client's request and a server's response. Unlike extensions, ISAPI filters can modify data as it enters *and* leaves the server, and thus have no parallel in CGI programming.

Just as we did for extensions, we discuss the architecture of filters and detail the information and variables available to the programmer. The simple example in the chapter is developed not for its functionality but to give a demonstration of the life-cycle of an ISAPI filter.

# Chapter 8: Automatic Document Selection

The number and diversity of browsers in use is a real headache for web designers–a page which looks great on one user's machine could well look quite different on that of another user. To solve this problem, the ISAPI filter developed in this chapter interrogates the client, to find out which version of HTML it supports, and sends an appropriate page.

Next, we develop a filter with the same functionality, but without using MFC; we come to realize, through the use of timing mechanisms, that our non-MFC version is faster. Because ISAPI filters need to be optimized, we won't be using MFC to create them again.

# Chapter 9: User Authentication

This chapter covers the implementation of our most advanced example ISAPI filter. The user authentication filter negates the need to set up an NT account for every user of your system. Instead, you can use a single account to handle multiple log-ins.

The 'heavy-duty' nature of this filter provides the stimulus for supplying more information about filter optimization, thread synchronization, memory management, and event logging.

# Chapter 10: Quick-fit Filters

After the hard work in Chapter 9, we round off the book with two short, efficient filters designed to make the lives of web administrators everywhere just a little bit easier.

Up first is a custom logging filter which allows the administrator to find out more about the clients visiting their site, and is presented in two versions: one writes the information to a new log file, the other sends it to the normal one. The second filter responds to requests for `.gif` files by interrogating the client to discover whether it supports the PNG standard. If it does, the HTTP request is changed dynamically and the `.png` file is sent instead.

# Appendices

The three appendices contain, respectively, the full source code for the Wrox ISAPI Debugger, a complete HTML tag reference, and a crash course in HTTP.

# ISAPI Extensions

In this chapter, we will look at how to call an ISAPI extension, what variables and information are available to it, and how an ISAPI extension sends information back to the client.

This chapter naturally falls into two parts. In the first part, we discuss the ISAPI specification and interface; we also look at some of the more advanced concepts of ISAPI programming. In the second part of this chapter, we see how MFC can simplify many aspects of ISAPI programming for us.

Those readers without a working knowledge of how to create DLLs need only skim the first part of this chapter, since MFC will handle most of the intricacies for you.

## The DLL Foundations

Every ISAPI extension is a DLL, with the following functions exported:

```
BOOL WINAPI GetExtensionVersion(HSE_VERSION_INFO  *pVer);
DWORD WINAPI HttpExtensionProc(LPEXTENSION_CONTROL_BLOCK  *lpEcb);
```

The **GetExtensionVersion()** function is only called the first time the extension is loaded. It provides information about the extension to the web server. However, this information is nothing more than a version number and a brief text description of the extension. It's encapsulated in the **HSE_VERSION_INFO** structure declared here:

```
typedef struct   _HSE_VERSION_INFO {

    DWORD  dwExtensionVersion;

    CHAR   lpszExtensionDesc[HSE_MAX_EXT_DLL_NAME_LEN];
} HSE_VERSION_INFO, *LPHSE_VERSION_INFO;
```

In general, the web server does nothing with this information, so we won't spend any more time on it.

## HttpExtensionProc

The function that does all the work is **HttpExtensionProc()**. It's called every time the extension is requested. As you can see from the prototype, the only parameter passed to it is a pointer to the ECB. This ECB structure is how all CGI/ISAPI information is passed in and out of our extension, and we'll discuss it in detail shortly.

Most ISAPI extensions finish when they return from **HttpExtensionProc()**, and return a value to indicate the success or failure of the call. However, there are instances when an extension may pass off the ISAPI request for another thread to process (for example, the extension may hand the processing off to a 'worker thread' that manages a queue of requests.) In this case, **HttpExtensionProc()** can return an **HSE_STATUS_PENDING** value, so that the web server knows that the call has been handed off to another thread. The list of possible **HttpExtensionProc()** return values, and their uses, is given here:

| Return Value | Context |
| --- | --- |
| **HSE_STATUS_SUCCESS** | The standard response when the extension has completed successfully. |
| **HSE_STATUS_SUCCESS_AND_KEEP_CONN** | Tells the server that the application is completed, but to hold the connection open if the client supports 'keep-alive'. However, the server does not *have* to keep the connection open. This option is rarely used. |
| **HSE_STATUS_ERROR** | Tells the server an error occurred in the extension. |
| **HSE_STATUS_PENDING** | Informs the server that the extension is still working on the request. This would occur when you create a separate thread to handle requests. The initial thread would exit by returning **HSE_STATUS_PENDING**. The spawned thread could then work on the request. It would call the **ServerSupportFunction()** described below when it completes. |

In the next section, we will see that MFC provides a wrapper for **HttpExtensionProc()**. Unfortunately, as of VC++4.2, MFC only supports **HSE_STATUS_SUCCESS** and **HSE_STATUS_ERROR** in its wrapper for **HttpExtensionProc()**. If you need other results to be returned, such as **HSE_STATUS_PENDING**, you can't use the default implementation of MFC—in fact, it would be very difficult to use MFC at all.

# DllMain()

As with any other DLL, you can declare a single function as an entry point for the DLL. This function is usually called **DllMain()**. The entry point is called once, when the library is first mapped into the address space of the parent process, and again each time a new thread is created (or an old one terminated) inside the process. This function is also called just before the DLL is unloaded from the processes address space. Since the **DllMain()** function is always the first function called when the library is loaded, and the last one called before unloading, it's ideal for any initialization and clean-up that you might need for your extension. There is, however, an interesting problem associated with this technique, which may be of interest to the advanced programmer. We shall now consider the intrigue of this problem in detail—less experienced programmers may skip this discussion if they wish, and re-enter when we come to consider some of the solutions on offer.

When the **DllMain()** function is used for this type of initialization and clean up, all calls to any DLL entry point function, in a given process, are serialized by NT. So, it happens that only one DLL entry point function can be running inside a given process at any one time. Therefore, no matter how many DLLs you have, only one **DllMain()** will run at a time.

> When `DllMain()` is called, all other thread creations and terminations are suspended until the call to `DllMain()` is finished.

As a result, it's difficult to perform certain types of 'clean up' in **`DllMain()`**. Let's investigate this situation by imagining the following scenario:

You have allocated some global variable during **`DllMain()`**'s **`DLL_PROCESS_ATTACH`** notification. Now, your DLL is being unloaded, and it receives the **`DLL_PROCESS_DETACH`** notification. If another thread is running at the same time, and the **`DLL_PROCESS_DETACH`** code frees up the global memory, it will cause problems. At first, you might try to wait until all the threads are finished before cleaning up. However, this 'solution' will quickly bring your web server to a halt.

To appreciate what's happening here, we need to understand the process by which NT handles calls to DLL entry point functions. This discussion moves us on to the topic of mutex objects, and other objects for controlling the multithreaded environment. These are discussed in greater detail, later in the book.

When NT creates a process, it creates a single mutex object to control access to DLL entry points. Whenever a thread needs to make a call to any DLL entry point, NT makes the thread wait until it has ownership of the mutex before it lets it execute any DLL entry point functions. Let's say that you have a **`DllMain()`** function that looks like this:

```
BOOL WINAPI DllMain(HMODULE hMod, DWORD fReason, LPVOID pvRes)
{
   switch (fReason)
   {
      case DLL_PROCESS_ATTACH:
       DisableThreadLibraryCalls(hMod);
       Sleep(10000);
       break;

      case DLL_THREAD_ATTACH:
         break;

      case DLL_PROCESS_DETACH:
         break;

      case DLL_THREAD_DETACH:
         break;
   }
   return TRUE;
}
```

This code is obviously useless, and also looks completely harmless. However, this simple DLL will suspend all ISAPI calls for 10 seconds; not just calls to this DLL, but all ISAPI calls to any DLL. The reason for this is that MSIIS creates a new thread for each ISAPI request. (MSIIS uses a thread from a pool of pre-existing threads for normal document requests.) Each time a new thread is created, NT must get exclusive access to the mutex, so that it can call the DLL entry point of each DLL currently loaded into the address space. Each entry point will be given a **`DLL_THREAD_ATTACH`** notification—provided that it hasn't turned this notification request off.

Even though we disabled thread attach and detach notification for this particular DLL, with the call to **`DisableThreadLibraryCalls()`**, NT will still wait for the mutex, since it may need to call the entry points for other DLLs.

Our example **DllMain()** function was, of course, contrived for the purposes of this demonstration, and would never be used in the real world. We therefore present the following function, as a challenge for you to determine what its behavior would be:

```
BOOL WINAPI DllMain(HMODULE hMod, DWORD fReason, LPVOID pvRes)
{
  switch (fReason)
  {
    case DLL_PROCESS_ATTACH:
      DisableThreadLibraryCalls(hMod);
      // DummyThread is some 'worker' thread
      hThread = CreateThread(NULL, 0, (LPTHREAD_START_ROUTINE) DummyThread,
(LPVOID)0, 0, &dwThreadId);
      break;

    case DLL_THREAD_ATTACH:
      break;

    case DLL_PROCESS_DETACH:
      // Wait for our thread to terminate before cleaning up
        WaitForSingleObject(hThread,INFINITE);
      // Clean up any global memory
      // ....
      // ....
      break;

    case DLL_THREAD_DETACH:
      break;
  }
  return TRUE;
}
```

### Analysis

If **DummyThread** hasn't exited by the time **DllMain()** is called with the **DLL_PROCESS_DETACH** notification, this DLL will wait forever. The reason for this is that when **DummyThread** exits, NT waits for the **DllMain()** mutex before completely terminating the thread. **DummyThread** will never get the mutex, because the thread that owns it is waiting for **DummyThread** to finish. In addition, no new threads (which the web server must be able to create if it is to handle any requests) can begin execution. And so this simple DLL will quickly bring all ISAPI extensions on your server to a halt.

Therefore, we may conclude that while it is perfectly acceptable to put initialization and clean-up code in **DllMain()**, you should be very careful if you're using any thread synchronization objects.

It's at this point that we can welcome back those that may have chosen to skip the above discussion.

To allow for a clean up routine before your extension is unloaded, an optional exported function has been introduced in MSIIS 2.0. The function is defined as:

```
BOOL WINAPI TerminateExtension(DWORD dwFlags)
```

After a DLL is loaded into the web server, that web server may need to unload it for some reason. It may need the memory, or it may simply be shutting down. In any case, the web server will need to unload your DLL, and you can then use **TerminateExtension()** to perform any house cleaning that you need doing, without having to worry about NT serializing anything behind your back.

`TerminateExtension()` takes a single parameter with the following values:

| dwFlags Value | Context |
|---|---|
| `HSE_TERM_ADVISORY_UNLOAD` | The server passes this parameter when it would like to unload your DLL, but it is asking first. If your function returns **TRUE**, it will be unloaded. **FALSE** will keep it in memory. |
| `HSE_TERM_MUST_UNLOAD` | As the name implies, the server is telling your DLL that it is going to be unloaded. |

# The Call

ISAPI extensions are called in exactly the same way as with CGI programs, except that instead of specifying an **.exe** file, you specify a **.dll** file.

When a call is made (i.e. **http://mydomain.com/scripts/myISAPI.dll?optional +parameters+here**)  the server first checks to see if **myISAPI.dll** is loaded. If this is the first time it's being called, or if it has been called but subsequently unloaded, then it will need to initiate a load.

Once the DLL is loaded, the entry point is called. This is usually **DllMain()**, but it can be any function you care to specify as the entry point. When **DllMain()** finishes, the server calls the **GetExtensionVersion()** function to get information about the ISAPI extension–such as a version number and a description. The server then calls the DLL's **HttpExtensionProc()** function to start the actual ISAPI extension.

If the DLL was already loaded, the server simply starts the request by calling the **HttpExtensionProc()** function. The **HttpExtensionProc()** takes, as its parameter, a pointer to an Extension Control Block (ECB). The ECB is used for getting incoming data and writing data back to the client.

# Extension Control Block Structure

The ECB is defined as follows (the **IN** and **OUT** comments indicate whether the data can be read or written):

```
typedef struct _EXTENSION_CONTROL_BLOCK {

    DWORD      cbSize;                              //IN
    DWORD      dwVersion;                           //IN
    HCONN      ConnID;                              //IN
    DWORD      dwHttpStatusCode;                    //OUT
    CHAR       lpszLogData[HSE_LOG_BUFFER_LEN];     //OUT
    LPSTR      lpszMethod;                          //IN
    LPSTR      lpszQueryString;                     //IN
    LPSTR      lpszPathInfo;                        //IN
    LPSTR      lpszPathTranslated;                  //IN
    DWORD      cbTotalBytes;                        //IN
    DWORD      cbAvailable;                         //IN
    LPBYTE     lpbData;                             //IN
    LPSTR      lpszContentType;                     //IN
```

```
      BOOL (WINAPI * GetServerVariable)
         (HCONN        hConn,
          LPSTR        lpszVariableName,
          LPVOID       lpvBuffer,
          LPDWORD      lpdwSize);

      BOOL (WINAPI * WriteClient)
         (HCONN        ConnID,
          LPVOID       Buffer,
          LPDWORD      lpdwBytes,
          DWORD        dwReserved);

      BOOL (WINAPI * ReadClient)
         (HCONN        ConnID,
          LPVOID       lpvBuffer,
          LPDWORD      lpdwSize);

      BOOL (WINAPI * ServerSupportFunction)
         (HCONN        hConn,
          DWORD        dwHSERRequest,
          LPVOID       lpvBuffer,
          LPDWORD      lpdwSize,
          LPDWORD      lpdwDataType);

} EXTENSION_CONTROL_BLOCK, *LPEXTENSION_CONTROL_BLOCK;
```

The following is a description of variables in the ECB structure:

| Variable | Context |
|----------|---------|
| **cbSize** | The size of the ECB. This is rarely used. |
| **DwVersion** | Version information. |
| **connID** | A number used by the HTTP server to identify this ECB. It is unique, and it should never be modified. |
| **DwHttpStatusCode** | The status that will be sent back to the HTTP server when the ISAPI extension is done. It can be one of:<br>**HTTP_STATUS_BAD_REQUEST**<br>**HTTP_STATUS_AUTH_REQUIRED**<br>**HTTP_STATUS_FORBIDDEN**<br>**HTTP_STATUS_NOT_FOUND**<br>**HTTP_STATUS_SERVER_ERROR**<br>**HTTP_STATUS_NOT_IMPLEMENTED** |
| **lpszLogData** | A buffer that contains log information. This is changed when you are implementing a custom logging scheme. |
| **LpszMethod** | The same as the regular CGI variable **REQUEST_METHOD**. It should be either **GET** or **POST**. |
| **LpszQueryString** | A URL-encoded string that is the same as the CGI **QUERY_STRING** variable. See ISAPI/CGI variables below for more information. |

*Table Continued on Following Page*

| Variable | Context |
|---|---|
| `LpszPathInfo` | The same as `PATH_INFO`. |
| `LpszPathTranslated` | The same as `PATH_TRANSLATED`. |
| `CbTotalBytes` | The same as `CONTENT_LENGTH`. |
| `CbAvailable` | The amount of data that is currently available from the client and saved in `lpdData`. Usually, this is the same as `cbTotalBytes`. If all the data isn't available, the ISAPI extension will need to call the `ReadClient` function, which is part of the ECB structure and is discussed below. |
| `LpbData` | The first 48K of total data sent over by the client. The actual size is indicated by `cbAvailable`. |
| `LpszContentType` | The same as `CONTENT_TYPE`. |

If you're a CGI programmer, you're probably wondering: "Where's the rest?". If you aren't a CGI programmer, you simply don't know what you're missing yet!

## ECB.GetServerVariable()

In order to get at any other information that the server passes us (such as the name of the remote host that is connected to us, the user's name and password, etc.) We need to call the `GetServerVariable()` function of the ECB. This function is defined as follows:

```
BOOL WINAPI GetServerVariable(
    HCONN hConn,
    LPSTR lpszVariableName,
    LPVOID lpvBuffer,
    LPDWORD lpdwSizeofBuffer
);
```

| Parameter | Meaning |
|---|---|
| `hConn` | This must be the same as that supplied by the ECB, or the server will read from the wrong ECB. |
| `LpszVariableName` | The name of the variable that you are looking for. A list of possible variables is given in the following table. |
| `LpvBuffer` | A pointer to the buffer that will hold the response. |
| `LpdwSizeofBuffer` | A pointer to the size of the `lpvBuffer` when the function is called. When the function returns, it indicates how many bytes were actually transferred into `lpvBuffer`. |

`lpszVariableName` should hold the CGI/ISAPI name of a variable that you would prefer to read. On the next page is a list of typical CGI/ISAPI variables. A typical call to find the information that you are looking for is as follows (in this case, `szBuffer` should contain the remote users address, i.e. 206.34.194.10 after the function returns):

```
bReturn = pECB->GetServerVariable (pECB->ConnID, "REMOTE_ADDR",   szBuffer,
&dwBufferSize);
```

A list of possible variables you can retrieve is given below:

### ISAPI/CGI Variables

| Variable | Context |
|---|---|
| ALL_HTTP | All information not assigned in these tables. See below for what might be contained here. |
| AUTH_TYPE | The method that's used to ask for a username and password (if one was required). In most cases this is **Basic**, but it can be **NTLM** if NT challenge-response is used. NT challenge-response requires that the client browser supports it. |
| CONTENT_LENGTH | The length (in characters) of the data being sent by the client using the **POST** method. |
| CONTENT_TYPE | The way that information is being sent over from the client, if using the **POST** method. |
| GATEWAY_INTERFACE | The version of the gateway interface. It should be **CGI/1.1**. |
| HTTP_ACCEPT | The types of data that the client will accept natively. For example, this could be: **image/gif, image/jpeg** to indicate that browser will display both GIF and JPEG images. A browser that also displays progressive JPEGS would show **image/gif, image/jpeg, image/pjpeg**. |
| HTTP_AUTHORIZATION | A Base-64 encoded username password combination, if **AUTH_TYPE = BASIC**. |
| LOGON_USER | The NT user for this request (after any password mapping has taken place). (Version 2.0). |
| PATH_INFO | Any part of the request that is after the script name and before the query string. In **http://www.myhost.com/scripts/myscript.dll/ mydir/myfile?parameter**, the **PATH_INFO** would be **/mydir/ myfile**. |
| PATH_TRANSLATED | If any of the directories in **PATH_INFO** are virtual (i.e. they aren't part of the physical directory structure, but map somewhere else), **PATH_TRANSLATED** would show the physical path to the directory. |
| QUERY_STRING | Anything that follows after the ? in the request. This string is URL-encoded. That is, blank spaces are converted to **+** signs and any non-alphanumeric characters are shown as hexadecimal preceded with a **%**. |
| REMOTE_ADDR | The IP address of the host requesting the document. It's derived from the IP packet, rather than the client actually telling us. |
| REMOTE_HOST | Host name of the host requesting the document. |
| REMOTE_USER | The name the user is using to access the server. |
| REQUEST_METHOD | The type of request that is being answered. Usually **GET** or **POST**. |
| SCRIPT_NAME | The name of the script file being requested. |

*Table Continued on Following Page*

| Variable | Context |
|---|---|
| **SERVER_NAME** | The name or IP address of the server. |
| **SERVER_PORT** | The port number which received the request. |
| **SERVER_PROTOCOL** | The type of protocol that is being used (usually **HTTP/1.0**). |
| **SERVER_SOFTWARE** | The type of software the server is running. |
| **URL** | Provides the base of the URL requested. (Version 2.0). |

If you are a CGI programmer, you're probably wondering about variables like **USER_AGENT** and **HTTP_COOKIE**. These, and anything else that doesn't fit into the above list, are put into **ALL_HTTP**. However, you can still retrieve them using the **GetServerVariable()** function. This allows for the use of custom header variables. Since not all browsers support these variables, some of the more commonly supported ones are listed separately here:

| Custom Header Variable | Context |
|---|---|
| **USER_AGENT** | The type of browser the client is using. |
| **HTTP_COOKIE** | Any cookies the client is sending over with the request. |
| **HTTP_REFERER** | The page that linked to this request. |

As the astute reader has probably noticed, there's some redundancy in the ECB structure. The variables that are put directly into the ECB structure are put there for ease of access. They can also be retrieved from the **GetServerVariable()** function. For example:

```
pECB->lpszQueryString;
```

is the same as **szBuffer** in

```
bReturn = pECB->GetServerVariable (pECB->ConnID, "QUERY_STRING",
    szBuffer, &dwBufferSize);
```

## *Writing Back to the Client*

Another function within the ECB structure is the **WriteClient()** function. As one might suspect, this is used to write data back to the client's browser. The function is declared as follows:

```
BOOL WriteClient(
    HCONN hConn,
    LPVOID lpvBuffer,
    LPDWORD lpdwSizeofBuffer,
    DWORD dwReserved
);
```

| Parameters | Meaning |
|---|---|
| hConn | Our familiar connection handle. |
| LpvBuffer | The data that you want to write to the client. |
| LpdwSizeofBuffer | On calling the function, this should contain the length of **lpvBuffer**. On return, it will contain the actual number of bytes written. Unless an error occurs, these two values will be the same. |
| DwReserved | This is reserved for future use, and should be set to **0**. |

A typical call to **WriteClient** would look like this:

```
bReturn = pECB->WriteClient (pECB->ConnID,  (LPVOID) rgBuff,  &cb, 0);
```

## Reading Additional Data

If all the data that the client has written using the **POST** method isn't made available to **lpbData** in the ECB (for instance, the data is larger than 48K), you will need to get the rest of the data by making one or more calls to the **ReadClient()** function of the ECB.

```
BOOL ReadClient(
    HCONN hConn,
    LPVOID lpvBuffer,
    LPDWORD lpdwSize
);
```

| Parameters | Meaning |
|---|---|
| hConn | The connection handle. |
| LpvBuffer | A place to put the additional information. |
| LpdwSize | On calling **ReadClient()**, **lpdwSize** should contain the size of **lpvBuffer**. On return, it will contain the actual number of bytes read. |

You should continue to call **ReadClient()** until the total number of bytes read equals **cbTotalBytes,** or no more data is returned. A typical way of handling this is as follows:

```
memcpy(lpszLargeBuffer, (LPCTSRT) ECB->lpdData, ECB->cbAvailable);

cbDataRead=ECB->cbAvailable;

while (cbDataRead < ECB->cbTotalBytes && ECB->ReadClient(ECB->ConnID,(LPVOID)
(lpszLargeBuffer + cbDataRead),&lpdwSize) && lpwdSize!=0)
{
    cbDataRead+=lpwdSize;
    lpwdSize=dwSizeOfLargeBuffer - cbDataRead;
}
```

The example above first copies any available data into **lpszLargeBuffer**. It then checks to see if the client indicated that more data is available. The reader should note that the value of the **ECB->cbTotalBytes** variable is decided by what the client's browser sends over in the **Content-Length:** header. A problem can occur if a user decides to upload a large amount of data but then cancels the upload half way through. When the client starts the transfer, he or she will send a large value for the

**Content-Length:** header, indicating the amount of data that the client intends to send. If our extension simply loops though until it receives this amount of data, we would get into trouble if the user canceled the upload–or the network connection was lost half way through. The reason for this is that, contrary to what you might expect, **ReadClient()** only returns **FALSE** when an error occurs. Network problems such as lost connections and user cancellations aren't considered errors. When a connection is lost, or the users terminates the upload, **ReadClient()** returns **TRUE**, copies no data into the buffer, and sets the **lpwdSize** parameter to 0. By checking for this condition, we're making sure that we aren't in an infinite loop waiting on a lost connection.

## Additional Features

The ECB **ServerSupportFunction()** function gives the programmer easy access to a few frequently used server functions. It's defined as follows:

```
BOOL ServerSupportFunction(
    HCONN hConn,
    DWORD dwHSERequest,
    LPVOID lpvBuffer,
    LPDWORD lpdwSize,
    LPDWORD lpdwDataType
);
```

| Parameter | Meaning |
|---|---|
| hConn | The connection handle. |
| DwHSERequest | The type of predefined request you're asking the server to perform. A list of defined requests available on all ISAPI-compliant servers is given in the table below. Your server may have additional types defined. |
| LpvBuffer | An optional status string for the request. If **NULL**, **200 OK** is used. This is useful for ending meaningful error messages to the browser. |
| LpdwSize | Only used when requesting **HSE_REQ_SEND_RESPONSE_HEADER**. On calling the function, it should contain the size of **lpvDataType**. On returning, it will contain the actual number of bytes written to the header. |
| LpdwDataType | Any optional headers you wish to return to the client, **NULL** if none. |

The **dwHSERequest** parameter should be one of the following definitions:

| dwHSERequest Value | Meaning |
|---|---|
| HSE_REQ_SEND_URL_REDIRECT_RESP | This sends a header back to the client asking his browser to load the URL specified. We will see this used in our first example. |
| HSE_REQ_SEND_URL | Has a similar effect to **HSE_REQ_SEND_URL_REDIRECT_RESP** above, but a different implementation. In this case, the server sends the client the document specified in the call to **ServerSupportFunction()**, rather than the document the client asked for. The document must reside on the same server, and the path to it must be absolute (beginning with a '**/**'). |

*Table Continued on Following Page*

| dwHSERequest Value | Meaning |
|---|---|
| HSE_REQ_SEND_RESPONSE_HEADER | Sends an HTTP server header back to the client. If data is given in **lpdwDataType**, this is included in the header packet. This would be useful for adding things such as HTTP cookies. |
| HSE_REQ_MAP_URL_TO_PATH | Upon its return, this function maps the logical path given by **lpvBuffer**, when the function is called to the physical path. For example, if **lpvBuffer** equals **"/mydir/home.html"** on entry, it would return **"c:\inetsrv\wwwroot\userdirs\mydir\home.html"**. |
| HSE_REQ_DONE_WITH_SESSION | Tells the server that the extension is done. This would be used, as mentioned in the table on **HttpExtensionProc()** return values, for a spawned thread, to let the server know that it's finished with a particular request. |

# A Simple Example

The following sample shows a simple non-MFC ISAPI extension that performs a basic ISAPI variable dump. While the code will certainly compile and run, it's given here more as an illustration.

To use this extension, create a normal DLL with AppWizard, and then create the following file. Save it as **SimpleDump.cpp**, and add it to the project.

```
/////////////////////////////////////////////////////////////////////
//    SimpleDump.cpp

#include <httpext.h>

#define BUFLEN      4096
#define DESCRIPT    64

void WriteHTML(EXTENSION_CONTROL_BLOCK *pECB,LPCSTR lpszOutput)
{
    DWORD dwLength=lstrlen(lpszOutput);
    pECB->WriteClient(pECB->ConnID,(PVOID)lpszOutput,&dwLength,0);
}

BOOL WINAPI GetExtensionVersion(HSE_VERSION_INFO *pVer)
{
    pVer->dwExtensionVersion = 1;

    strncpy(pVer->lpszExtensionDesc,
            "Exclusive DllMain",
            HSE_MAX_EXT_DLL_NAME_LEN);
    return TRUE;
}

DWORD WINAPI HttpExtensionProc(EXTENSION_CONTROL_BLOCK *pECB)
{
```

```
TCHAR szTempBuffer[BUFLEN];
DWORD dwBufferSize = BUFLEN;


// First send the content-type header
strcpy(szTempBuffer,"Content-type: text/html\r\n\r\n");
DWORD dwHeaderSize = strlen(szTempBuffer);
pECB->ServerSupportFunction(pECB->ConnID, HSE_REQ_SEND_RESPONSE_HEADER,
    NULL, &dwHeaderSize, (LPDWORD) szTempBuffer);

// Now get and print all the server variables

if (pECB->GetServerVariable (pECB->ConnID,
      "ALL_HTTP",szTempBuffer,&dwBufferSize))
{
   WriteHTML(pECB,"ALL_HTP = ");
   WriteHTML(pECB,szTempBuffer);
}


if (pECB->GetServerVariable (pECB->ConnID,
      "AUTH_TYPE",szTempBuffer,&dwBufferSize))
{
   WriteHTML(pECB,"<BR>AUTH_TYPE = ");
   WriteHTML(pECB,szTempBuffer);
}

if (pECB->GetServerVariable (pECB->ConnID,
      "CONTENT_LENGTH",szTempBuffer,&dwBufferSize))
{
   WriteHTML(pECB,"<BR>CONTENT_LENGTH = ");
   WriteHTML(pECB,szTempBuffer);
}

if (pECB->GetServerVariable (pECB->ConnID,
      "CONTENT_TYPE",szTempBuffer,&dwBufferSize))
{
   WriteHTML(pECB,"<BR>CONTENT_TYPE = ");
   WriteHTML(pECB,szTempBuffer);
}

if (pECB->GetServerVariable (pECB->ConnID,
      "GATEWAY_INTERFACE",szTempBuffer,&dwBufferSize))
{
   WriteHTML(pECB,"<BR>GATEWAY_INTERFACE = ");
   WriteHTML(pECB,szTempBuffer);
}

if (pECB->GetServerVariable (pECB->ConnID,
      "HTTP_ACCEPT",szTempBuffer,&dwBufferSize))
{
   WriteHTML(pECB,"<BR>HTTP_ACCEPT = ");
   WriteHTML(pECB,szTempBuffer);
}

if (pECB->GetServerVariable (pECB->ConnID,
      "HTTP_AUTHORIZATION",szTempBuffer,&dwBufferSize))
{
```

```
    WriteHTML(pECB,"<BR>HTTP_AUTHORIZATION = ");
    WriteHTML(pECB,szTempBuffer);
}

if (pECB->GetServerVariable (pECB->ConnID,
    "LOGON_USER",szTempBuffer,&dwBufferSize))
{
    WriteHTML(pECB,"<BR>LOGON_USER = ");
    WriteHTML(pECB,szTempBuffer);
}

if (pECB->GetServerVariable (pECB->ConnID,
    "PATH_INFO",szTempBuffer,&dwBufferSize))
{
    WriteHTML(pECB,"<BR>PATH_INFO = ");
    WriteHTML(pECB,szTempBuffer);
}

if (pECB->GetServerVariable (pECB->ConnID,
    "PATH_TRANSLATED",szTempBuffer,&dwBufferSize))
{
    WriteHTML(pECB,"<BR>PATH_TRANSLATED = ");
    WriteHTML(pECB,szTempBuffer);
}

if (pECB->GetServerVariable (pECB->ConnID,
    "QUERY_STRING",szTempBuffer,&dwBufferSize))
{
    WriteHTML(pECB,"<BR>QUERY_STRING = ");
    WriteHTML(pECB,szTempBuffer);
}

if (pECB->GetServerVariable (pECB->ConnID,
    "REMOTE_ADDR",szTempBuffer,&dwBufferSize))
{
    WriteHTML(pECB,"<BR>REMOTE_ADDR = ");
    WriteHTML(pECB,szTempBuffer);
}

if (pECB->GetServerVariable (pECB->ConnID,
    "REMOTE_HOST",szTempBuffer,&dwBufferSize))
{
    WriteHTML(pECB,"<BR>REMOTE_HOST = ");
    WriteHTML(pECB,szTempBuffer);
}

if (pECB->GetServerVariable (pECB->ConnID,
    "REMOTE_USER",szTempBuffer,&dwBufferSize))
{
    WriteHTML(pECB,"<BR>REMOTE_USER = ");
    WriteHTML(pECB,szTempBuffer);
}

if (pECB->GetServerVariable (pECB->ConnID,
    "REQUEST_METHOD",szTempBuffer,&dwBufferSize))
{
    WriteHTML(pECB,"<BR>REQUEST_METHOD = ");
```

```
      WriteHTML(pECB,szTempBuffer);
}

if (pECB->GetServerVariable (pECB->ConnID,
      "SCRIPT_NAME",szTempBuffer,&dwBufferSize))
{
   WriteHTML(pECB,"<BR>SCRIPT_NAME = ");
   WriteHTML(pECB,szTempBuffer);
}

if (pECB->GetServerVariable (pECB->ConnID,
      "SERVER_NAME",szTempBuffer,&dwBufferSize))
{
   WriteHTML(pECB,"<BR>SERVER_NAME = ");
   WriteHTML(pECB,szTempBuffer);
}

if (pECB->GetServerVariable (pECB->ConnID,
      "SERVER_PORT",szTempBuffer,&dwBufferSize))
{
   WriteHTML(pECB,"<BR>SERVER_PORT = ");
   WriteHTML(pECB,szTempBuffer);
}

if (pECB->GetServerVariable (pECB->ConnID,
      "SERVER_PROTOCOL",szTempBuffer,&dwBufferSize))
{
   WriteHTML(pECB,"<BR>SERVER_PROTOCOL = ");
   WriteHTML(pECB,szTempBuffer);
}

if (pECB->GetServerVariable (pECB->ConnID,
      "SERVER_SOFTWARE",szTempBuffer,&dwBufferSize))
{
   WriteHTML(pECB,"<BR>SERVER_SOFTWARE = ");
   WriteHTML(pECB,szTempBuffer);
}

WriteHTML(pECB,"<p>");


// Now output the data in the ECB structure itself.

WriteHTML(pECB,"lpszLogData = ");
WriteHTML(pECB,pECB->lpszLogData);

WriteHTML(pECB,"<BR>lpszMethod = ");
WriteHTML(pECB,pECB->lpszMethod);

WriteHTML(pECB,"<BR>lpszQueryString = ");
WriteHTML(pECB,pECB->lpszQueryString);

WriteHTML(pECB,"<BR>lpszPathInfo = ");
WriteHTML(pECB,pECB->lpszPathTranslated);

WriteHTML(pECB,"<BR>lpszLogData = ");
WriteHTML(pECB,pECB->lpszLogData);
```

```
    WriteHTML(pECB,"<BR>lpbData = ");
    WriteHTML(pECB,(LPCSTR)pECB->lpbData);

    WriteHTML(pECB,"<BR>lpszContentType = ");
    WriteHTML(pECB,pECB->lpszContentType);

    return HSE_STATUS_SUCCESS;
}
```

Next, create, save, and add the following **SimpleDump.def** file to your project:

```
LIBRARY SimpleDump

DESCRIPTION 'SimpleDump v.01'

EXPORTS

    HttpExtensionProc
    GetExtensionVersion
```

You will now be able to compile the project. Once complete, copy the resulting DLL into the **Scripts** directory on your IIS server. It's now ready to use. Enter the following URL into your browser:

**http://www.your.server.com/scripts/simpledump.dll**

You should get something similar to the screenshot below:

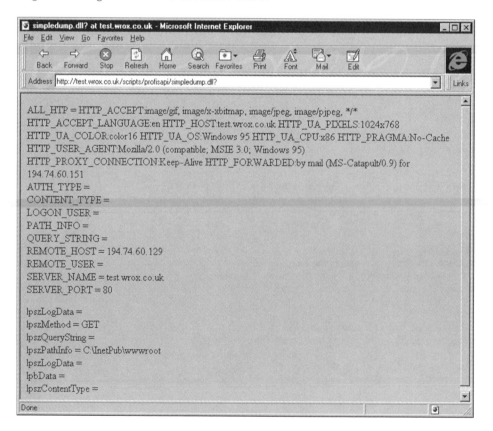

*Note that we have placed our extensions within a subdirectory of **Scripts** to make management of the extensions easier.*

# MFC for ISAPI

In order to make ISAPI programming a little easier, Microsoft has included some ISAPI classes in MFC 4.1. The ones that apply to ISAPI extensions are **CHttpServer**, **CHttpServerContext**, and **CHtmlStream**.

## CHttpServer

**CHttpServer** is the main class used by MFC ISAPI extensions. The first time your request is called, a **CHttpServer** object is created to handle it. Once it is created, it uses the **CHttpServerContext** class to handle the individual requests, each of which runs as its own thread. Thus, there's only one instance of **CHttpServer** for each extension, but there can be many **CHttpServerContext** instances.

The primary function of **CHttpServer** is to handle the interface between the web server and your extension. The **CHttpServer** takes the request for the web server, passes it through a parse map, and calls the appropriate function with the appropriate parameters for you. The mechanism for doing this, as well as the other member functions of **CHttpServer**, will be covered in detail in the next chapter.

## CHttpServerContext

The **CHttpServerContext** class is the class that is passed to each function that processes a web request. By looking at the member function of the **CHttpServerContext** class, you will see that it's simply a thin wrapper for the ECB discussed above. The class, however, doesn't give us all the functionality of the ECB, so a pointer to the actual ECB is included—as seen below, in the description of **CHttpServerContext**.

| Members | Meaning |
|---|---|
| **m_pECB** | In case we need to access the ECB directly, a pointer is provided here. |
| **m_pStream** | A pointer to an HTML stream, discussed below. |
| **CHttpServerContext()** | The constructor. |
| **GetServerVariable()** | Same as **m_pECB->GetServerVariable()** except that you don't need to pass the connection id as a parameter: the **CHttpServerContext** class takes care of that for us. |
| **WriteClient()** | Same as **m_pECB->WriteClient()** except as noted above. |
| **ReadClient()** | Same as **m_pECB->ReadClient()** except as noted above. |
| **ServerSupportFunction()** | Same as **m_pECB->ServerSupportFunction()** except as noted above. |
| **Operator <<** | As opposed to using the **WriteClient()** function, we can use the overridden **<<** operator. This makes outputting HTML very simple. |

# CHtmlStream

This class is used by **CHttpServer** to write data back to the client. It's created in the **CHttpServer::ConstructStream()** function, and passed to us as a member of the **CHttpServerContext** class. The **CHtmlStream** class maintains an in-memory HTML buffer, and automatically creates more memory when needed and frees it up when it's finished. While it does have some member functions which can allow you to increase the size of the buffer by hand, there are no functions for reading the buffer. Most of our interaction with this class will be with the << operator, which writes data into the string and performs formatting operations on numerical data being inserted. The only other function of interest to us in this class is the constructor. If you override the **CHttpServer::ConstructSream()** function, you can call the constructor of the **CHtmlStream** class directly using **CHtmlStream(UINT nGrowBytes)**, where **nGrowBytes** is the amount of memory allocated in each block. You might want to change this for an extension which outputs a long response.

# The Dark Side of MFC

While the MFC ISAPI classes mentioned help to make our lives easier, we should now take a moment to look at what problems await us. First of all, there are some bugs in the MFC ISAPI code. You should consult the Microsoft KnowledgeBase regularly to ensure that you know what they are, and how to fix them.

A note of caution about MFC code that is not ISAPI-specific: once again, it is the issue of thread-safety. Several problems exist which might causes threads to interfere with each other. Among these are the use of global and static variables. If one thread uses a global variable, it might get changed by another thread, and then used again by the original thread. As you can imagine, this could lead to serious problems. Since, in many cases, you don't know what is going on inside the MFC code, you should thoroughly test any ISAPI application that uses non-ISAPI MFC code. This is especially true when the extension accesses a database, as we will discuss in the chapter on database access. (The MFC ODBC database classes were not thread-safe until VC++ 4.2.) So, while we use MFC here in some of our examples, you should pay special attention to any cautions that are given.

# Extending MFC

While MFC does a lot, it doesn't do everything. We will assume that you're familiar with C++ object-oriented programming, and provide simple descriptions and explanations for the additional classes we will use here in the book. The source code for all classes is on the Wrox Press web site (**www.wrox.com**), but this source will not be presented in the book until it is used in an example. This way, the classes will be presented in the context of solving a particular deficiency in the MFC classes.

A side note for the extended classes: these classes are intended to instruct the reader in how ISAPI/CGI programming works, and to provide usable code for your own applications. Our emphasis, however, is on instruction. There are certainly places in these classes where performance could be increased but only at the cost of obscuring the actual functioning of the class. Since the classes are included here primarily to instruct, feel free to optimize them as you see fit. With that said, the following classes will be used in this book:

| Class | Usage |
|---|---|
| **CDataPool** | Handles a pool of database connections, so that you don't need to open and close a connection for each request. |
| **CHttpBase** | Provides generic HTTP functions which are used by some of the other classes. |
| **CHttpCookie** | Facilitates client-side cookies |
| **CWroxHttp** | Derived from **CHttpServer**, this gives us the flexibility to pass any number of form items to a function. |
| **CHttpForm** | When used with **CWroxHttp**, this handles the retrieval of data inputted to forms. |
| **CISAPISocket** | Derived from **Csocket**, this class helps us perform sockets programming inside an ISAPI extension. |

# Summary

ISAPI extensions are DLLs that run in the process space of the web server itself. Each ISAPI extension has two mandatory exported functions: **GetExtensionVersion()** and **HttpExtensionProc()**, plus an optional DLL entry point function, usually called **DllMain()**.

**GetExtensionVersion()** is called only once when the DLL is loaded, and is only used to provide version information about the DLL. **HttpExtensionProc()** is called for each ISAPI request, and does the work of processing the request.

The optional **DllMain()** function can be used for initialization and clean-up, but care should be taken, since all calls to **DllMain()** functions in a process are serialized by NT. All communication between the web server and the ISAPI extension takes place through an Extension Control Block (ECB) data structure.

While MFC provides convenient wrappers for **GetExtensionVersion()**, **HttpExtensionProc()**, and the ECB structure, it doesn't cover everything that an ISAPI extension needs to do. Fortunately, MFC provides a solid base from which we will develop extended ISAPI classes.

# Navigational Redirection

Now that we have an overview of the ISAPI specification, and know a little about how MFC helps us implement it, we'll get on to the tried and tested method of learning how to program: by example.

In this chapter, we'll develop an HTML navigational control that lets a user select a topic from a drop-down combo box, and then takes them to the desired topic when they click a GO! button. You're probably familiar with this control, as Microsoft use one like it on their web site. While MFC does most of the programming for us in this simple case, we'll still look at what is going on 'behind the scenes', so that we'll be better able to expand on the MFC framework in future chapters.

## Design of the Extension

We'll use AppWizard to create an ISAPI extension that will be called by the following fragment of hypertext:

```
<form action="/scripts/MFCRedir.dll" method="GET">
<select name="dest">
<option value="/default.htm">Default Home Page
<option value="http://www.microsoft.com">Microsoft
<option value="http://home.netscape.com">Netscape
</select>
<input type="SUBMIT" value="GO!">
</form>
```

The above **<form>** tag could also read **<form action="/scripts/MFCRedir.dll" method="POST">**. There are subtle differences between the **GET** and **POST** methods, which we'll get to in a minute. Before we go anywhere near the AppWizard, however, we need to have an understanding of the request sent to the server.

## Parameters and Commands

The above hypertext would send the following request to the server:

**http://myserver.com/scripts/MFCRedir.dll?dest=%2Fdefault.htm**

This request actually contains two separate pieces: a URL and a parameter. The web server uses the first question mark in the request as the separator; everything up to the question mark is the URL (**http://myserver.com/scripts/MFCRedir.dll**, in this case), while everything after it is simply passed on to the file pointed to by the URL. It is what happens to this passed-on information that's of interest to us at the moment.

Since we are calling an ISAPI DLL, the server generates an ECB structure for us, filling in the various members with the appropriate data. For example, the **lpszQueryString** will be set to **dest=/ default.htm**. The ECB structure is then passed on to the **HttpExtensionProc()** for processing.

The query string, in this case, is simply a parameter, or rather a **named parameter**. It is named because of the **dest=** portion of the string. In this case, it's not absolutely necessary because there's only one parameter; we could have just as easily used the link

```
http://myserver.com/scripts/MFCRedir.dll?%2Fdefault.htm
```

However, if we were to pass two parameters, say

```
http://myserver.com/scripts/
MFCRedir.dll?page=%2Fdefault.htm&server=www.microsoft.com
```

then the reason for using names becomes apparent—you can never know the order the parameters are going to be passed in.

> Notice how the parameters are separated by an ampersand. This is the standard way of delimiting the parameters in the query. If you send an ampersand as part of the value, it is converted into hexadecimal notation.

A single CGI script can have more than one command contained within it, and the same holds true for ISAPI extensions. A command is included in the query string by placing the command name before the parameters and separating it from the parameters with a question mark, as in:

```
http://myserver.com/scripts/MFCRedir.dll?jump?dest=%2Fdefault.htm
```

The query string would then become **jump?dest=/default.htm**, which passes **/default.htm** as a parameter to the **jump** command contained within **MFCRedir.dll**.

Why is this a good thing? The answer is quite simply that it allows you to share code. Consider writing a database access extension. You might want to implement the two most basic operations, reading and writing, as two separate extensions. However, the code which opens and closes the database would be the same in both cases. If you put both operations into the same extension, you can simply specify which of the two you want to use with the command.

# GET and POST

At this time, we must take a quick sidestep to discuss the **GET** and **POST** methods and how they apply to MFC ISAPI programming. While, in theory, it shouldn't matter which one we use, browser inconsistencies require that we take some caution. Many browsers, such as Netscape 2.0, would take this hypertext:

```
<form action="http://mydomain.com/db.dll?read" method="GET">
Enter table:
<input type="text" name=table value="mytable"><br>
<input type="submit" value="read">
</form>
```

and produce the following URL request:

```
http://mydomain.com/db.dll?table=mytable
```

Other browsers, however, (e.g. Microsoft Internet Explorer) produce the following request for the same HTML code:

```
http://mydomain.com/db.dll?read?table=mytable
```

Obviously, only the second version would work. The solution is always to use the **POST** method when submitting information from a form. This is a good practice anyway, because the **GET** method has a limit on the MSIIS of 1024 characters, which would preclude many longer forms. Unfortunately, there are many cases where one simply can't use the **POST** method (e.g. linking an imagemap to different ISAPI extensions). In these cases, you'll have to use **GET**, and then use some other way of passing the command to the extension (like a parameter of **command=read**).

How does all of this relate to the MFC? Well, we'll come to that just as soon as we have a project to play around with. Let's get on with it!

# Looking at the Code

To start with, create a new project and select the ISAPI Extension Wizard. If you want your source code to match up with the samples here, you'll need to use the name **MFCRedir**. Simply accept all the defaults (e.g. Generate a Server Extension, MFC as a shared DLL) and click Finish.

## MFCRedir.h

The functions are prototyped in the **MFCRedir.h** file shown below. For simple extension requests such as this one, there is very little that needs to be changed here.

```
// MFCREDIR.H - Implementation file for your Internet Server
//    MFCRedir Extension

class CMFCRedirExtension: public CHttpServer
{
public:
    CMFCRedirExtension();
    ~CMFCRedirExtension();

    BOOL GetExtensionVersion(HSE_VERSION_INFO* pVer);

    // TODO: Add handlers for your commands here.
    // For example:

    void Default(CHttpServerContext* pCtxt);

    DECLARE_PARSE_MAP()
};
```

There isn't a lot happening in the header, just the usual definitions that we normally see. The only point of interest is the **DECLARE_PARSE_MAP()** command. This is used in much the same way that **DECLARE_MESSAGE_MAP()** is used in other MFC classes. It adds the functions required to access the parse map into the class definition, as well as the parse map itself. We'll show how the parse map is generated in a moment.

## *MFCRedir.cpp*

If you are familiar with CGI programming, you are used to getting the query string as a single entity from either the **QUERY_STRING** environment variable or the command line, depending on whether the request was a **GET** or **POST** type, respectively. It was then up to you to decode the string, extracting the information that you needed all by yourself. With MFC, this is no longer the case. The parse map macros are there to do all the hard work for us, extracting the command, if present, and even assigning parameters to variables. All of this requires the correct use of the macros, so let's start by having a look at the source code generated for us:

```
// MFCREDIR.CPP - Implementation file for your Internet Server
//    MFCRedir Extension

#include "stdafx.h"
#include "MFCRedir.h"

/////////////////////////////////////////////////////////////////////
// The one and only CWinApp object
// NOTE: You may remove this object if you alter your project to no
// longer use MFC in a DLL.

CWinApp theApp;

/////////////////////////////////////////////////////////////////////
// command-parsing map

BEGIN_PARSE_MAP(CMFCRedirExtension, CHttpServer)
   // TODO: insert your ON_PARSE_COMMAND() and
   // ON_PARSE_COMMAND_PARAMS() here to hook up your commands.
   // For example:

   ON_PARSE_COMMAND(Default, CMFCRedirExtension, ITS_EMPTY)
   DEFAULT_PARSE_COMMAND(Default, CMFCRedirExtension)
END_PARSE_MAP(CMFCRedirExtension)

/////////////////////////////////////////////////////////////////////
// The one and only CMFCRedirExtension object

CMFCRedirExtension theExtension;

/////////////////////////////////////////////////////////////////////
// CMFCRedirExtension implementation

CMFCRedirExtension::CMFCRedirExtension()
{
}

CMFCRedirExtension::~CMFCRedirExtension()
{
}

BOOL CMFCRedirExtension::GetExtensionVersion(HSE_VERSION_INFO* pVer)
{
   // Call default implementation for initialization
   CHttpServer::GetExtensionVersion(pVer);

   // Load description string
```

```
    TCHAR sz[HSE_MAX_EXT_DLL_NAME_LEN+1];
    ISAPIVERIFY(::LoadString(AfxGetResourceHandle(), IDS_SERVER, sz,
                                        HSE_MAX_EXT_DLL_NAME_LEN));
    _tcscpy(pVer->lpszExtensionDesc, sz);
    return TRUE;
}


///////////////////////////////////////////////////////////////////////
// CMFCRedirExtension command handlers

void CMFCRedirExtension::Default(CHttpServerContext* pCtxt)
{
    StartContent(pCtxt);
    WriteTitle(pCtxt);

    *pCtxt << _T("This default message was produced by the Internet");
    *pCtxt << _T("Server DLL Wizard. Edit your CMFCRedirExtension::Default()");
    *pCtxt << _T(" implementation to change it.\r\n");

    EndContent(pCtxt);
}


// Do not edit the following lines, which are needed by ClassWizard.
#if 0
BEGIN_MESSAGE_MAP(CMFCRedirExtension, CHttpServer)
    //{{AFX_MSG_MAP(CMFCRedirExtension)
    //}}AFX_MSG_MAP
END_MESSAGE_MAP()
#endif    // 0


///////////////////////////////////////////////////////////////////////
// If your extension will not use MFC, you'll need this code to make
// sure the extension objects can find the resource handle for the
// module.  If you convert your extension to not be dependent on MFC,
// remove the comments arounn the following AfxGetResourceHandle()
// and DllMain() functions, as well as the g_hInstance global.

/****

static HINSTANCE g_hInstance;

HINSTANCE AFXISAPI AfxGetResourceHandle()
{
    return g_hInstance;
}

BOOL WINAPI DllMain(HINSTANCE hInst, ULONG ulReason, LPVOID lpReserved)
{
    if (ulReason == DLL_PROCESS_ATTACH)
    {
        g_hInstance = hInst;
    }

    return TRUE;
}

****/
```

At this time, you should be able to build and run the ISAPI extension which the AppWizard constructed for you. To do so, simply build the project and move the **MFCRedir.dll** into your server's scripts directory. Open up your favorite Internet browser and call **http://yourserver.com/scripts/ MFCRedir.dll**. You should get a response that reads:

This default message was produced by the Internet Server DLL Wizard. Edit your CMFCRedirExtension::Default() implementation to change it.

> *If you have trouble executing this script, you should read the sections 'Building and Testing the MFCRedir Extension' and 'Common Problems' at the end of this chapter.*

## CWinApp

When you take a look at the code generated for you, you'll notice a **CWinApp** object being created. Don't worry about this: your extensions won't be opening up a window! The reason this is included is that MFC needs a Windows object for a lot of its functions to work. You should only remove the **CWinApp** instantiation if you're not using *any* MFC code.

## The Parse Map

The parse map is a method that MFC uses to allow different functions inside the same DLL to be called as ISAPI extensions. It also provides a method for taking HTML form variables and passing them as parameters to the function being called.

The next step in using parse maps is to understand their syntax. The parse map macro consists of the following functions: **BEGIN_PARSE_MAP**, **ON_PARSE_COMMAND**, **ON_PARSE_COMMAND_PARAMS**, **DEFAULT_PARSE_COMMAND**, and **END_PARSE_MAP**.

### BEGIN_ and END_PARSE_MAP

**BEGIN_PARSE_MAP** naturally signals the beginning of the macro. It takes as its parameters the class that will have its functions mapped, and the parent of that class. The parent class must be **CHttpServer**, or a class derived from it.

**END_PARSE_MAP** takes as its only parameter the same class that was declared to be mapped in **BEGIN_PARSE_MAP**.

### ON_PARSE_COMMAND

**ON_PARSE_COMMAND** takes as its parameters the name of the function that will be called, the class of which the function is a member, and any parameters that will be passed to the function from the parameters section of the parse map string. The spelling of the function name must be the same as in the command portion of the parse map string. Also, the number of parameters must match exactly, or you must specify defaults. Defaults and other parse map topics will be covered in the next chapter.

**ON_PARSE_COMMAND** expects you to declare what type of parameters will be passed. Acceptable types shown on the next page:

| Type Macro | Meaning |
|------------|---------|
| ITS_LPSTR | A pointer to a string |
| ITS_I2 | A short |
| ITS_I4 | A long |
| ITS_R4 | A float |
| ITS_R8 | A double |
| ITS_EMPTY | You will pass no arguments at all |

In **MFCRedir**, we need to pass one value: the destination we wish to go to. Naturally, this is passed as a string. You should edit your parse map in **MFCRedir.cpp** to look like this:

```
BEGIN_PARSE_MAP(CMFCReDirExtension, CHttpServer)
    ON_PARSE_COMMAND(Default, CMFCReDirExtension, ITS_LPSTR)
DEFAULT_PARSE_COMMAND(Default, CMFCReDirExtension)
END_PARSE_MAP(CMFCReDirExtension)
```

Here we define the **Default()** command that is a member of **CMFCReDirExtension** and takes one string buffer as an additional parameter. Note that this is an *additional* parameter; all functions called by the parse map must have as their *first* parameter a pointer to the **CHttpServerContext** class, for reasons we'll get to in just a moment.

## CHttpServer::GetExtensionVersion

The **GetExtensionVersion()** member is defined as follows:

```
BOOL CMFCRedirExtension::GetExtensionVersion(HSE_VERSION_INFO* pVer)
{
    // Call default implementation for initialization
    CHttpServer::GetExtensionVersion(pVer);

    // Load description string
    TCHAR sz[HSE_MAX_EXT_DLL_NAME_LEN+1];
    ISAPIVERIFY(::LoadString(AfxGetResourceHandle(), IDS_SERVER, sz,
                                            HSE_MAX_EXT_DLL_NAME_LEN));
    _tcscpy(pVer->lpszExtensionDesc, sz);
    return TRUE;
}
```

This function simply provides the server with information about our extension. There is rarely any need to change it.

## CHttpServer::Default

The **Default()** member is one of the more important functions in the class. The AppWizard generates the following code for us:

```
void CMFCRedirExtension::Default(CHttpServerContext* pCtxt)
{
    StartContent(pCtxt);
    WriteTitle(pCtxt);
```

```
    *pCtxt << _T("This default message was produced by the Internet");
    *pCtxt << _T(" Server DLL Wizard. Edit your CMFCRedirExtension::Default()");
    *pCtxt << _T(" implementation to change it.\r\n");

    EndContent(pCtxt);
}
```

Here we should note several features about the **Default()** function implementation. First of all, it takes a pointer to a **CHttpServerContext** object as its only parameter. All MFC ISAPI extensions will have this parameter at least, though most will have more; we'll be changing the definition to allow more parameters when we write our own extensions. The **CHttpServerContext** class is this function's link back to the web server, and thus back to the client. All reading from and writing to the client must be done though the **CHttpServerContext** object. As you will see, this **CHttpServerContext** object will follow us everywhere we go in MFC ISAPI.

If you're a CGI programmer, you may be wondering why we need this object around. When you write out to the client in a simple batch CGI script, you can simply use '**echo "hello web world."**' Why can't MFC simply make us an **echo()** or **print()** function that writes to the client?

Remember, ISAPI is multithreaded. The reason for the **CHttpServerContext** object is to uniquely identify our output to the web server. At any one time, multiple threads could be calling the same write function. How then does the web server know which output was supposed to go to which client? The answer is that the web server creates the ECB discussed in the previous chapter and passes it to each request. MFC encapsulates the ECB inside a **CHttpServerContext** object and passes you a pointer to it. Thus, you must pass it to any function that wishes to read from or write to the client.

The second point to note is that the code is telling us to make changes here. Most of the time, this is where you would place the functionality of your extension, as this is the function called when there are no commands in the query string.

> Obviously, **Default()** would no longer be the default command if you were to modify the **DEFAULT_PARSE_COMMAND** entry in the parse map.

If you use commands, you should place code here that will handle the situation when the browser fails to send the command part on submitting a form (as we have shown to be the case above); for example, telling the user to update their browser to the latest version. A more serious solution would be to parse the parameters to deduce which command is being attempted, and then make the appropriate call. What you actually do in the **Default()** function is dependent on what your extension does.

## CHttpServer::StartContent

This first thing the **Default()** function does is make a call to **StartContent(pCtxt)**. Since **CHttpServer::StartContent()** writes data to the client, it passes a pointer to the **CHttpServerContext** object that was created to handle this request. In most CGI/ISAPI programs, the first thing you need to do is tell the client the type of data that your program will be returning. To do this, you need to write **Content-Type: text/html\r\n** into the headers that are going to be sent back to the client, which is exactly what **CHttpServer::StartContent()** does. If you look at the MFC source code, you will see that it is identical to **AddHeaders(pCtxt, "Content-Type: text/html\r\n");**

## The Stream

While we will cover the **CHttpServerContext** class in much more detail as we progress, what we want to touch on here is how the **CHtmlStream** class relates to it. Although **CHtmlStream** pretty much stays hidden from the programmer, it handles most standard output to the client.

Unlike the **CHttpServerContext::WriteClient()** member function, **CHtmlStream** does not write data to the client immediately. Instead, when you input data into **CHtmlStream**, it places it into an in-memory buffer. The class does the dirty work of allocating memory as you write into it. When your extension is finished, **CHttpServerContext** (using **CHttpServerContext::WriteClient()**) will write out anything that is held inside its **CHtmlStream** object, and **CHtmlStream** will free up any memory that was allocated for the stream. You don't need to know the exact mechanics of **CHtmlStream**, but you will use it quite frequently in the form of the overloaded operator **<<**. The **<<** operator is overridden by **CHttpServerContext** so that it sends any string output into the HTML stream, much like the way the familiar **<<** operator does for **cout**.

*There is no **>>** operator.*

Thus, the line

```
*pCtxt << _T("This default message was produced by the Internet");
```

writes This default message was produced by the Internet into the stream. When the extension finishes, it will be sent back to the client.

### Unicode

Don't be confused by the **_T()** macro: it's used for Unicode programming. Unicode is a character set in which each single character is represented by a 16-bit value, as opposed to the standard 8-bit value that you are, no doubt, familiar with. By allocating 16 bits to each character, the Unicode character set can represent 65536 different characters. This large character set greatly facilitates programming for an international market, in that it can represent any character in any language.

If you have **_UNICODE** defined, the **_T()** macro will convert the enclosed string to a Unicode string. If **_UNICODE** is not defined, the **_T()** macro does nothing and you could just as easily have left it off.

In ISAPI programming, there is a paradox when it comes to Unicode. The MFC classes for ISAPI programming do not support Unicode (as of version 4.2, at least), but all Win32 API calls require that their string parameters be in Unicode. This does not mean that you can't call Win32 API functions from inside your ISAPI extensions, it's just that when you do call them with an ANSI (8-bit) string, NT first converts the string to Unicode and then calls the API function. When an API call returns a string value, NT first converts it from Unicode and then returns the value. While this extra layer of converting back and forth between ANSI and Unicode is totally transparent to the programmer, it does still take a little time and memory.

> As of MFC 4.2, if you do have **_UNICODE** defined, you will see an **ERROR: ISAPI does not yet support Unicode** message from the compiler.

In other words, the **_T("")** macro currently does absolutely nothing and whether or not you use it is entirely up to you. However, you should start getting into the practice of using Unicode in all your programs, as that is clearly the direction in which NT programming is headed.

## Additional HTML Functions

The **WriteTitle()** and **EndContent()** functions write HTML tags into the stream so that they will be sent to the client. These functions do nothing that could not be done using the **CHtmlStream** << operator and are provided by MFC only for convenience. Using only the << operator we can rewrite the following code:

```
WriteTitle(pCtxt);
*pCtxt << _T("This default message was produced by the Internet");
*pCtxt << _T(" Server DLL Wizard. Edit your CMFCRedirExtension::Default()");
*pCtxt << _T(" implementation to change it.\r\n");
EndContent(pCtxt);
```

to read:

```
*pCtxt << _T("<html><head>");
*pCtxt << _T("<title> Default MFC Web Server Extension</title></head><body>");
*pCtxt << _T("This default message was produced by the Internet");
*pCtxt << _T(" Server DLL Wizard. Edit your CMFCRedirExtension::Default()");
*pCtxt << _T(" implementation to change it.\r\n");
*pCtxt << _T("</body></html>");
```

If you want to supply a different title than Default MFC Web Server Extension, you can override the **CHttpServer::GetTitle()** so that it returns a different string. Personally, I find it easier just to write the **<title>My Title</title>** using the << operator. In fact, the << operator should be the preferred method, as you may have several functions inside the same DLL, and each one might want to write out a different title. This would be impossible using the MFC **WriteTitle()** function, as **GetTitle()** could only be overridden once.

## Removing MFC Support

In the AppWizard-generated code, you probably noticed a large section of commented-out code that has instructions about making an non-MFC extension. Most of the time you'll want to use MFC, so there is no need to work with this section, and it can safely be deleted. If you do wish to remove MFC support from your application, it is probably better just to start from scratch, as the AppWizard puts in far too much MFC-specific code. Instead of hacking through the AppWizard code to try to strip out any references to MFC, you can simply use the following 'template' to create non-MFC based extensions:

```
#include <httpext.h>

BOOL WINAPI DllMain(HMODULE hMod, DWORD fReason, LPVOID pvRes)
{
   switch (fReason) {
   case DLL_PROCESS_ATTACH:
      break;

   case DLL_THREAD_ATTACH:
      break;

   case DLL_PROCESS_DETACH:
      break;

   case DLL_THREAD_DETACH:
      break;
   }
```

```
    return TRUE;
}


BOOL WINAPI GetExtensionVersion(HSE_VERSION_INFO *pVer)
{
    pVer->dwExtensionVersion = 1;

    strncpy(pVer->lpszExtensionDesc, "Your description here",
                                     HSE_MAX_EXT_DLL_NAME_LEN);
    return TRUE;
}


DWORD WINAPI HttpExtensionProc(EXTENSION_CONTROL_BLOCK *pECB)
{
    // Your custom code here.
    return HSE_STATUS_SUCCESS;
}
```

# Adding the Redirection Functionality

Now we'll deal with the changes to the definition of the `Default()` function we mentioned a little while ago. First, edit the `CMFCRedirExtension::Default()` prototype in the `MFCRedir.h` file so that it looks like this:

```
void Default(CHttpServerContext* pCtxt, LPCTSTR pstrParameter);
```

Next, edit the implementation of `CMFCRedirExtension::Default()` so that it looks like this:

```
void CMFCRedirExtension::Default(CHttpServerContext* pCtxt, LPCTSTR pstrParameter)
{
    // The GET method has a limit of 1024 bytes

    TCHAR* pszDestination;

    pszDestination = strstr(pstrParameter,"=");


    if (pszDestination!=NULL)
    {
        // Skip the = sign;
        pszDestination++;
        pCtxt->ServerSupportFunction(HSE_REQ_SEND_URL_REDIRECT_RESP,
                              pszDestination, NULL, NULL);
    }
    else
    {
        StartContent(pCtxt);
        WriteTitle(pCtxt);
        *pCtxt << _T("No url pair (name=value) specified");
        EndContent(pCtxt);
    }
}
```

Let's take a look at what this function does. First, it finds the equals sign in the parameter, which should look something like **dest=http://www.microsoft.com** or **dest=/default.htm**. We are not interested in anything to the left of the equals sign; we could have used any name for the form variable, and the parse map would pass it as the parameter. For example, if we replace the line of hypertext

```
<select name="dest">
```

with

```
<select name="different">
```

then, rather than getting **dest=http://www.microsoft.com**, we would be passed **different=http://www.microsoft.com**. We will see in the next chapter how to use parse maps for specific named variables.

If the parameter does not contain an **=**, something must be wrong, and we output an error using the familiar functions.

## CHttpServer::ServerSupportFunction

Once we have the destination that the user wants to go to, we make a call to the server to ask it to redirect the client for us. The actual redirection is done by **CHttpServerContext::ServerSupportFunction()**, which is prototyped as:

```
BOOL ServerSupportFunction(DWORD dwHSERRequest,
                           LPVOID lpvBuffer,
                           LPDWORD lpdwSize,
                           LPDWORD lpdwDataType);
```

You will notice that this **ServerSupportFunction()** is a simple wrapper for the ECB's **ServerSupportFunction()** described in the previous chapter. We pass **HSE_REQ_SEND_URL_REDIRECT_RESP** to ask the server to issue a redirect for us. We also pass the destination we want the client redirected to. Since we are not going to be reading anything back from the client, and **lpvBuffer** must be a null-terminated string when calling **HSE_REQ_SEND_URL_REDIRECT_RESP**, we can send **NULL** for **lpwdSize**. Similarly, since **lpwdDataType** is only used with **HSE_REQ_SEND_RESPONSE_HEADER**, we pass **NULL** for **lpdwDataType**. The server support function then writes a header to the client that contains **Location: http://your.redirect.domain.here.com**. When the client browser sees this, it requests the appropriate document. The actual header and body that the server writes back to the client is:

```
HTTP/1.0 302 Object moved
Location: http://www.microsoft.com
Server:  Microsoft-Internet-Information-Server/1.0
MIME-version: 1.0
Context-Type: text/html
Content-Length: 152

<head><title>Document moved</title></head>
<body><h1>Object Moved</h1>This document may be found
                  <a href="http://www.microsoft.com">here</a></body>
```

What usually happens, of course, is that your browser picks up the **302** in the header and automatically jumps to the URL specified in the **Location:** header. You'll only see this body if your browser doesn't support redirection.

# Building and Testing MFCRedir

We are now ready to build our first real ISAPI Extension. To do this, simply build the project and move the **MFCRedir.dll** into your **scripts\ProfISAPI** directory. (We'll put it in a subdirectory to avoid cluttering.) Create a document called **ReDirTest.html** in your web server's root directory (**wwwroot** by default) that reads:

```
<html><head></head>
<body>
<form action="/scripts/profisapi/MFCRedir.dll" method="GET">
<select name="dest">
<option value="/default.htm">Default Home Page
<option value="http://www.microsoft.com">Microsoft
<option value="http://home.netscape.com">Netscape
</select>
<input type="SUBMIT" value="GO!">
</form>
</body>
</html>
```

From your browser, load **http://your.domain.here.com/ReDirTest.html**. If all goes well, clicking on the GO! button will take you elsewhere. In case of errors, make sure the DLL is in a directory with executable permissions and that the anonymous HTTP user (i.e. **IUSR_YOURMACHINE**) has rights to execute the DLL.

# Debugging an ISAPI Extension

Hopefully, this example compiled and ran the first time through. You will probably not always be so lucky. There are several options available to you when debugging an ISAPI extension–which you choose depends on what software you have and on the type of extension you are developing. The options available are:

▲ Debug interactively on your development machine. This requires you to be running NT Server on the machine you are developing on. This is the best 'real world' environment to debug in. Unfortunately, since the browser does not show you any headers, if you are developing an application that manipulates headers, you'll be in the dark.

▲ Debug remotely from another workstation. This allows the NT Server to be running on a different machine from the one you're developing on. This is essentially the same as the above option, except that it is a little harder to set up. Also, note that only one person can be debugging remotely at one time.

▲ Use the Wrox ISAPI Debugger (see Appendix A, or download it from the Wrox Press web site). This is a fast way to debug in any environment. It shows all headers, and lets you check your DLL's loading and unloading procedures easily. The problem is that it's not a real web server and so doesn't have 100% of the functionality. You should always test your extension in a real environment before you finally deploy it.

# Interactive Debugging on Your Development Machine

To start with, you will need to give yourself rights to act as part of the operating system, and generate security audits. To do this, open the User Manager for Domains program. Select Policies | User Rights. Check Show Advanced User Rights. From the drop-down menu, select Act as part of the operating system and then click Add.... Add the users or group you want to be able to debug and select Add. Repeat this procedure for Generate security audits as well. Remember, you must log off and log back on for these changes to take effect.

Stop all Internet Services from running, including gopher and ftp. To do this, use the Internet Service Manager. If you are doing frequent debugging, you may want to switch the services to Manual startup, so that you don't have to stop them each time.

In the Visual C++ IDE, with the project open, select Build | Settings..., then switch to the Debug tab and make sure the General category is selected. Enter the path to your Internet server executable in the Executable for debug session field. In most cases, this will be `c:\Inetsrv\Server\Inetinfo.exe` if you have MSIIS version 1.0. If you have NT 4.0, it will probably be installed in `c:\Winnt\System32\Inetsrv\Server\Inetinfo.exe`. Enter -e w3svc in the Program arguments field.

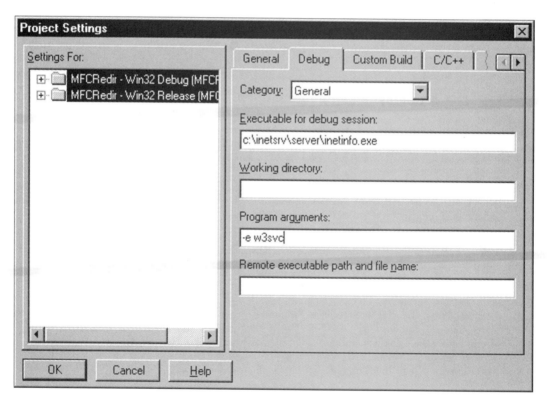

Select the Link tab and enter the path where you want your finished DLL to be run from in the Output file name field. This should be something like `c:\inetsrv\scripts\mfcredir.dll`.

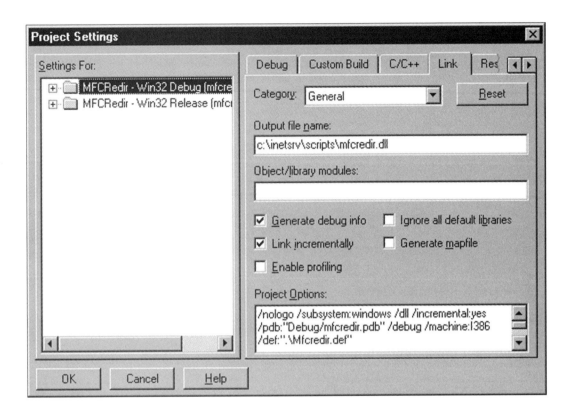

In order to prevent the server from caching the DLLs, you need to set the `HKEY_LOCAL_MACHINE\SYSTEM\CurrentControlSet\Services\W3SVC\Parameters\` `CacheExtensions` registry entry. Change the **DWORD** value to **0** so that the server will unload each DLL after each call. This will allow you to debug any clean-up code that you put in the destructors for your classes. We don't have any in this example, but we will later. Note that you should use this option only for testing/debugging, as it will greatly degrade performance. You should also test with the value set on (i.e. **1**) to make sure that your DLL doesn't require it to be reset after every call.

Now that you have it set up to debug, simply select *F5* to start a debugging session. (Be sure to set any breakpoints you might want.) Once the program is compiled and waiting, switch to your favorite browser and call your ISAPI DLL as normal. Once you call it, have some patience: it takes a couple of seconds for it to get going. If all goes well, the debugger should pop up at your first break point and let you start debugging.

> Once you get used to this type of interactive debugging, you will notice that it takes a while to start up each time. This is because NT has to initialize all of its sockets routines. If, when you're not debugging, you have other Internet services running (such as ftp or gopher), the web server will start up much faster.
>
> The web server itself must always be shut down before you start to debug using this method.

# Remote Debugging of an ISAPI Extension

In the event that you don't have NT Server running on your development machine, you can still interactively debug your application using the following technique.

> *In this example, we will call the machine running NT Server the **server** and the one running Windows 95 or NT workstation the **workstation**. I'm also assuming the following configuration:*
>
> *The server has the MSIIS set up in `c:\Inetsrv`; the actual IIS executable is at `c:\inetsrv\server\inetinfo.exe`, and the scripts directory is `c:\inetsrv\scripts`.*
>
> *The workstation has mapped a network drive `x:` to `\\SERVER\C`.*

On the server, set up the user account described in local debugging (i.e. a user with rights to act as part of the operating system and generate security audits). This user must be the one logged on to the server while debugging is taking place.

If the server does not already have them on it, you need to copy the following files from the workstation to the server: **Msvcmon.exe, Msvcrt40.dll, Tln0com.dll, Tln0t.dll, Dmn0.dll**. These will be in the **Msdev\Bin** and **System32** directories.

You should create a directory on the server and place all the files listed above into it, except for **Msvcrt40.dll** which should be placed in the server's **System32** directory. As with local debugging, you should make sure that all IIS services on the server are shut down. You should also make sure that DLL caching is turned off, as mentioned above. When the server is ready, run **Msvcmon.exe** on the server. For the settings, select Network (TCP/IP), then Settings. Enter the workstation's IP address or hostname in the appropriate box (the hostname must be a valid DNS entry, not simply the Windows name for the computer); you may also optionally specify a password. Click OK, then Connect. The server is now configured and waiting to start the debug process.

On the workstation, you will need to load up the project you want to debug in Visual C++. Select Tools | Remote Connection. Make sure Win32 is selected, then select Network(TCP/IP) and click Settings. Enter the server's IP address or hostname in the appropriate box, as well as any password you entered on the server. Once this is done, select Build | Settings. Select the Debug tab, and make sure you are in the General category. Fill in the boxes as follows:

Executable for debug session:                  **x:\Inetsrv\Server\Inetinfo.exe**
(The location of the MSIIS relative to the workstation)

Working directory:                             (Leave blank)

Program arguments:                             **-e w3svc**

Remote executable path and file name:          **c:\Inetsrv\Server\Inetinfo.exe**
(The location of the MSIIS relative to the server)

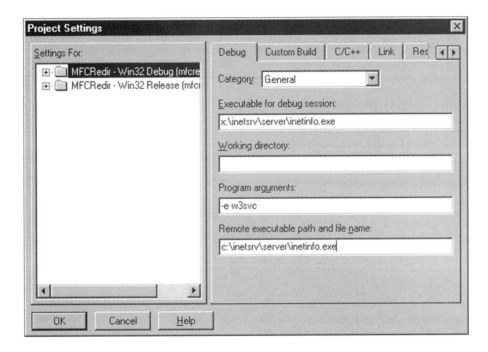

Once these options are set, select the Additional DLLs option from the Category box. Click inside the Local Name box, and type the location of the DLL extension relative to the workstation. In this case, it will be **x:\Inetsrv\Scripts\MFCRedir.dll**. Then click in the Remote Name box, and type the location of the DLL relative to the server, in this case, **c:\Inetsrv\Scripts\MFCRedir.dll**. Lastly, make sure the Try to locate other DLLs box is *not* checked.

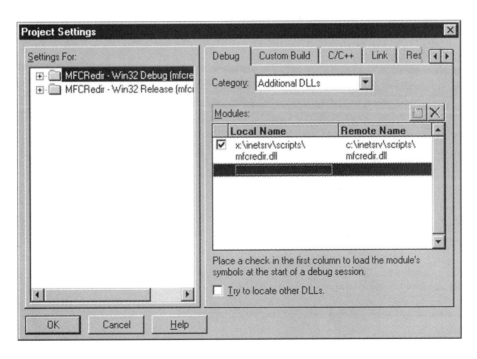

Now, scroll over to the Link tab on the Project Settings and make sure the General category is selected. Change the Output file name to be the path of the DLL relative to the workstation (**x:\Inetsrv\Scripts\MFCRedir.dll**). This way you don't have to copy the file over after each rebuild. Set any breakpoints you wish to evaluate, and build and debug the application as normal.

# The Wrox ISAPI Debugger

To help with your debugging, I have included an ISAPI debugger on the Wrox Press web site. The source code and a brief discussion are in Appendix A. Once you are familiar with ISAPI programming, it will be well worth your time to look over the code for the debugger, as it will give you a better idea of exactly how ISAPI works.

To use the debugger, you need to copy it to the computer you are developing on. I am assuming that since you are developing on the machine, you will have all the MFC and run-time libraries that you need. You should note that this debugger was written using MFC 4.2, and will not work with ISAPI extensions written with previous versions. If Microsoft releases a new MFC library that is not compatible with 4.2, you will need to recompile the debugger if you want it to work with your new non-4.2 compatible ISAPI extensions.

The debugger works using the principle that everything is passed to it on the command line. The first parameter the debugger expects is the location of the DLL you wish to debug. After that, you can pass to it any HTTP variable and its value in the form **HTTP_VARIABLE: <value>.** All the HTTP variables use their actual names (as given in the previous chapter). Thus, to set the **QUERY_STRING** to **variable1=test&variable2=this+is+variable2**, you would pass

**QUERY_STRING:variable1=test&variable2=this+is+variable2**

on the command line. If you set **METHOD:POST**, the **QUERY_STRING** would be passed to **lpbData**, the **cbTotalBytes** and **cbAvailable** variables would be set to the length of **QUERY_STRING**, and **lpszQueryString** would be set to **NULL** just as if your DLL were called with a **POST** method.

The reason for passing everything on the command line is that the debugger allows you the option of setting what will be passed. This way, you won't need to retype in all the parameters you need to set each time. For example, let us say that we want to use the Wrox ISAPI debugger for the example we completed earlier in this chapter. I will assume that you have the debugger installed at **c:\Wrox\Isapi\Debugger\Isapidebug.exe** and that your DLL is being written to **c:\Inetsrv\Scripts\Mfcredir.dll**. We want to call the DLL using the **POST** method and pass it the **QUERY_STRING** of **destination=http://www.microsoft.com**. To do this, set your Executable for debug session parameter to **c:\Wrox\Isapi\Debugger\Isapidebug.exe** and your Program arguments parameter to **c:\Inetsrv\Scripts\Mfcredir.dll QUERY_STRING:destination=http://www.microsoft.com METHOD:POST**, as seen on the following page.

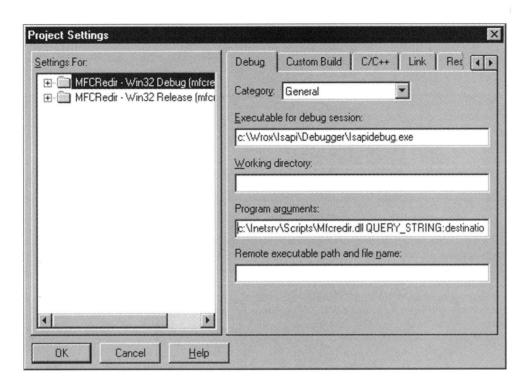

As soon as you start the debugger, the Wrox ISAPI debugger should open up and look like this:

You will notice that it placed all the information you entered into the debugger into the appropriate boxes. You can edit the DLL, Method, PathInfo, and Query entries. All others are read-only and can be set only by passing the appropriate HTTP variable on the command line. Also, just because the HTTP variable is not shown does not mean that you can't use it. There are just too many HTTP variables to fit on the screen, so I used only some of the more common ones. However, if you pass **SERVER_TYPE:My+Custom+Server+v1.001**, it will pass this along to the DLL. (Note: you must use the **+** (plus) sign instead of a space.)

To use the Wrox ISAPI debugger, first click the DLL Loaded box. This will load your DLL, or give you an error. Once the DLL is loaded, click Submit to send the request to the DLL; the output will appear in the Response box. If you want to debug the unloading of the DLL, simply click the DLL Loaded checkbox again. Clicking Quit also unloads the DLL before the program exits.

## Common Problems

While this book assumes that you know how to set up and configure the MSIIS, there are a few things that commonly go wrong when trying to run ISAPI extensions. Below are some common error messages and their solutions.

| Message | Solution |
| --- | --- |
| HTTP/1.0 500 Server Error (The specified module could not be found.) | Make sure that the DLL is copied into your **Scripts** directory. If you didn't tell the linker to write it into your **Scripts** directory, you will have to move it by hand after each rebuild. |
| HTTP/1.0 403 Access Forbidden (Execute Access Denied - This Virtual Directory does not allow objects to be executed.) | Make sure that your **Scripts** directory has execute permissions set. This would be configured in the Microsoft Internet Service Manager. |
| Error: Access is Denied. (After it asks for a username and password) | Check that the file has execute permissions for the web server account. |

# Summary

MFC and the AppWizard let us write a functioning ISAPI extension with very little code. The key features are in the **CHttpServerContext** and **CHtmlStream** classes, and the parse map macros. The **CHttpServerContext** class provides the actual interface to the web server, and the **CHtmlStream** lets us easily direct text output to the client by use of the familiar **<<** operator. The parse map macros take the data sent over by the client via either the **GET** or **POST** method, parse it for you, and pass the resulting form variables as parameters to the appropriate function.

Once we have built an ISAPI extension, there are three methods of debugging it. First, you can interactively debug from the same machine on which you're developing. If you don't have NT Server as a development machine, you can debug remotely. Alternatively, you can use the Wrox ISAPI debugger to debug on a machine that doesn't have NT Server or access to a working web server.

# Accessing Databases

The CGI or ISAPI programs that you are most likely to come across on the Internet are those that link client browsers to server databases. Whether it's a major search engine's index of millions of web pages or simply a list of outlets for a local retailer, if you have data in a database, you need a way to put it on the Internet.

In my introduction, I touted ISAPI as being the next evolutionary step above CGI. Hopefully, I was not so convincing that you threw out all your CGI programming books because, as we'll see, ISAPI database programming isn't for everyone. The problems associated with ISAPI programming arise with thread safety and we will address these first before we get into the actual how-to of writing ISAPI extensions that use databases.

Once we've covered the basics of database access, we'll introduce several topics dealing with thread synchronization and we'll use these to create the **CDataPool** class that will help us manage our ISAPI database connections. Even if you don't plan to write a database extension, you should still cover the thread synchronization material as it's essential ISAPI programming and you'll come across it again, later in the book.

## ODBC, COM, and DAO

When an ISAPI extension is running, it must share resources with the parent process (the ISAPI server itself) and other ISAPI extensions running in other threads. The problem here is that many database access methods rely on public resources for their implementation. For example, let us say that one thread opens a DAO database and executes a query. While this query is executing, another person 'hits' the site with a similar query. When your ISAPI extension initializes your DAO object, it will erase the previous DAO object, and the first user's query will be lost. Unfortunately, the problem isn't just limited to DAO. You will encounter similar problems with any data access method that uses COM (Component Object Model). See Microsoft's TN067 document for an official description of the difficulties. As noted by Microsoft, the solution to the problem is not to use DAO in an ISAPI extension, but to implement a thread-safe ODBC driver (almost all drivers for client-server databases such as Oracle and Microsoft's SQL Server are thread-safe). Thread-safe ODBC drivers are being developed continually, and if one is available for the type of database you wish to access then this solves half of your problem.

> *A more experienced Win32 programmer might be wondering if we could solve the problem simply by synchronizing threads so that only one thread would have a DAO object or non-thread-safe ODBC driver open at one time. While this is possible, it is also (in my opinion) undesirable. If we synchronize the threads, we can have at most one person querying the database at one time. If you're running a small database application where it's reasonable to expect that you will rarely have more than one person accessing the database at one time, this obviates the need for the improved performance and scalability of ISAPI. Also, all ISAPI programs must use the same method for synchronization. This would severely limit the compatibility of your ISAPI extension with others.*

The other half of the problem is that ODBC also uses some public resources in its initialization. The specifics are that one application should have, at most, one ODBC environment allocated to it. Since the web server is the only application we're running (all our extensions are simply threads), all ISAPI extensions must use the same ODBC environment. Fortunately, MFC takes care of all this for us, as we will see shortly.

## Alternatives to ISAPI

If you really must have access through DAO, or if no-one makes a thread-safe ODBC driver for the type of database you wish to access, you still have several alternatives at your disposal. The first is, as mentioned above, to synchronize all your threads so that no more than one can be accessing the database at any one time. However, as I've already noted, most programmers should not take this approach. The second option is to use traditional CGI programming or an ISAPI-to-CGI interface which runs a separate process for each request. Yet another alternative is to use an ISAPI extension to call an out-of-process OLE server. You can create such out-of-process OLE servers with Visual Basic—they make an excellent interface to Microsoft Access databases. Lastly, you can create a separate service to handle all your database requests. This is the method used by programs such as dbWeb, but it's beyond the scope of this book.

If, however, you are looking for a high-performance database solution capable of scaling itself well under a large number of simultaneous queries, then ISAPI is what you're looking for. Now, with all that behind us, let's see how easy it is to actually write an ISAPI extension with database access.

## The User Database

In this example, we'll start to develop a user database application which will demonstrate both reading from and writing to a database. This sample is meant to be coupled with an ISAPI filter that we will develop in the second part of the book. When you have completed both this sample and the complementing filter sample, you will have a site that requires users to register before they can gain access to specific sections that you designate as protected. We're also including a way to display the contents of the database. While you will probably not implement this reading function on a real site, it's being used here to illustrate how to read data from a database and display it on the Internet.

The sample database included on the Wrox web site for this application is in Microsoft Visual FoxPro format because the current version of the Visual FoxPro ODBC drivers are thread-safe and can be downloaded from Microsoft's web site. If you have an older version of the FoxPro ODBC driver, it should still work with this application, but it will not be thread-safe and should only be used for development (consequently you will need to create your own FoxPro table, however, as the one on the Wrox web site works only with Visual FoxPro). In order to develop this application using the ClassWizard to handle your database classes, you will need to set up the proper ODBC System Data Source Name (DSN) before you begin.

> *In a live web site situation, you would probably prefer to use SQL Server rather than Visual FoxPro as your database. This is fine; you can change the DSN entry to use SQL Server and point it to your database. Provided the table names and fields are the same, you won't even have to recompile the extension. This is one of the advantages of using ODBC.*

# Configuring ODBC

If you haven't done so already, you should download the Visual FoxPro drivers from Microsoft's site and install them. (To find the drivers on Microsoft's site, go to **http://www.microsoft.com/kb** to search the Knowledge Base. Select the Download a Driver, Patch or Sample File image, then select Microsoft Visual FoxPro as the category, and find the Visual FoxPro ODBC driver in the resulting list.) Once you've installed the drivers, you'll need to configure a System DSN for the Internet server to access it. You can't use the normal User Data Sources for the MSIIS as these are user-specific.

From the ODBC administrator, click System DSN... then Add.... Select the Microsoft Visual FoxPro driver from the list. The data source name should be **WroxData**, and you can type in a brief description if you like. For the path, type in the name of the directory (not the full filename) you copied the database files to; be sure to have Free Table Directory selected as well. Also, it is very important that you select the Options button and make sure the Fetch data in background is *not* selected–the driver will not work properly with ISAPI extensions otherwise. Once these options are set, click OK, and we're done with the ODBC setup.

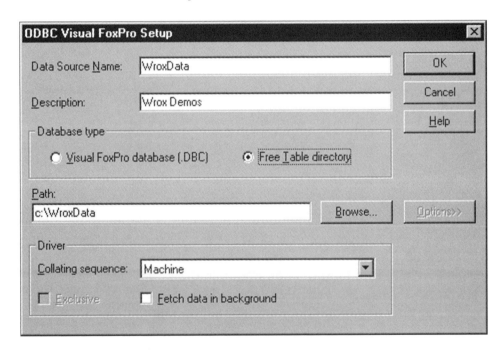

The table is part of the source code that you can download from the Wrox Press web site. You can, if you like, create the table using the following command:

```
create table user (username char(20), password char(10), ntuser char(20), ntpass
char(20), name char(30), age integer, address1 char(50), address2 char(50), city
char(30), state char(2), zip char(5), phone char(15), fax char(15), email char(50))
```

# The HTML

The input mechanism will take data from the following form:

```
<html>
<head>
<title>User Database</title>
</head><body>
<form action="/scripts/MFCData.dll?write" method="POST">
Name: <br>
<input type=text name=name size=20><br>
Age: (optional) <br>
<input type=text name=age size=2><br>
Address:<br>
<input type=text name=address1 size=50><br>
<input type=text name=address2 size=50><br>
<input type=text name=city size=40>
<input type=text name=state size=2>
<input type=text name=zip size =5><br>
Phone (optional):<br>
<input type=text name=phone size=15><br>

Fax (optional):<br>
<input type=text name=fax size=15><br>
Email:<br>
<input type=text name=email size=50><br>
<hr>
Desired UserName:<br>
<input type=text name=username size=10><br>
Desired Password (At least 4 characters):<br>
<input type=text name=password size=10><br>
<hr>
<input type=submit>
</body></html>
```

# Requirements

In addition to simply taking data from the form and writing it to a database, we need to perform several checks on the data before we insert it into the table. For a start, we have to make sure the user name is unique. We also need to make sure that the password is at least four characters and that the user inputs data for some of the items on the form.

The extension that produces the output will simply list information from the database in tabular format.

# Getting Started

Once again, we'll be using the ISAPI wizard and MFC to help us with our development. Create a new project as in the last chapter. (The name will need to be **MFCData** if you are working along with the source.) Once the ISAPI wizard has finished, you can safely remove the large section of commented-out lines at the end of the **MFCData.cpp** file.

## Required Header Files

By default, the AppWizard doesn't add database support for your ISAPI extension. To add it, you must include the **afxdb.h** file into your project by adding **#include <afxdb.h>** to your **stdafx.h** file. The finished file will look like this:

```
// stdafx.h: include file for standard system include files,
//  or project specific include files that are used frequently, but
//     are changed infrequently
//

#include <afx.h>
#include <afxwin.h>
#include <afxmt.h>        // for synchronization objects
#include <afxext.h>
#include <afxisapi.h>
#include <afxdb.h>
```

## More on Parse Maps

Now that everything is set up, we're ready to start programming. Just below the **#include** statements in **MFCData.cpp**, we need to fix up the parse maps by adding a mapping for both the **Read** and **Write** commands and deleting the **Default** command from our map. We touched on parse maps in the last chapter, but in this chapter, we'll cover just about everything that they do (which, as we'll see in the next chapter, is often not enough).

The **Read** command takes only the required pointer to the **CHttpServerContext** object as a parameter. The function displays some information on every user in the database in a tabular format. The parse map command for it is as follows (note that the **ITS_EMPTY** is required when no parameters are present):

```
ON_PARSE_COMMAND(Read, CMFCDataExtension, ITS_EMPTY)
```

We'll also specify **Read** as the default command by changing the **DEFAULT_PARSE_COMMAND** macro to:

```
DEFAULT_PARSE_COMMAND(Read, CMFCDataExtension)
```

The **Write** command, on the other hand, has several required and a couple of optional parameters with varying data types. When parameters will be passed to the function, two commands are used to define the parse map. The first, **ON_PARSE_COMMAND**, tells the macro what function to call, what class it's in, and what data types the parameters will be. Here are the parameter types that are supported by the parse map macros:

| Data Type Constant | Meaning |
| --- | --- |
| ITS_EMPTY | No arguments |
| ITS_I2 | Short |
| ITS_I4 | Long |
| ITS_R4 | Float |
| ITS_R8 | Double |
| ITS_PSTR | String |

To simplify parsing of the form variables, you should use the **ON_PARSE_COMMAND_PARAM**. This macro lists which HTML form variables will be mapped to which parameters. The order in which parameter types are listed in the **ON_PARSE_COMMAND** matches the order of the parameters listed in the **ON_PARSE_COMMAND_PARAMS** command. (Note: this has nothing to do with what order they are placed in the HTML form.)

For example, consider passing the values that a user enters for his or her name and age from an HTML form to an extension. Your **ON_PARSE_COMMAND** could look like this:

```
ON_PARSE_COMMAND(MyFunction, CMyExtension, ITS_PSTR ITS_I2)
```

and the function declaration like this:

```
void MyFunction(CHttpServerContext* pCtxt, LPCTSTR name, short age)
```

> You should note the lack of commas between the types in the ON_PARSE_COMMAND. This allows us to make use of C++ automatic string concatenation.

This code would work fine, provided that the browser passes calls to the extension with the URL:

```
http://my.server.com/scripts/MyExtension.dll?MyFuncton?name=John+Doe&age=23
```

A potential problem is that some browsers may shuffle the order in which variables are passed. For example, by reversing the order in which the name and age form variables are placed on the **QUERY_STRING**, the **short age** would get mixed up with the **LPCTSTR name** and an exception would be raised. Fortunately, the **ON_PARSE_COMMAND_PARAMS** overcomes this by allowing you to specify a name to match with the data type specified in the **ON_PARSE_COMMAND**.

In our little example, we would supply the line:

```
ON_PARSE_COMMAND_PARAMS("name age")
```

immediately after the **ON_PARSE_COMMAND** line. The parser would then pass the value of the HTML form variable **name** as the first, **LPCTSTR**, parameter and the value of **age** as the second, **short**, parameter. Thus, no matter in what order the client browser passes the HTML form data, the **ON_PARSE_COMMAND_PARAMS** will make sure that each value is passed as the appropriate parameter.

The **ON_PARSE_COMMAND_PARAMS** also supplies defaults for any optional variables. A variable is optional if it isn't necessary to have the form specify it for the extension to work. However, the variable can still be blank. If the browser sends over any value for the variable, including the empty string, the parse map will use it. In our example, we will require that all the lines on the form be filled in except for the phone, fax and age fields. In the parse map, however, we will only specify the phone and fax fields as being optional.

This will allow us to demonstrate the difference between optional fields and empty fields. If the HTML form is missing the **<input type=text name=phone size=15>** tag or the **<input type=text name=fax size=15>** tag, the extension will simply fill the value **none** in for us and pass it to our function as a parameter just as if the user had typed in **none** in the field. The **ON_PARSE_COMMAND** does this because we will specify phone and fax as optional fields. If, however, you're missing the **<input type=text name=age size=2>** tag, you'll probably get a 'Document Contains No Data' message from your browser when you try to run the extension because **age** is defined as a mandatory parameter. If the browser doesn't send an age field, the parse map doesn't have enough variables to pass to the calling function. (The same type of error would occur when too many variables are passed.)

As a side note, when debugging parse maps, you will frequently receive a 'Document Contains No Data' message, for the reasons noted above. When this occurs, you should check the count of your mandatory and optional parameters in **ON_PARSE_COMMAND_PARAMS** and make sure that they line up with the data types specified in **ON_PARSE_COMMAND.** If you wish to provide a more meaningful response than 'Document Contains No Data', you can associate a string value with **AFX_IDS_HTTP_BAD_REQUEST** in the string table for the extension. Alternatively, you can override the **CHttpServer::OnParseError()** function if you need a more customized parse error handler.

The format for optional parameters is **name=default** and, like default parameters for functions, must appear at the end of the definition. In this case, our macros would look like this:

```
ON_PARSE_COMMAND(Write, CMFCDataExtension, ITS_PSTR ITS_I2
    ITS_PSTR ITS_PSTR ITS_PSTR
    ITS_PSTR ITS_PSTR ITS_PSTR
    ITS_PSTR ITS_PSTR ITS_PSTR
    ITS_PSTR)
ON_PARSE_COMMAND_PARAMS("name age address1 address2 city "
    "state zip email username password phone=none fax=none")
```

> Note that there is a white space after `city` in the `ON_PARSE_COMMAND_PARAMS` statement.

This macro will cause the **ON_PARSE_COMMAND** to call the **Write()** function in **CMFCDataExtension** with twelve parameters, all of them being strings except the second which is a short. The server will require a form field for all of the parameters except phone and fax for which it will fill in with **none** if the form doesn't use these variables. If the phone and fax variables are used anywhere on the form, and the user doesn't type anything in for them, they will come over as empty strings rather than as **none**.

Also, make sure that you delete the **ON_PARSE_COMMAND** for the **Default** command and any corresponding code for it, i.e. its definition in the **CMFCDataExtension** class and its implementation in the **MFCData.cpp** file. Your finished parse map should look like this:

```
BEGIN_PARSE_MAP(CMFCDataExtension, CHttpServer)

    ON_PARSE_COMMAND(Read, CMFCDataExtension, ITS_EMPTY)
    ON_PARSE_COMMAND(Write, CMFCDataExtension, ITS_PSTR ITS_I2
        ITS_PSTR ITS_PSTR ITS_PSTR
        ITS_PSTR ITS_PSTR ITS_PSTR
        ITS_PSTR ITS_PSTR ITS_PSTR
        ITS_PSTR)
    ON_PARSE_COMMAND_PARAMS("name age address1 address2 city "
        "state zip email username password phone=none fax=none")
    DEFAULT_PARSE_COMMAND(Read, CMFCDataExtension)
END_PARSE_MAP(CMFCDataExtension)
```

# Declarations

Now that our parse map is in place, we need to add some things to the **CMFCDataExtension** class. To start with, we need to add our **Read()** and **Write()** functions. To do this, right click the **CMFCDataExtension** class in the ClassView, select Add a Function and add a **public** function as follows:

```
void Write(CHttpServerContext* pCtxt, LPCTSTR name, SHORT age,
       LPCTSTR address1, LPCTSTR address2,
       LPCTSTR city, LPCTSTR state, LPCTSTR zip,
       LPCTSTR email, LPCTSTR username, LPCTSTR password,
       LPCTSTR phone, LPCTSTR fax);
```

Repeat this for **void Read(CHttpServerContext* pCtxt);**

We are now finished with the **CMFCDataExtension** class declaration. Your **MFCData.h** file should look something like this:

```
// MFCDATA.H - Header file for your Internet Server
//    MFCData Extension

#include "resource.h"

class CMFCDataExtension: public CHttpServer
{
public:
   void Read(CHttpServerContext* pCtxt);
   void Write(CHttpServerContext* pCtxt, LPCTSTR name, SHORT age,
      LPCTSTR address1, LPCTSTR address2, LPCTSTR city,
      LPCTSTR state, LPCTSTR zip, LPCTSTR email,
      LPCTSTR username, LPCTSTR password, LPCTSTR phone, LPCTSTR fax);
   CMFCDataExtension();
   ~CMFCDataExtension();

// Overrides
   // ClassWizard generated virtual function overrides
      // NOTE - the ClassWizard will add and remove member functions here.
      //    DO NOT EDIT what you see in these blocks of generated code!
   //{{AFX_VIRTUAL(CMFCDataExtension)
   public:
   virtual BOOL GetExtensionVersion(HSE_VERSION_INFO* pVer);
   //}}AFX_VIRTUAL

   // TODO: Add handlers for your commands here.
   // For example:

   DECLARE_PARSE_MAP()

   //{{AFX_MSG(CMFCDataExtension)
   //}}AFX_MSG
};
```

# Writing the Data

Even though it's the more complex function, we will start with writing the data, because it's logical to write before we read. As we mentioned earlier, we do need to enforce some restrictions before we insert data into our database. First, we want the user to have filled in all the information that we require (everything except the phone and fax). Second, we want the password to be longer than three characters. Lastly, we can't allow a duplicate user name in our database.

To accomplish this, you need the following code (which is broken up with explanatory text):

```
void CMFCDataExtension::Write(CHttpServerContext* pCtxt, LPCTSTR name,
                    SHORT age, LPCTSTR address1, LPCTSTR address2,
                    LPCTSTR city, LPCTSTR state, LPCTSTR zip, LPCTSTR email,
                    LPCTSTR username, LPCTSTR password, LPCTSTR phone,
                    LPCTSTR fax)
{
    CString stringSql;

    StartContent(pCtxt);            //Write header and title info
    WriteTitle(pCtxt);


    //Make sure the user has typed something for the fields that we want

    if (*name=='\0' || *address1=='\0' || *address2=='\0' || *city=='\0' ||
        *state=='\0' || *email=='\0' || *username=='\0' || *password=='\0')
    {
        *pCtxt<< _T("Please fill in all required items<br>\r\n");
        EndContent(pCtxt);
        return;
    }

    //  Check the password

    if (CString(password).GetLength()<4)
    {
        *pCtxt << _T("Please enter a longer password<br>\r\n");
        EndContent(pCtxt);
        return;
    }
}
```

Once we've verified that the user entered all the appropriate fields and entered a long enough password, we need to open up a connection to the database. In this case, we'll use **CDatabase::OpenEx()**, which is a new addition to MFC 4.2. Like the familiar **CDatabase::Open()**, **OpenEx()** opens a connection to the database. The reason that we use **CDatabase::OpenEx()** for ISAPI programming is the addition of the **CDatabase::noOdbcDialog** parameter. When using the regular **CDatabase::Open()** function, if the parameters don't specify enough information to make the ODBC connections (for example, you left out the user name or password), MFC will automatically open an ODBC connection dialog to request more information from the user. While this is a nice feature for a typical application, we certainly don't want dialog boxes opening up on the web server expecting user input. (Actually, since the web server runs as a service, no dialog box would be displayed unless you set the Interact with Desktop option in the Services Control Panel.)

```
// Create and open the database
CDatabase Db;
Db.OpenEx("DSN=WroxData;",CDatabase::noOdbcDialog);
```

Once the database connection is open, we're ready to start using it. The first task is to find out if the user name has already been used by someone else. The easiest way to do this is to attempt to select the record with user name supplied from the table. If we get back an empty recordset, then we are OK to add this user. To perform the select, we need to use a **CRecordset** derived class, **CUserRecordset**, which we'll get to a bit later in the chapter.

The main point to note in the following code is that we have surrounded the database access code with a **try** block, catching any database exceptions that occur. You will notice that this becomes a bit of a recurring theme in our code. If you haven't had experience of exception handling, don't worry, we'll cover the basics after we've finished looking at the function.

```
// We can't have duplicate user names in the database, so we check to see
// if this user name exists first.

CUserRecordset rsUser(&Db);
stringSql.Format("Select * from user where username='%-.10s'",username);

try
{
    rsUser.Open(CRecordset::snapshot, stringSql);
}
catch (CDBException* pEx)
{
    *pCtxt << _T("Error Selecting from table:");

    TCHAR szErrorMessage[1024];

    if (pEx->GetErrorMessage(szErrorMessage, sizeof(szErrorMessage)))
    {
        *pCtxt << szErrorMessage;
        *pCtxt << _T("\r\n");
    }
    EndContent(pCtxt);
    return;
}
```

To check for an empty recordset, we use the **IsBOF()** function from **CRecordset**. This will only be **TRUE** if there are no records in the set, as when the recordset is first opened the cursor points to the first record (i.e. **IsBOF()** will be **FALSE**). If this is the case (we do have an empty recordset), we write the details to the database with a simple SQL statement, and report back to the user the success of the operation, if indeed it was successful.

```
if (rsUser.IsBOF()) // The user name does not exist, so we insert it.
                    // Not all drivers are supported by the AddNew, Update methods,
                    // so, we write our own sql statement to insert the data.
{
    // Make sure the field names aren't too big for the columns.
    stringSql.Format("Insert into user (username, password,"
        "name, age,address1, address2, city, state, zip,"
        "phone,fax,email,ntuser,ntpass) VALUES ('%-.20s','%-.10s','%-.30s',"
        "%d,'%-.50s','%-.50s','%-.30s','%-.2s','%-.5s','%-.15s',"
```

```
            "'%-.15s','%-.50s','webuser','webpass')",username, password, name, age,
            address1, address2, city, state, zip,phone,fax,email);

        try
        {
            Db.ExecuteSQL(stringSql);
        }
        catch (CDBException* pEx)
        {
            *pCtxt << _T("Error inserting into table");
            TCHAR szErrorMessage[1024];

            if(pEx->GetErrorMessage(szErrorMessage, sizeof(szErrorMessage)))
            {
                *pCtxt << szErrorMessage;
                *pCtxt << _T("<br>\r\n");
                *pCtxt << stringSql;
            }
            EndContent(pCtxt);
            return;
        }
    }
    else
    {
        *pCtxt << _T("The username you selected is already taken.");
        EndContent(pCtxt);
        rsUser.Close();
        Db.Close();
        return;
    }
    rsUser.Close();
    Db.Close();
    *pCtxt << _T("Thank you for your submission. Your information has been added"
                " to our database.<p>");
    EndContent(pCtxt);
}
```

If you aren't familiar with C++ exception handling, you may be wondering about the **try** and **catch** commands in the above code. While a complete coverage of these commands is beyond the scope of this book, we will see quite a bit of them in ISAPI programming, so we'll have a quick look at them here.

## C++ Exception Handling

There are many unexpected situations which might occur when a program is running. You might run out of memory, run out of disk space, try to read or write protected memory, etc. Rather than writing code that constantly checks and handles errors, C++ incorporates a powerful but simple-to-use method of dealing with errors or exceptions. One should note that C++ exception handling is different from structured exception handling. We'll cover structured exception handling later, but for now we'll limit ourselves to standard C++ exception handling which uses the **try**, **catch**, and **throw** commands.

As you can probably guess from the code presented above, the format for the **try**/**catch** block is:

```
try
{
    // block of code you wish to execute
```

```
    // something might go wrong in it though
}
catch (error-type variable)
{
    // Code to execute if error-type exception is raised
}
catch (different-error-type variable)
{
    // Code to execute if different-error-type exception is raised
}
catch (…)
{
    // Catch everything else
}
// Code execution resumes here unless we exited one of the catch routines
```

The **try** block of code is nothing more than code that we want to try to execute, but that we suspect may give rise to some type of error. If an error does occur, an exception is thrown. The type of exception depends on the type of error, and we can even create our own exception types and cause them to be raised with the **throw** command. Thus, not all exceptions are actual errors, but rather user-defined responses to unexpected situations. In the above example, the exception we're trying to catch is defined inside MFC as a **CDBException**. A **CDBException** isn't an error in the same sense that trying to write to protected memory is. If an unexpected result is returned by one of the ODBC database calls that the **CRecordset** class encapsulated, the **CDBException** is thrown.

If we catch the particular type of exception with the **catch** command, the code inside the **catch** block is executed. Program execution resumes after the termination of all the catch blocks unless one of the **catch** blocks returns (as we do in our example) or passes the exception on to the next higher **try/catch** block by using the **throw** command. The **throw** command is used to cause an exception to be raised. This is done to indicate that an error has occurred and to pass control back to the next higher **try/catch** block. We will see this done later in the chapter when we're using nested **try/catch** blocks.

In the above example, we're only interested in database-specific errors, as those are the only ones we can do anything about. However, we could **catch** any type of error by using a **catch (...)** command. By using the ellipsis for the catch type, we catch any unexpected situations which might arise.

The MSIIS surrounds the call to your ISAPI extension with a **try/catch** block so that any errors that you don't catch are passed up to the server. However, the server doesn't clean up after you; it simply terminates the request and gives the client an error message. Typically, the client gets a 'Document Contains No Data' message. If you need to free up memory or close resources, the server will not do this for you and unhandled exceptions can lead to memory leaks.

## The Recordset

Looking at the **Write()** function, you will notice an instance of **CUserRecordset** called **rsUser**. The easiest way to check to see if a record is in the database is to open a **CRecordset** object using a **select** statement and see if any records are returned. In this case we use **CUserRecordset**, which is the same recordset we will use when we read the data back to the client.

To create the **CUserRecordset** class, open the ClassWizard and then select Add Class... | New.... The name of the class is **CUserRecordset** and the base class is **CRecordset**. For the database options, you should select the ODBC source which we created above for our Visual FoxPro table (**WroxData**). You should also select the Snapshot type and the option to bind all columns. Once the class is created, you should have two files. The header looks like this:

```
// UserRecordset.h: header file
//

/////////////////////////////////////////////////////////////////////////////
// CUserRecordset recordset

class CUserRecordset: public CRecordset
{
public:
    CUserRecordset(CDatabase* pDatabase = NULL);
    DECLARE_DYNAMIC(CUserRecordset)

// Field/Param Data
    //{{AFX_FIELD(CUserRecordset, CRecordset)
    CString    m_username;
    CString    m_password;
    CString    m_ntuser;
    CString    m_name;
    long    m_age;
    CString    m_address1;
    CString    m_address2;
    CString    m_city;
    CString    m_state;
    CString    m_zip;
    CString    m_phone;
    CString    m_fax;
    CString    m_email;
    CString    m_ntpass;
    //}}AFX_FIELD


// Overrides
    // ClassWizard generated virtual function overrides
    //{{AFX_VIRTUAL(CUserRecordset)
    public:
    virtual CString GetDefaultConnect();    // Default connection string
    virtual CString GetDefaultSQL();    // Default SQL for Recordset
    virtual void DoFieldExchange(CFieldExchange* pFX);  // RFX support
    //}}AFX_VIRTUAL

// Implementation
#ifdef _DEBUG
    virtual void AssertValid() const;
    virtual void Dump(CDumpContext& dc) const;
#endif
};
```

while the implementation file should look like this:

```
// UserRecordset.cpp: implementation file
//

#include "stdafx.h"
#include "MFCData.h"
#include "UserRecordset.h"

#ifdef _DEBUG
```

```
#define new DEBUG_NEW
#undef THIS_FILE
static char THIS_FILE[] = __FILE__;
#endif

/////////////////////////////////////////////////////////////////////////
// CUserRecord

IMPLEMENT_DYNAMIC(CUserRecordset, CRecordset)

CUserRecordset::CUserRecordset(CDatabase* pdb)
  : CRecordset(pdb)
{
   //{{AFX_FIELD_INIT(CUserRecordset)
   m_username = _T("");
   m_password = _T("");
   m_ntuser = _T("");
   m_name = _T("");
   m_age = 0;
   m_address1 = _T("");
   m_address2 = _T("");
   m_city = _T("");
   m_state = _T("");
   m_zip = _T("");
   m_phone = _T("");
   m_fax = _T("");
   m_email = _T("");
   m_ntpass = _T("");
   m_nFields = 14;
   //}}AFX_FIELD_INIT
   m_nDefaultType = snapshot;
}


CString CUserRecordset::GetDefaultConnect()
{
   return _T("ODBC;DSN=WroxData");
}


CString CUserRecordset::GetDefaultSQL()
{
   return _T("[user]");
}
```

While it may seem unnecessary to mention all this ClassWizard-generated code here, there is a very important note to watch for in the **DoFieldExchange()** method of any ISAPI **CRecordset**, namely that the number and order in which the fields are listed in **DoFieldExchange()** must match up exactly with the order in which they are returned from the **select** statement. If not, your ISAPI extension may appear simply to 'freeze' when you run it and will raise an exception in **dbcore.cpp** if you try to debug it.

```
void CUserRecordset::DoFieldExchange(CFieldExchange* pFX)
{
   //{{AFX_FIELD_MAP(CUserRecordset)
   pFX->SetFieldType(CFieldExchange::outputColumn);
   RFX_Text(pFX, _T("[username]"), m_username);
```

```
    RFX_Text(pFX, _T("[password]"), m_password);
    RFX_Text(pFX, _T("[ntuser]"), m_ntuser);
    RFX_Text(pFX, _T("[name]"), m_name);
    RFX_Long(pFX, _T("[age]"), m_age);
    RFX_Text(pFX, _T("[address1]"), m_address1);
    RFX_Text(pFX, _T("[address2]"), m_address2);
    RFX_Text(pFX, _T("[city]"), m_city);
    RFX_Text(pFX, _T("[state]"), m_state);
    RFX_Text(pFX, _T("[zip]"), m_zip);
    RFX_Text(pFX, _T("[phone]"), m_phone);
    RFX_Text(pFX, _T("[fax]"), m_fax);
    RFX_Text(pFX, _T("[email]"), m_email);
    RFX_Text(pFX, _T("[ntpass]"), m_ntpass);
    //}}AFX_FIELD_MAP
}


/////////////////////////////////////////////////////////////////////////////
// CUserRecordset diagnostics

#ifdef _DEBUG
void CUserRecordset::AssertValid() const
{
    CRecordset::AssertValid();
}

void CUserRecordset::Dump(CDumpContext& dc) const
{
    CRecordset::Dump(dc);
}
#endif //_DEBUG
```

These ClassWizard-generated files contain information about the variables in the database. There is no need to edit anything here. All they do is map columns selected from the database into public variables in the **CUserRecordset** class.

In this example, we only use **CUserRecordset** when reading from the database. We could also have used this class to write to the database by using the **AddNew()** and **Update()** member functions of **CRecordset**, but as not all drivers support these methods, I chose to use the **ExecuteSQL()** function to write the insert statement directly. This function is universally supported and eliminates the need to create a **CRecordset** object if you aren't going to read data back from the database.

While the ClassWizard creates the **CUserRecordset** class for you, it doesn't tell your main implementation file that it needs it. To do this, add **#include "UserRecordset.h"** to **MFCDataExtension.cpp**. The top of the file should now read:

```
// MFCDATA.CPP - Implementation file for your Internet Server
//     MFCData Extension

#include "stdafx.h"
#include "MFCData.h"
#include "UserRecordset.h"
```

# Reading the Data

Once the data is in the database, we might want a way to read it back. In this case, a simple function that queries our ODBC database using the recordset we created above will suffice. The code follows below:

```
void CMFCDataExtension::Read(CHttpServerContext* pCtxt)
{

    CDatabase   Db;
    Db.OpenEx("DSN=WroxData;",CDatabase::noOdbcDialog);
    CUserRecordset rsUser(&Db);
```

After opening the database connection, we need to obtain the data from the table so that we can display it. Unlike in the **Write()** function, where we passed a SQL statement to the **Open()** function, we only need to use **Open()** without any parameters. This causes **Open()** to use the **GetDefaultSQL()** override that ClassWizard so generously created for us, selecting all the records in the table–just what we want.

```
    try
    {
        rsUser.Open();                    //The default SQL string in this case
                                          // gives us the whole table
    }
    catch (CDBException* pEx)
    {
        *pCtxt << _T("Error Selecting from table:");

        TCHAR szErrorMessage[1024];

        if (pEx->GetErrorMessage(szErrorMessage, sizeof(szErrorMessage)))
        {
            *pCtxt << szErrorMessage;
            *pCtxt << _T("\r\n");
        }
        return;
    }
```

After making sure that we have some records to display, writing out the data to the client becomes a simple matter of looping through the recordset. We check the 'End Of File' condition (**IsEOF()**) before outputting the field values stored in the member variables of our **CUserRecordset** class. The **MoveNext()** function causes these variables to be updated with the next record's values or sets the 'End Of File' flag if we have reached the end of the recordset.

```
    if (!rsUser.IsBOF())                  // We found some records
    {
        StartContent(pCtxt);
        WriteTitle(pCtxt);
        *pCtxt << _T("<table border=3>");
        while (!rsUser.IsEOF())
        {
            *pCtxt << _T("<tr><td rowspan=4 valign=top>") << rsUser.m_name
                << _T("<td>") << rsUser.m_email
                << _T("<tr><td>") <<rsUser.m_address1
                << _T("<tr><td>") <<rsUser.m_address2
                << _T("<tr><td>") <<rsUser.m_city << _T(" ") << rsUser.m_state
```

```
            << _T(" ") << rsUser.m_zip;
        rsUser.MoveNext();
    }
    *pCtxt << _T("</table>");
    EndContent(pCtxt);
    }
    rsUser.Close();
    Db.Close();
}
```

You should now be able to build your application. See the *Building and Testing the* **MFCData** *Extension* section at the end of the chapter for additional information. While the program should work without any trouble, you'll notice that each request opens the database, reads or writes, and then closes the database. Chances are, if you're doing ISAPI programming, you're interested in performance and don't want the additional overhead associated with creating a new connection for each request. Another drawback to this approach is that it doesn't have a method to limit database access. Let's say that you have a high-traffic site that performs frequent database queries. During peak hours, the above method will submit all queries to the database for execution. This will cause all the queries to run more slowly. If enough people are querying the database, all of the queries will time out and everyone will get error messages. Instead, you should put a limit on the number of simultaneous queries that can be running at one time, so that after this limit, the server simply tells the client it is too busy or waits until some queries are finished before submitting new ones. While your hardware doesn't allow you to please everyone during peak hours, at least as many users as possible will get answers back.

# CDataPool Class

In order to give you the performance and control that you need over your database connections, we'll introduce the **CDataPool** class. The **CDataPool** class opens up a pool of connections to an ODBC data source when the function is first called. It then gives out open connections to each request that asks for one. If all the connections are in use, the **CDataPool** class will put the threads to sleep until a free connection is available or a time out safeguard occurs. By putting the threads to sleep, they take no CPU time and the server is then able to handle a heavy load.

# Thread Safety

The central issue to the **CDataPool** object is to make sure that only one thread has access to one connection at a time. The technique of controlling which threads have access to data at certain times is called **thread synchronization**, and Win32 provides us with several tools to help us do this. The four main thread synchronization objects are **critical sections**, **mutexes**, **semaphores**, and **events**. We'll examine critical sections and semaphores here, and take a look at mutexes and events elsewhere in the book.

As a note to the reader, MFC does provide implementations for thread synchronization objects. However, I don't feel that the MFC implementation of these objects simplifies multithreaded programming in any way. In most cases, the MFC implementation provides only a very thin wrapper which does little more than change the name of the call. Since we will need to use thread synchronization objects later in the book in non-MFC applications, the presentation here only uses the Win32 API.

## Critical Sections

A critical section is simply a structure that, when coupled with the Win32 API calls for dealing with critical sections, allows only one thread at a time to access a piece of data. While another thread owns it, a critical section will put to sleep all other threads which are trying to access it. Once the thread is out of the critical section, the next thread will be woken up and allowed to enter it. If multiple threads are waiting to enter a critical section, NT will decide for you which one will be allowed to enter once the critical section is freed, based on the priority level of each waiting thread.

To use a critical section, you must declare a **CRITICAL_SECTION** variable with a scope such that all threads that need to be synchronized by it have access. In many applications, it is simply declared as a global variable, but in our ISAPI extensions, it is usually encapsulated in a class as we'll see later with **CDataPool**.

Before we can use a critical section, it must be initialized. After we are done, we should free it up by deleting it. The Win32 API calls for these functions are self-explanatory and take as their parameters the address of a critical section:

```
InitializeCriticalSection(&csPool);
DeleteCriticalSection(&csPool);
```

In order to ensure that our thread is the only one that currently holds the critical section, we need to call the **EnterCriticalSection()** function, again passing the address of the critical section. All other threads that call **EnterCriticalSection()** will be put to sleep until the thread that owns it calls **LeaveCriticalSection()** with the same parameter again.

From the above discussion, and in the **CDataPool** class that will be listed shortly, you should see that critical sections are fairly easy to use. They are also very fast, which is why we'll see them used frequently in this book. It is imperative that the thread leaves the critical section when it is done with it; if it doesn't, all other threads that try to access it will be put to sleep indefinitely.

## The Semaphore

The semaphore is a kernel object that can do everything that the critical section can and more. The main enhancement that the semaphore offers is the ability to count resource use. The critical section simply lets one thread have access. The semaphore, on the other hand, can let a fixed number of threads have access to some data and put other threads to sleep until any one of the threads signals that it is done. Another advantage that the semaphore offers is the ability to time out after waiting for a given number of milliseconds. We will see this used in our ISAPI programs to return an error message to the client rather than putting the thread to sleep forever. The semaphore can also be used to synchronize threads across multiple processes; however, as all ISAPI extensions run in the same process, we will not cover this aspect here.

As with critical sections, semaphores exist in one of two states: signaled and non-signaled. In the non-signaled state, the thread sleeps waiting for the semaphore to be freed up. In the signaled state, the thread is allowed to execute.

As the semaphore offers much greater flexibility over the critical section, using it is a little more difficult. To create a semaphore, you need to create a handle and then assign it to a semaphore by using the **CreateSemaphore()** function prototyped here:

```
CreateSemaphore(LPSECURITY_ATTRIBUTES lpSemaphoreAttributes,
                LONG lInitialCount, LONG lMaximumCount, LPCTSTR lpName)
```

The security attributes are used to determine whether the handle can be inherited by child processes. In this book, we will not be passing any handles to child processes, so we will always pass a **NULL** for this value. The **lInitialCount** parameter specifies the start up count for the semaphore, and **lMaximumCount** specifies the maximum count of available resources. For example, let's say that we want 10 open connections, but only want 5 of them to be initially available for use. We would pass 5 and 10 respectively. The **lpName** parameter is used to uniquely identify this semaphore to the system. Thus, if you use the same name for two semaphores, the handle the **CreateSemaphore()** function returns will indeed be for the same semaphore, even if the call was made in different processes. You should always use names that you know will be unique, unless you intend to use the same semaphore for synchronization purposes. You can also create a semaphore with a **NULL** name. In this case, the semaphore can only be accessed by using the handle that the **CreateSemaphore()** function returns, but it will be guaranteed not to clash with any other semaphore names.

In order to access a semaphore, we must call either **WaitForSingleObject()** or **WaitForMultipleObjects()**. **WaitForMultipleObjects()** is only used when you also need to wait for more than one object (either another semaphore or different type of synchronization object). We'll cover **WaitForSingleObject()** here, and hold off on covering **WaitForMultipleObjects()** until we actually need to use it later in the book.

The prototype for **WaitForSingleObject()** is

```
DWORD WaitForSingleObject(HANDLE hHandle, DWORD dwMilliseconds)
```

where **hHandle** is a handle to the object to wait for, and **dwMilliseconds** is the number of milliseconds to wait before timing out. If **dwMilliseconds** is **INFINITE**, the call will never time out. When the call returns, it has one of three values:

| Return Value | Meaning |
|---|---|
| **WAIT_ABANDONED** | Applies to mutex objects in which the owning thread terminated before it released the object. |
| **WAIT_OBJECT_0** | The call succeeded, and you now have possession of the object. |
| **WAIT_TIMEOUT** | The call timed out, and you do not have possession of the object. |

The **WaitForSingleObject()** decrements the available count of the semaphore upon a successful return. Thus, if you call **CreateSemaphore(NULL,3,3,"MyName")** and then call **WaitForSingleObject()** four times, the wait will return **WAIT_OBJECT_0** for the first three, but will not return the fourth time until one or more objects is released.

To release semaphores, you need to call the **ReleaseSemaphore()** function prototyped here:

```
BOOL ReleaseSemaphore(HANDLE hSemaphore, LONG lReleaseCount,
                      LPLONG lpPreviousCount)
```

The **hSemaphore** is the handle to the semaphore. **lReleaseCount** is the amount you want to increment the semaphore count and **lpPreviousCount** is the value the semaphore count was at before this function was called.

The **ReleaseSemaphore()** function returns **TRUE** if the requested number of semaphores were freed up. Otherwise, it returns **FALSE** and doesn't free up anything. So, if you pass **lReleaseCount()** a value that would cause the semaphore to exceed its maximum count, the function returns **FALSE** and does nothing. You should note that there's no way to determine the current count of a semaphore by using the **ReleaseSemaphore()** function without changing the current count. The **lpPreviousCount** will contain the previous count of the semaphore only when the count changes.

Unlike the critical section, the semaphore doesn't have to be released by the same thread that captured it. In fact, you don't even have to call **WaitForSingleObject()** or **WaitForMultipleObjects()** before you can call **ReleaseSemaphore()**. If you create the semaphore with its initial count less than the maximum count, you can release a semaphore when a thread enters a section, and capture it when it leaves. This implements a way to count how many threads are currently in a certain section of code. We'll use this technique when we make our user-authentication filter in the second part of the book.

Lastly, when you're done with a semaphore object, you need to delete it. This is done with a call to **CloseHandle()** in which you pass the handle to the semaphore you wish to delete.

# CDataPool Declaration

Now that you have some idea of the synchronization objects we are about to use, it's time to start adding flesh to the bones of our idea. The initial starting point is the declaration of the **CDataPool** class, shown here:

```
////////////////////////////////////////////////////////////
/// DataPool.h


#define POOL_TIME_OUT           20000
#define POOL_DEFAULT_CONNECTIONS   5

class CDataPool
{
public:
    CDataPool(LPSTR lpzODBCConnect,INT nQueryTimeOut, LPSTR lpszSemName,
              INT nDBPoolCount=POOL_DEFAULT_CONNECTIONS);
    ~CDataPool();

    INT GetConnection(CDatabase **pDB);
    void FreeConnection(INT nDbIndex);
    void ResetConnection(CDatabase* pDB);
    void DisplayError(CHttpServerContext* pCtxt, CDBException* pEx);

private:
    CDatabase    **m_dbPool;
    BOOL    **m_bPoolIndex;
    HANDLE    m_hSemPool;
    CRITICAL_SECTION    m_csPool;
    INT    m_nPoolSize;
    CString m_strConnect;
};
```

The prototypes of the member functions show that we will instantiate the object by passing it our ODBC connection string, the ODBC time out, the name we should call our semaphore, and the number of connections we want to open. We have several member functions which allow us to acquire, free, and reset connections, and we have a function to display ODBC errors.

We also have several private members for handling the connections and thread access. The first is a pointer to an array of **CDatabase** objects. This is the actual pool of connections we are managing. We use a pointer to a pointer here as we will be generating a dynamic array of pointers. The second member, also a pointer to a pointer, is a matching array of **BOOL** objects which we will use to indicate which of the connections are currently being used by threads.

The next two members are the handles to the controlling semaphore and a critical section for restricting access to the code which accesses the **m_bPoolIndex** member, as we'll see shortly. The final two members simply store the pool size and the connection string used to open the databases.

# CDataPool Implementation

Most of the work is done in the constructor. It creates and opens all the database connections and then initializes the semaphore and critical section. The semaphore is used to ensure that no more than the maximum number of users have database connections at any one time. The critical section is used for accessing the shared variable **m_bPoolIndex**, which is the array that tells which connections are in use. The code for this is:

```
#include "stdafx.h"
#include "DataPool.h"


CDataPool::CDataPool(LPSTR lpzODBCConnect,INT nQueryTimeOut, LPSTR lpszSemName,
                     INT nDBPoolCount)
{
    m_dbPool = new CDatabase*[nDBPoolCount];
    m_bPoolIndex = new BOOL*[nDBPoolCount];
    m_nPoolSize = nDBPoolCount;
    m_strConnect = lpzODBCConnect;
    for (int x=0; x<m_nPoolSize;x++)
    {
        m_dbPool[x] = new CDatabase;
        m_dbPool[x]->SetQueryTimeout(nQueryTimeOut);
        m_dbPool[x]->OpenEx(lpzODBCConnect,CDatabase::noOdbcDialog);
        m_bPoolIndex[x]=new BOOL;
        *m_bPoolIndex[x]=FALSE;
    }
    m_hSemPool = CreateSemaphore(NULL, m_nPoolSize,,_nPoolSize, lpszSemName);
    InitializeCriticalSection(&m_csPool);
}
```

We will see why the critical section is needed by looking at what might happen if we didn't use it. Imagine that two threads (on two different processors) start executing **GetConnection** at the same time. Assume that there are enough free database connections for both of them. They would both increment the same number of times until they found an open connection, and then both would pass back the same pointer to the same **CDatabase** object. Once the threads try to use this **CDatabase** object, they will either write over the other's data or receive an error, as only one query at a time can be executing on a connection for ODBC datasources such as SQL Server.

> *With Oracle, on the other hand, you aren't limited to a single query. If you are using Oracle you really don't need this **CDataPool** object. Instead, you could open the database in the **CMFCDataExtension** constructor, close it in the destructor, and use it as a private variable of the class simultaneously for all threads.*

The destructor does the exact opposite of the constructor. The first task we need to perform is grabbing all the connections ourselves. If we don't do this, we could very easily end up with threads trying to access connections that we have subsequently shut down. Once this has been done, we rip through the pool, closing the connections and deleting the **CDatabase** and **BOOL** objects we previously created. After all the connections are done away with, we delete the pointer arrays before finally removing the synchronization objects.

```
CDataPool::~CDataPool()
{
    CDatabase*    pDb;
    INT    nConnectionIndex;

    for (int x=0; x<m_nPoolSize;x++)
        nConnectionIndex=GetConnection(&pDb);
    for (x =0; x<m_nPoolSize;x++)
    {
        m_dbPool[x]->Close();
        delete m_dbPool[x];
        delete m_bPoolIndex[x];
    }
    delete [] m_dbPool;
    delete [] m_bPoolIndex;
    DeleteCriticalSection(&m_csPool);
    CloseHandle(m_hSemPool);
}
```

The **GetConnection()** function takes as a parameter the address to a **CDatabase** object and returns the connection index number if the call was successful–otherwise, it returns **-1**.

```
INT CDataPool::GetConnection(CDatabase **pDB)
{
    if (WAIT_TIMEOUT==WaitForSingleObject(m_hSemPool, POOL_TIME_OUT))
        return -1;
    EnterCriticalSection(&m_csPool);
    for (int x=0; x<m_nPoolSize && *m_bPoolIndex[x]==TRUE;x++);
    *m_bPoolIndex[x]=TRUE;
    LeaveCriticalSection(&m_csPool);
    *pDB=m_dbPool[x];
    return x;

}
```

**FreeConnection()** frees up the connection index that it is passed. It doesn't do any checking to see if the index is valid.

```
void CDataPool::FreeConnection(INT nDbIndex)
{
    EnterCriticalSection(&m_csPool);
    *m_bPoolIndex[nDbIndex]=FALSE;
    LeaveCriticalSection(&m_csPool);
    ReleaseSemaphore(m_hSemPool, 1, NULL);
}
```

The **ResetConnection()** function simply closes the connection before reopening it. This is useful for error conditions where we want to make sure the connection is left in a known and tidy state.

```
void CDataPool::ResetConnection(CDatabase* pDB)
{
   pDB->Close();
   pDB->OpenEx(m_strConnect,CDatabase::noOdbcDialog);
}
```

Lastly, the **DisplayError()** function displays any associated error message for an exception to the client.

```
void CDataPool::DisplayError(CHttpServerContext* pCtxt, CDBException* pEx)
{
   TCHAR szErrorMessage[1024];

   if (pEx->GetErrorMessage(szErrorMessage, sizeof(szErrorMessage)))
   {
      *pCtxt << szErrorMessage;
      *pCtxt << _T("\r\n");
   }
}
```

# Using CDataPool

The following code shows how you can use the **CDataPool** class to do the same thing that the above example achieves. Only the **MFCDataExtension.cpp** implementation file is given here, as it is the only one with substantial changes. However, you'll also need to add the line **#include "DataPool.h"** to the top of **MFCDataExtension.h**. (Make sure that the path containing **DataPool.h** is contained in your include directory list, or copy the files into your project directory.) You'll also need to add this code,

```
private:
   CDataPool*   pDataPool;
```

to the **CMFCDataExtension** class declaration.

*In the following listing, we have highlighted the new code that is required to use the **CDataPool** class.*

```
// MFCDATA.CPP - Implementation file for your Internet Server
//     MFCData Extension

#include "stdafx.h"
#include "MFCData.h"
#include "UserRecord.h"

/////////////////////////////////////////////////////////////////////
// The one and only CWinApp object
// NOTE: You may remove this object if you alter your project to no
// longer use MFC in a DLL.

CWinApp theApp;

/////////////////////////////////////////////////////////////////////
// command-parsing map

BEGIN_PARSE_MAP(CMFCDataExtension, CHttpServer)

   ON_PARSE_COMMAND(Read, CMFCDataExtension, ITS_EMPTY)
```

```
    ON_PARSE_COMMAND(Write, CMFCDataExtension, ITS_PSTR ITS_I2
        ITS_PSTR ITS_PSTR ITS_PSTR
        ITS_PSTR ITS_PSTR ITS_PSTR
        ITS_PSTR ITS_PSTR ITS_PSTR
        ITS_PSTR)
    ON_PARSE_COMMAND_PARAMS("name age address1 address2 city "
        "state zip email username password phone=none fax=none")
    DEFAULT_PARSE_COMMAND(Read, CMFCDataExtension)
END_PARSE_MAP(CMFCDataExtension)



/////////////////////////////////////////////////////////////////////
// The one and only CMFCDataExtension object

CMFCDataExtension theExtension;


/////////////////////////////////////////////////////////////////////
// CMFCDataExtension implementation

CMFCDataExtension::CMFCDataExtension()
{
    pDataPool = new CDataPool("DSN=WroxData;",30,"MFCData1",3);
}

CMFCDataExtension::~CMFCDataExtension()
{
    delete pDataPool;
}

BOOL CMFCDataExtension::GetExtensionVersion(HSE_VERSION_INFO* pVer)
{
    // Call default implementation for initialization
    CHttpServer::GetExtensionVersion(pVer);

    // Load description string
    TCHAR sz[HSE_MAX_EXT_DLL_NAME_LEN+1];
    ISAPIVERIFY(::LoadString(AfxGetResourceHandle(),
            IDS_SERVER, sz, HSE_MAX_EXT_DLL_NAME_LEN));
    _tcscpy(pVer->lpszExtensionDesc, sz);
    return TRUE;
}

/////////////////////////////////////////////////////////////////////
// CMFCDataExtension command handlers

// Do not edit the following lines, which are needed by ClassWizard.
#if 0
BEGIN_MESSAGE_MAP(CMFCDataExtension, CHttpServer)
    //{{AFX_MSG_MAP(CMFCDataExtension)
    //}}AFX_MSG_MAP
END_MESSAGE_MAP()
#endif   // 0
```

## *The New Write() Function*

```
void CMFCDataExtension::Write(CHttpServerContext* pCtxt, LPCTSTR name, SHORT age,
                    LPCTSTR address1, LPCTSTR address2, LPCTSTR city,
                    LPCTSTR state, LPCTSTR zip, LPCTSTR email,
                    LPCTSTR username, LPCTSTR password, LPCTSTR phone,
                    LPCTSTR fax)
{
    INT nConnectionIndex;

    CString stringSql;

    StartContent(pCtxt);            //Write header and title info
    WriteTitle(pCtxt);


    //Make sure the user has typed something for the fields that we want

    if (*name=='\0' || *address1=='\0' || *address2=='\0' || *city=='\0' ||
        *state=='\0' || *email=='\0' || *username=='\0' || *password=='\0')
    {
        *pCtxt<< _T("Please fill in all required items<br>\r\n");
        EndContent(pCtxt);
        return;
    }

    //  Check the password

    if (CString(password).GetLength()<4)
    {
        *pCtxt << _T("Please enter a longer password<br>\r\n");
        EndContent(pCtxt);
        return;
    }


    // The database is already open, we just need a pointer to it
    CDatabase* pDb;

    if((nConnectionIndex = pDataPool->GetConnection(&pDb))<0)
    {
        *pCtxt << _T("Error allocating connection.");
        EndContent(pCtxt);
        return;
    }
```

While the use of the **CDataPool** class here is relatively simple, the important thing to note is the added **try/catch** blocks for handling errors. If an exception occurs after we get the connection but before we free it, and we don't have a handler for it, the exception would be passed up to the next **try/catch** block. In this case, it would be the **try/catch** that the server surrounds its call to ISAPI extensions with. Program execution would thus be transferred out of our extension and the database connection would never be freed. If this happened a couple of times, all of our connections would be tied up and everything would return errors.

```
    // We need to make sure that we free up the connection
    // when we are done with it
    try
    {
```

```
CUserRecordset rsUser(pDb);
stringSql.Format("Select * from user where username='%-.10s'",username);
try
{
    rsUser.Open(CRecordset::snapshot, stringSql);

}
catch (CDBException* pEx)
{
    // Use our new member function to display the error to the client
    pDataPool->DisplayError(pCtxt,pEx);
    // Pass the error on up to the next try
    throw pEx;
}

if (rsUser.IsBOF())
{
    // Make sure the field names aren't too big for the columns.
    stringSql.Format("Insert into user (username, password,"
      "name, age,address1, address2, city, state, zip,"
      "phone,fax,email,ntuser,ntpass) VALUES ('%-.20s','%-.10s','%-.30s',"
      "%d,'%-.50s','%-.50s','%-.30s','%-.2s','%-.5s','%-.15s',"
      "'%-.15s','%-.50s','webuser','webpass')",username, password, name, age,
       address1, address2, city, state, zip,phone,fax,email);

    try
    {
        pDb->ExecuteSQL(stringSql);
    }
    catch (CDBException* pEx)
    {
        pDataPool->DisplayError(pCtxt,pEx);
        throw pEx;
    }
}
else
{
    *pCtxt << _T("The username you selected is already taken.");
    rsUser.Close();
    // Free up the conneciton for the next request
    pDataPool->FreeConnection(nConnectionIndex);
    EndContent(pCtxt);
    return;
}

// We can only reference variables created inside a try block
// while still inside that same try block.
rsUser.Close();
}
```

In the following code, you should notice that in the **catch(...)** block, the extension calls the **ResetConnection()** method of **CDataPool**. When you write your own database access ISAPI extensions, you will probably want to do something similar. The reason is that the **CDataPool** class keeps connections open for speed of access. However, network connections can be lost, database servers occasionally need to be restarted, or some important connection parameter could have been changed on a previous call and not changed back to the default status. In any of these cases, the web server simply closes the existing connection and attempts to reopen a new one. Admittedly, not every ODBC error requires that the connection is reset. However, if your extension is programmed properly, the only ODBC errors you should get would be server ones and would probably require that the connection is reset.

```
// catch the CDBException that we may have thrown
// as well as any other type of connections
catch(...)
{
    pDataPool->ResetConnection(pDb);
    pDataPool->FreeConnection(nConnectionIndex);
    *pCtxt << _T("Freeing up Connection..");
     EndContent(pCtxt);
    return;
}
pDataPool->FreeConnection(nConnectionIndex);
*pCtxt << _T("Thank you for your submission. Your information has been added"
            " to our database.<p>");
EndContent(pCtxt);
}
```

## The New Read() Function

The implementation for the new **Read()** function is now given below. The same techniques are used for reading data as in writing. That is, we must use **try**/**catch** blocks to ensure that any resources we use are freed up, and we reset the connection in case of errors. For your own extensions, you may want to try to re-execute the SQL statement after the connection has been reset. By doing this, the client won't get an error in the event that resetting the connection solves the problem.

```
void CMFCDataExtension::Read(CHttpServerContext* pCtxt)
{

    CDatabase*    pDb;
    INT nConnectionIndex;

    if((nConnectionIndex = pDataPool->GetConnection(&pDb))<0)
    {
        *pCtxt << _T("Error allocating connection.");
        return;
    }


    try
    {
        CUserRecordset rsUser(pDb);
        try
        {
            rsUser.Open();              //The default SQL string in this case
        }                              // gives us the whole table
        catch (CDBException* pEx)
        {
            pDataPool->DisplayError(pCtxt,pEx);
            throw pEx;
        }
        if (!rsUser.IsBOF())                       // We found some records
        {
            StartContent(pCtxt);
            WriteTitle(pCtxt);
            *pCtxt << _T("<table border=3>");
```

```
        while (!rsUser.IsEOF())
        {
            *pCtxt << _T("<tr><td rowspan=4 valign=top>") << rsUser.m_name
                    << _T("<td>") << rsUser.m_email
                    << _T("<tr><td>") <<rsUser.m_address1
                    << _T("<tr><td>") <<rsUser.m_address2
                    << _T("<tr><td>") <<rsUser.m_city << _T(" ") << rsUser.m_state
                    << _T(" ") << rsUser.m_zip;
            rsUser.MoveNext();
        }
        *pCtxt << _T("</table>");
    }
    rsUser.Close();
}
catch (...)
{
    pDataPool->ResetConnection(pDb);
    pDataPool->FreeConnection(nConnectionIndex);
    *pCtxt <<   _T("Freeing up Connection..");
    EndContent(pCtxt);
    return;
}
pDataPool->FreeConnection(nConnectionIndex);
EndContent(pCtxt);
}
```

As a final note on using permanent connections to ODBC databases, you should not set any persistent options that you do not reset later. For example, if you make a call to a **SET ROWCOUNT 10** on SQL Server, you should make a call to **SET ROWCOUNT 0** before you are done with the connection. If you don't, the other threads that use the same connection will have their row count also limited to 10.

## Building and Testing the MFCData Extension

Now that your application is complete, you can build it and run it. Be sure the ODBC datasource is configured as a system datasource (as described above) before testing it. If you have DLL caching turned off (**HKEY_LOCAL_MACHINE\SYSTEM\CurrentControlSet\Services\W3SVC\ Parameters\CacheExtensions** set to 0), you can set breakpoints inside the destructor events to make sure that you are cleaning up everything properly. If you want to see that the new connections are not being opened up with each call to the DLL, you will need to set DLL caching to 1 and call the DLL two consecutive times without stopping the debugger. The first time it will open all the connections; the second time it will simply give you the first free one.

# Summary

Connecting to a database in the multithreaded environment is much more complex than in an application that uses only a single thread. You must make sure that the ODBC driver that you're using is specifically designed to work in the multithreaded environment and that your code is thread-safe itself.

Although multithreaded ODBC programming is more difficult, it can provide some worthwhile advantages. Not only do you get the usual benefits of an ISAPI extension over the cumbersome CGI executable, but you can also use persistent connections to provide extremely fast response times.

In order to take advantage of persistent connections, threads must be synchronized so that only one thread is using one connection at a time. To do this, you must use thread synchronization objects such as critical sections and semaphores. The critical section is used to ensure that only one thread has access to the critical section at any given time. The semaphore is used to count how many threads are using a given resource.

# Using Cookies

Now that we've covered the basics of MFC ISAPI programming, we're ready to move on to some topics that MFC doesn't cover completely. To do this, we'll use some of our own classes. One of these classes will be a derivation of **CHttpServer** which will enhance its functionality. The others will be general purpose HTTP classes that will make it a little easier to write ISAPI extensions.

While the main purpose of this chapter is to introduce our new classes, we'll be doing so around the framework of a simple extension, which uses all of the new classes as well as the **CDataPool** class introduced in the last chapter. In this chapter, we'll be developing a simple 'Custom page' extension which allows browsers that support the **HTTP-COOKIE** mechanism to save a custom list of sites they like to visit.

## Design of the Extension

The extension will take a request and first see if the client has already made a custom page. If the client doesn't have a custom page, the request will direct the client to the following HTML page (for this example to work, you'll need to put this page in your **wwwroot** directory and call it **Custom.html**):

```
<html>
<head><title>Wrox Press custom page example</title></head>
<body>
<center>
<h1>Customize Your Page</h1>
</center>

<form action="/scripts/WroxCookie.dll?SaveCookie" method="post">
Enter the links you want on your homepage:<br>
Name:<input type=text name="name"> URL:<input type=text name="url" size=30><br>
Name:<input type=text name="name"> URL:<input type=text name="url" size=30><br>
Name:<input type=text name="name"> URL:<input type=text name="url" size=30><br>
Name:<input type=text name="name"> URL:<input type=text name="url" size=30><br>
Name:<input type=text name="name"> URL:<input type=text name="url" size=30><br>
<input type=submit>
</form>
</body>
</html>
```

On subsequent calls to the request, the extension will give the client his or her own custom page in the following form:

```
<html>
<head><title>Wrox Press custom page example</title></head>
<body>
<center>
```

```
<h1>Your Custom Page</h1>
</center>

<a href="http://www.microsoft.com>Microsoft's Page</a><br>
<a href="http://home.netscape.com>Netscape's Home Page</a><br>
</body>
</html>
```

where Netscape and Microsoft are sites filled in by the user.

Since **HTTP-COOKIES** are becoming more and more popular, it's important not to inundate the client with cookie information. To prevent this happening, we'll store only a key on the client's side. The actual links will be stored in a database on the server. When the client passes the cookie key, the extension will look up his or her information in the database and generate a custom page on the fly.

It's left to the reader, as a rather simple task, to allow the user to edit his or her custom page once it has been created.

# HTTP Cookies

HTTP cookies are a way to save information on the client side that is selectively given back to the server depending on the request. Not all browsers support cookies and many do allow the client to turn them off. However, many popular web features make use of client-side cookies, so we'll cover their usage here.

When the client saves a cookie, the browser writes it to the client's hard drive and returns it to the server under the conditions outlined in the **Set-Cookie** command described below. The client sends it to the server by inserting it into the request header using the following format:

**Cookie: Cookie_name=Cookie_value; Next_cookie=Next_value**

Multiple cookies can be sent from the client to the server; they are separated from each other by a semicolon.

The request for the client to save a cookie is sent over in the response header of a request to the server. Typically, the client has requested a CGI or ISAPI extension and the server responds by giving the client a header containing the following information:

**Set-Cookie: Cookie_name=Cookie_value; expires=date; path=/mydir;**
**domain=www.mydomain.com; secure**

The name of the cookie helps identify it; it's used to retrieve your specific cookie as the client may have sent several of them over. If the client already has a cookie by the same name for the same path and domain, the cookie will be overwritten with the new value. The value is the information stored under that cookie name. A typical browser will allow up to 4K to be stored for each cookie. However, as using cookies this large could result in a major inconvenience for the user, you should keep your cookies as small as possible.

The **expires** clause must contain a validly formatted date. While different browsers support different formats for the date, all browsers should support the following:

**Wdy, DD-Mon-YYYY HH:MM:SS  GMT**

If an expiration date isn't specified, the cookie will expire when the client shuts down their browser. If an expiration data in the past is specified, the cookie will be erased.

The **path** information specifies what path and subpaths the client will return the cookie for. For example, if the path is **/**, the client will return the cookie for all requests to your domain, which is probably not what you want. The path **/scripts/cookies** would tell the client to send over the cookie for all calls to the **/scripts/cookies** directory and any directories underneath it. If no path is specified, the path is set to the same path as the request that set the cookie.

The **domain** specifies to which domains the cookie will be sent. The domain matches the rightmost domains to see if a match occurs. Thus, **myhost.yourdomain.www.mycompany.com** will match **www.mycompany.com**.

▲ Domain names must have at least 2 or 3 periods in them for the client to set them. This is to prevent people setting **.com** as the domain and inundating the web with cookies.

▲ The domain requires at least 2 periods if it is in one of the following top level domains: **com**, **edu**, **net**, **org**, **gov**, **mil**, **int**. The domain requires at least 3 periods if it is in any other.

▲ Only hosts within the domain listed are allowed to set cookies for the domain.

▲ If the **secure** tag is listed, the cookie will only be sent over a secure connection.

# Shortcomings of MFC

In our example, MFC's most obvious shortcoming is that it doesn't have any special methods for dealing with cookies. This is actually a rather minor concern. The biggest problem lies in the form's input variables. While we can use the **PARSE_MAP** macros to pass our form information to our functions, what happens if we want to increase the number of URLs that the client can submit? We have to edit the code and recompile the extension. This is certainly out of the question when we're writing extensions with input forms that the users might need to adjust themselves.

Another problem is the ability, or rather the inability, of the parse map to handle multiple selection list boxes. This is a major MFC shortcoming and one which we'll fix within this chapter.

To solve these problems, we'll use the following classes:

# CHttpBase

There are many general purpose functions that are used in various ISAPI functions. So that we have easy access to these functions, we'll create a base class from which we will derive other ISAPI classes. The declaration of this **CHttpBase** class is given below (**HttpBase.h**):

```
#ifndef _HTTPBASE
#define _HTTPBASE


class CHttpBase
{
public:
    CHttpBase(CHttpServerContext *pInCtxt);
```

```
    CHttpBase();
    ~CHttpBase();
    void UrlDecode(CString *pstringUrlValue);
    void UrlEncode(CString *pstringUrlValue);
    BOOL GetFromString(LPCSTR pszSearchIn, const LPCSTR pszSearchFor,
                const LPCSTR pszTokens,CString *pstringValue);
protected:
    CHttpServerContext    *pCtxt;
    int HexToInt(TCHAR tc);

};


#endif
```

As you will notice, this class has two constructors. This is in case you derive a class that doesn't use **CHttpServerContext**. The constructor simply saves any relevant information in private variables.

## Constructors and Destructor

The implementation for the constructors and destructor is in **HttpBase.cpp**:

```
//////////////////////////////////////////////////////////////////
// Implementation file for CHttpBase
#include "stdafx.h"
#include "HttpBase.h"

CHttpBase::CHttpBase(CHttpServerContext *pInCtxt)
{
    pCtxt = pInCtxt;
}

CHttpBase::CHttpBase()
{
    pCtxt = NULL;
}

CHttpBase::~CHttpBase()
{
}
```

## GetFromString()

I included the **GetFromString()** function in this class as I found myself using it frequently. It's a simple string-parsing function and we'll see it used in the **CHttpCookie** class that we list later.

```
BOOL CHttpBase::GetFromString(LPCSTR pszSearchIn, const LPCSTR pszSearchFor,
                    const LPCSTR pszTokens,CString *pstringValue)
{
    char *pszStartAt;
    char *pszEndAt;
    char *pszValue;
    INT   nLength;

    if((pszStartAt = strstr(pszSearchIn, pszSearchFor))==NULL)
        return FALSE;
    if ((pszEndAt = strpbrk(pszStartAt,pszTokens))==NULL)
```

```
    {
        *pstringValue = pszStartAt;
    }
    else
    {
        nLength = pszEndAt-pszStartAt;
        pszValue = new char[nLength+1];
        strncpy(pszValue, pszStartAt, nLength);
        *(pszValue+nLength)='\0';
        *pstringValue = pszValue;
        delete pszValue;
    }
    return TRUE;
}
```

## HexToInt()

The **HexToInt()** is a simple function that does what its name implies; it's used only for the **UrlDecode()** function.

```
int CHttpBase::HexToInt(TCHAR tc)
{
    if (tc >= _T('0') && tc <= _T('9'))
        return (tc - _T('0'));

    if ((tc>= _T('a') && tc<= _T('f')) ||
        (tc>= _T('A') && tc<= _T('F')))
        return (tolower (tc) - _T('a') + 10);

    return -1;
}
```

## UrlDecode() and UrlEncode()

If you're a CGI programmer, you'll be very familiar with the **UrlDecode()** function. However, if you're meeting this function for the first time, you'll have probably noticed that when you submit a form, the URL that it goes to (if it was done using the **GET** method) contains a bunch of **%** and **+** signs. Before a browser sends text to the server, it **UrlEncode**s the data. This consists of changing all white spaces to **+** signs and replacing any non-alphanumeric character with a **%** sign followed by its hexadecimal value. Thus the " (double quotation mark) becomes **%**22. In the previous examples, MFC has taken care of the decoding for us. However, we're now overriding some of the MFC implementation and will be required to do our own decoding. An MFC maven might note that there are MFC functions which will URL-decode data for us. While this is true, I am still including the code here as I use it in non-MFC extensions that require that data be URL-decoded. In addition, we sometimes need to URL-encode data before it is sent back to the client. This situation might occur when you're building a link to an ISAPI extension dynamically. Neither **CHtmlStream** nor **CHttpServerContext::WriteClient()** have any mechanism to URL-encode data going to the client, so you'll need to encode the data yourself. I will illustrate exactly what needs to be encoded before it's sent to the client and what doesn't by means of a couple of simple examples.

When you're simply returning data to the client, you don't need to encode it. You should simply send it over using **WriteClient()** or the **CHtmlStream**. For example:

```
*pCtxt << _T("Jack & Jill");
```

If, however, you're building a link to an ISAPI/CGI script and wish to place parameters in the link, you should always encode the parameters. For example, consider the following:

```
*pCtxt << _T("<a href=\"/scripts/myisapi.dll?name=Jack&Jill\">Click here</a>");
```

In this case, the browser will not encode the data on the link and will send over a **QUERY_STRING** of **name=Jack&Jill** which will be interpreted as two separate parameters which isn't what we intended. Thus, the proper link should look as follows:

```
*pCtxt << _T("<a href=\"/scripts/myisapi.dll?name=Jack%26Jill\">Click here</a>");
```

which is exactly what **UrlEncode()** would have given us. (Note: **%26** is the hex encoding for the **&** sign.)

As a final example, if you're dynamically building a form, you shouldn't encode the data as all browsers automatically encode form data. Thus, if we have

```
*pCtxt << _T("<form method=GET action=/scripts/myisapi.dll>");
*pCtxt << _T("<input type=hidden name=RIGHT value=\"Jack&Jill\");
*pCtxt << _T("<input type=hidden name=WRONG value=\"Jack%26Jill\");
*pCtxt << _T("<input type=submit");
*pCtxt << _T("</form>");
```

when the client clicks the submit button, both hidden forms will automatically be encoded and the **QUERY_STRING** will look as follows:

**RIGHT=Jack%26Jill&WRONG=Jack%2526Jill**

When your extension decodes this, it will have **RIGHT=Jack&Jill** and **WRONG=Jack%26Jill**. The same would have occurred if we had used the **POST** method rather than the **GET**.

The functions to encode and decode are given here:

```
void CHttpBase::UrlDecode(CString *pstringUrlValue)
{
    TCHAR    chCurrentChar;
    TCHAR    chTempChar;
    int      nValue;
    int nLength;
    int nCurrentPos = 0;
    CString    stringNew;

    nLength = pstringUrlValue->GetLength();
    while (nCurrentPos<nLength)
    {
        chCurrentChar = pstringUrlValue->GetAt(nCurrentPos);
        if (chCurrentChar=='+')
            chCurrentChar=' ';
        if (chCurrentChar=='%')
        {
            if (nCurrentPos+2<nLength)          // We still have more characters
            {
                chCurrentChar=pstringUrlValue->GetAt(++nCurrentPos);
```

```
            if ((nValue=HexToInt(chCurrentChar))==-1)
            {
                // Not a valid URL encoded string
                return;
            }
            chTempChar = (TCHAR) (nValue << 4);

            chCurrentChar=pstringUrlValue->GetAt(++nCurrentPos);
            if ((nValue=HexToInt(chCurrentChar))==-1)
            {
                // Not a valied URL encoded string
                return;
            }

            chTempChar |= (TCHAR) (nValue);
            chCurrentChar = chTempChar;
        }
        else
        {
            return;
        }
    }
    stringNew+=chCurrentChar;
    nCurrentPos++;
    }
    *pstringUrlValue=stringNew;
}


void CHttpBase::UrlEncode(CString *pstringUrlValue)
{
    TCHAR    chCurrentChar;
    CString   stringNew;
    TCHAR    achHex[2];

    int nLength=pstringUrlValue->GetLength();
    int nCurrentPos=-1;

    while (++nCurrentPos<nLength)
    {
        chCurrentChar = pstringUrlValue->GetAt(nCurrentPos);
        if (chCurrentChar == ' ')
        {
            stringNew+="+";
            continue;
        }
        if ((chCurrentChar>= _T('0') && chCurrentChar<= _T('9')) ||
            (chCurrentChar>= _T('a') && chCurrentChar<= _T('z')) ||
            (chCurrentChar>= _T('A') && chCurrentChar<= _T('Z')))
        {
            stringNew+=chCurrentChar;
            continue;
        }
        sprintf(achHex,"%x",chCurrentChar);
        stringNew+='%'+achHex;
    }

    *pstringUrlValue=stringNew;
}
```

# CHttpCookie

Our class to deal with **HTTP-COOKIES** is declared here in **HttpCookie.h**:

```
#include "HttpBase.h"

#define START_COOKIE_SIZE    512
#define MAX_COOKIE_SIZE   4096

class CHttpCookie: private CHttpBase
{
public:
    CString CreateCookie(CString stringName, CString stringValue, int nDays=0,
        CString stringPath="", CString stringDomain="", BOOL bIsSecure=FALSE);
    CHttpCookie(CHttpServerContext *pCtxt);
    ~CHttpCookie();

    BOOL GetCookie(LPCSTR pszName, CString *pstringCookie);

    CString    m_stringCookie;
};
```

## Constructor and Destructor

When the class is instantiated, it first gets all the **HTTP-COOKIE** variables sent over from the client. It tries to fit them into the **START_COOKIE_SIZE** buffer. If the client is sending over large cookies, it will expand the buffer up the **MAX_COOKIE_SIZE**. If you expect larger cookies, you'll need to change the size of these values. However, you shouldn't be using cookies that size under normal circumstances. This file is **HttpCookie.cpp**:

```
#include <stdafx.h>
#include "HttpCookie.h"

CHttpCookie::CHttpCookie(CHttpServerContext *pCtxt): CHttpBase(pCtxt)
{
    CHAR szTemp[START_COOKIE_SIZE];
    DWORD cbSize;

    cbSize = sizeof(szTemp);
    if (pCtxt->GetServerVariable("HTTP_COOKIE",szTemp,&cbSize))
    {
        m_stringCookie = szTemp;
        return;
    }

    if (ERROR_INSUFFICIENT_BUFFER==GetLastError() && cbSize<=MAX_COOKIE_SIZE)
    {
        // There could be large cookies in the header,
        // so we try a larger size
        TCHAR*    pszHttpCookie;

        pszHttpCookie = new CHAR[cbSize+1];
        cbSize = sizeof(*pszHttpCookie)*(cbSize+1);

        if(!pCtxt->GetServerVariable("HTTP_COOKIE",pszHttpCookie, &cbSize))
            *pszHttpCookie='\0';
```

```
        else
            pszHttpCookie[cbSize]='\0';
        m_stringCookie = pszHttpCookie;
        delete [] pszHttpCookie;
        return;
    }
    // If there data still won't fit, we aren't interested in it
    // If you expect large cookies, set MAX_COOKIE_SIZE larger than 4k
    m_stringCookie="";
}
```

The destructor does nothing, as the cookie is held in a **CString** object which frees itself up when the class is deleted.

```
CHttpCookie::~CHttpCookie()
{
}
```

There are only two other functions that are needed: one to get a specific cookie, and one to create a new cookie.

## GetCookie()

In order to get the cookie, we call **GetFromString()** and have it break on; which is how cookies are delimited when sent over from the client. When the cookie is matched by **GetFromString**, it is in the form **COOKIE_NAME=COOKIE_VALUE**. We cut out the value and return it:

```
BOOL CHttpCookie::GetCookie(LPCSTR pszName, CString *pstringCookie)
{
    CString stringTempCookie;
    int    nStartCut;

    // Get the Whole cookie we are looking for
    if(!GetFromString(m_stringCookie, pszName,";",&stringTempCookie))
        return FALSE;

    // Get rid of the stuff before the =
    if ((nStartCut=stringTempCookie.Find("="))>=0)
        *pstringCookie=stringTempCookie.Right(stringTempCookie.GetLength()-nStartCut-1);
    return TRUE;
}
```

## CreateCookie()

To create a new cookie, you must write a header with the following format:

**Set-Cookie: NAME=VALUE; expires=DATE; path=PATH; domain=DOMAIN_NAME; secure**

As noted above, the only required items to set a cookie are the name and value. Our function incorporates this, as these are the only required parameters to the function. If you do specify any additional information to the function, it will properly format it for you and return the string required to create the cookie. Once you have this string, you will need to call the **AddHeader()** function to actually send it to the client.

If you call **CreateCookie()** with a negative number for the number of days until expiration, it will return a valid cookie to send to the client. When you send this cookie to the client, it will erase the original cookie from the client as the expiry date is in the past.

```
CString CHttpCookie::CreateCookie(CString stringName, CString stringValue,
                        int nDays, CString stringPath, CString stringDomain,
                        BOOL bIsSecure)
{
    CString retString;

    CTime Expires = CTime::GetCurrentTime();
    CTimeSpan Extend(nDays,0,0,0);
    Expires+=Extend;

    // All Cookies must have name=value
    retString = "Set-Cookie: "+stringName+"="+stringValue;

    // The default is to expire at the end of the session,
    // but we can tell the browser to hold it longer
    if (nDays!=0)
        retString=retString+"; expires="+Expires.FormatGmt("%A, %d-%b-%Y %H:%M:%S GMT");

    //  We can also specify a different path.
    if (stringPath!="")
        retString=retString + "; path="+stringPath;

    //  Or a different domain
    if (stringDomain!="")
        retString=retString + "; domain="+stringDomain;

    // Only transmit the cookie over a secure connection.
    if (bIsSecure)
        retString = retString +"; secure ";

    retString = retString +"\r\n";
    return retString;

}
```

# CHttpForm

Any extension that wants to deal flexibly with forms must use a class similar to **CHttpForm**. **CHttpForm** is worthless without **CWroxHttp**, but we'll give its description here; you'll see how **CWroxHttp** uses it shortly. **CHttpForm** is declared in **HttpForm.h** as:

```
// HttpForm.h
//

#include "HttpBase.h"


struct FORM_FIELDS {
   FORM_FIELDS *pNextField;
   CString    lvalue;
   CString rvalue;
};
```

```
class CHttpForm: private CHttpBase
{
public:
    CHttpForm(CHttpServerContext* pCtxt);
    ~CHttpForm();

    BOOL FormFields(LPCSTR pszName, CString* pstringValue,int nCount=1);
    BOOL FormFieldsByNumber(CString* pstringLvalue, CString* pstringRvalue, int
nCount);
    int    m_nFieldCount;
    CString   m_stringQueryString;

private:
    FORM_FIELDS *pFieldBase;
    void ParseQueryString();
    void AddFormItem(FORM_FIELDS **pCurrentField, CString lvalue, CString rvalue);

};
```

## Constructor

When **CHttpForm** is instantiated, it parses through the query string to create a linked list of form items. The perceptive reader might think that the method given below would only work if the form is called with a **GET** method. However, we'll see why this isn't the case when we look at **CWroxHttp**. In the meantime, here's **HttpForm.cpp**:

```
#include "stdafx.h"
#include "HttpForm.h"

CHttpForm::CHttpForm(CHttpServerContext * pCtxt)
{
    m_nFieldCount=0;
    m_stringQueryString = pCtxt->m_pECB->lpszQueryString;

    // Get Rid of the '?'
    int QPosition = m_stringQueryString.Find('?');
    if (QPosition>=0)
    {
        m_stringQueryString = m_stringQueryString.Right(
            m_stringQueryString.GetLength()-QPosition-1);
    }
    ParseQueryString();
}
```

The reason it must first search for the **?** before deleting it is that you may have called the default procedure, in which case there will be no **?** in the query string.

## ParseQueryString()

The **ParseQueryString** function does the work of parsing up and decoding the form values by looking for **&** signs to signify the splitting of pairs and **=** signs to indicate the splitting of the name and value.

```
void CHttpForm::ParseQueryString()
{
```

```
int nCurrentPos = 0;
int nLength = m_stringQueryString.GetLength();

// Make sure we have something to parse
if (nLength ==0)
{
   pFieldBase=NULL;
   return;
}

CString    stringLValue;
CString stringRValue;
BOOL    bIsLValue=TRUE;
FORM_FIELDS *pCurrentFields=NULL;
CHAR    chCurrentChar;

// Loop though a character at a time
while (nCurrentPos < nLength)
{
    chCurrentChar = m_stringQueryString[nCurrentPos];

    // Look for pairs seperated by & or end of string
    if (chCurrentChar=='&' || nCurrentPos==(nLength-1))
    {
        // We found a new one
        if (nCurrentPos==(nLength-1) && chCurrentChar!='=')
           stringRValue+=chCurrentChar;

        bIsLValue = TRUE;
        AddFormItem(&pCurrentFields, stringLValue, stringRValue);
        stringLValue="";
        stringRValue="";
        nCurrentPos++;
        continue;
    }
    // Switching sides from left to right
    if (chCurrentChar=='=')
    {
        bIsLValue = FALSE;
        nCurrentPos++;
        continue;
    }
    if (bIsLValue)
    {
        stringLValue+=chCurrentChar;
    }
    else
    {
        stringRValue+=chCurrentChar;
    }
    nCurrentPos++;
  }
}
```

## AddFormItem()

When the **ParseQueryString** function has parsed out a pair, it needs to insert it into our linked list of
**FORM_FIELDS** structures by using the following function:

```
void CHttpForm::AddFormItem(FORM_FIELDS **pCurrentField, CString lvalue, CString
rvalue)
{

    if (*pCurrentField == NULL)
    {
        *pCurrentField = new FORM_FIELDS;
        pFieldBase = *pCurrentField;
    }
    else
    {
        (*pCurrentField)->pNextField = new FORM_FIELDS;
        *pCurrentField=(*pCurrentField)->pNextField;
    }

    // Defined in CHttpBase
    UrlDecode(&lvalue);
    UrlDecode(&rvalue);
    (*pCurrentField)->lvalue = lvalue;
    (*pCurrentField)->rvalue = rvalue;
    (*pCurrentField)->pNextField = NULL;
    m_nFieldCount++;
}
```

## FormFields()

Once the data is stored in the linked list, **CHttpForm** has two methods for retrieving information: by name or by number. The most common method is to retrieve by name. Let's say that you have a list box which asks people which Internet browser they use. Of course, it will allow the user to select more than one, as he or she might use several different types. The HTML would look like this:

```
<select multiple name="browser">
<option>Microsoft
<option>Netscape
<option>NCSA
</select>
```

As you already know, the use of a standard MFC parse map on this type of input is unrealistic. However, we can obtain the values from **CHttpForm** by a call to the member function **FormFields()**. We would pass it the name of the form item we're looking for (in this case, **browser**), an address to a **CString** that will contain the value on return, and the number of the occurrence we're looking for. Let's say that in the above browser example, the user select Netscape and NCSA. We'll use a **CString** object called **stringName** to hold our values.

**FormFields("browser", stringName,1)** returns **TRUE** and **stringName** is "Netscape".

**FormFields("browser", stringName,2)** returns **TRUE** and **stringName** is "NCSA".

**FormFields("browser", stringName,3)** returns **FALSE** and **stringName** is "".

Thus, to get all the selected items you simply need to loop though until **FormFields()** returns **FALSE**. You can also use **FormFields(formItem, stringName)** to get non-multiselect items such as text boxes or radio buttons.

The **FormFields()** function is given below. You can see that all it does is scan through the linked list of name value pairs until it finds the **nCount** occurrence of the name you are looking for.

```
BOOL CHttpForm::FormFields(LPCSTR pszName, CString* pstringValue, int nCount)
{
    FORM_FIELDS    *Field=pFieldBase;
    int    nCurrentCount=0;

    if (pFieldBase==NULL)
    {
        *pstringValue = "";
        return FALSE;
    }

    // Loop through all the FORM_FIELDS
    do
    {
        // Find one that matches
        if (!strcmp(Field->lvalue,pszName))
        {
            // Check to see if its number we asked for
            if (++nCurrentCount==nCount)
            {
                *pstringValue = Field->rvalue;
                return TRUE;
            }
        }
        Field=Field->pNextField;
    } while (Field!=NULL);

    *pstringValue = "";
    return FALSE;
}
```

## FormFieldsByNumber()

In case you don't know the name of the form variable you're looking for, you can always call **FormFieldsByNumber()** and pass it the number of the form item you're looking for. Since browsers sometimes mix up the order in which they send over information on a form, you shouldn't assume that the first item you listed in your HTML form will be returned by **FormFieldsByNumber(CString, CString, 1)**. The main use for **FormFieldsByNumber()** is to list all elements of a form regardless of their names. The function is given here:

```
BOOL CHttpForm::FormFieldsByNumber(CString* pstringLValue, CString* pstringRValue, int
nCount)
{
    int CurrentCount=1;
    FORM_FIELDS    *Field=pFieldBase;

    *pstringLValue = "";
    *pstringRValue = "";

    if (pFieldBase==NULL || nCount>m_nFieldCount)
    {
        return FALSE;
    }
```

```
    // Loop through the FORM_FILEDS until we have the number we asked for
    while (CurrentCount++<nCount && Field!=NULL)
    {
        Field=Field->pNextField;
    }

    if(Field!=NULL)
    {
        *pstringLValue = Field->lvalue;
        *pstringRValue = Field->rvalue;
    }
    return TRUE;
}
```

## Destructor

Lastly, since the **CHttpForm** creates the linked list, it needs to clean it up when it is done with it. This is taken care of in the destructor:

```
CHttpForm::~CHttpForm()
{
    FORM_FIELDS    *Field = pFieldBase;
    FORM_FIELDS *NextField;

    while(Field!=NULL)
    {
        NextField=Field->pNextField;
        delete Field;
        Field=NextField;
    }
}
```

# CWroxHttp

**CWroxHttp** is a very small but useful class. It greatly extends the MFC ISAPI classes in just a few lines of code because it lets MFC do everything for it. **CWroxHttp** is defined as follows in **WroxHttp.h**:

```
// WroxHttp.h: header file
//


class CWroxHttp: public CHttpServer
{

public:
    int CallFunction(CHttpServerContext* pCtxt, LPTSTR pszQuery,  LPTSTR pszCommand);
    CWroxHttp();
    virtual ~CWroxHttp();
};
```

## CallFunction()

You'll notice that **CallFunction()** is an overridden function of the **CHttpServer** class. The trick is to take advantage of everything that MFC does for us, but still get it to do what we want. The first thing we need to do is to be able to have a variable number of form items without having to change the actual number of parameters our functions take. Of course, we still want to take advantage of the parse map macros as they let us keep all our functions in one DLL without using tiresome **if** statements. This greatly simplifies code management as well as improving speed of execution. The way to do this is to override **CallFunction()** as follows:

```
int CWroxHttp::CallFunction(CHttpServerContext* pCtxt, LPTSTR pszQuery,   LPTSTR
pszCommand)
{
    TCHAR    szTempQueryString[1024];       // Create our dummy "QUERY_STRING"
    LPTSTR    pszTempQuery;
    INT    nCount=0;
    LPSTR    lpszPlaceHolder;
    INT    nRetVal;

    lpszPlaceHolder = pCtxt->m_pECB->lpszQueryString;  // Save the current state
    pszTempQuery = szTempQueryString;            // We need the pointer for CallFunction
    *pszTempQuery = '\0';                  // If the client didn't specify
                                //?command? in the URL, use the default
    if (pszCommand == NULL) {
        while (*(pszQuery+nCount)!='\0')         // Loop through the REAL QUERY_STRING
        {
            if (*(pszQuery+nCount++)=='?')        //  Find the command delimiter '?'
            {
                strncpy(pszTempQuery,pszQuery,nCount);  // Make our dummy have the command
                *(pszTempQuery+nCount)='\0';        // followed by a '?' then '\0'
                break;
            }
        }
    }
    else
    {
        strcpy(pszTempQuery,pszCommand);
        strcat(pszTempQuery,"?");
        pCtxt->m_pECB->lpszQueryString=pszQuery;
    }

    // Make MFC think that client specified only the command, no parameters.
    // All the information we
    try {
        nRetVal = CHttpServer::CallFunction(pCtxt, pszTempQuery,   NULL);
        pCtxt->m_pECB->lpszQueryString = lpszPlaceHolder;
    }
    catch (...) {
        // In case an error occured, we need to put this back so the server
        // can free up the memory.
        pCtxt->m_pECB->lpszQueryString = lpszPlaceHolder;
        throw;
    }
    return nRetVal;
}
```

The way this works is that **CWroxHttp** handles the **CallFunction()** by intercepting the **pszQuery** and **pszCommand** parameters that MFC uses to call the parse map macro and substitutes them with what we want. If the client called this request with a **GET** method, **pszQuery** points to the actual ECB structure. If we edit it directly, we'll have changed the client's request and will not be able to get any of the information passed over. To avoid this, we use our own variable **szTempQueryString** and a pointer to it **pszTempQuery**.

Let's say we received a request for **http://myhost.com/scripts/myisapi.dll?read?name=Michael** using the **GET** method. The **pszQuery** variable would point to "read?name=Michael". We want the part before the **?**, so the **CHttpServer::CallFunction()** function will call the **read()** function. We don't want to have to take any parameters, however, so we simply truncate anything after the **?**. This leaves the parse map macros intact except that each function must have **ITS_EMPTY** for its parameter no matter what the form sends over.

If the extension was called with the **POST** method, **pszQuery** would point to the same data and **szCommand** would be **read?**. However, when called with the **POST** method, **pszQuery** points to its own memory location, not back to the ECB structure. The problem that occurs when the client uses the **POST** method is that the MFC code has already read all the data from the client. If you remember from the chapter on HTTP variables, the **POST** method only gives the first 48K of data. Anything after that needs to be picked up with subsequent calls to **ReadClient()**. However, once the data is read, it can't be read again. MFC has read this data, and stored it in the area pointed to by **pszQuery**. We can't pass **pszQuery** directly to our ISAPI function as it only takes the pointer to the **CHttpServerContext** variable as a parameter. The solution is temporarily to point the extension control blocks **lpszQueryString** to the data pointed to by **pszQuery**. There's no harm in doing this, as we point it back when we're done with it. This will have no effect on methods that call this extension using the **GET** method.

Since **szCommand** doesn't contain any information we need, we simply pass **NULL** to **CHttpServer::CallFunction()**. By passing **NULL**, the **CHttpServer::CallFunction()** looks for the method to call in the **pszTempQuery** parameter which we pass it. The **CHttpServer::CallFuntion()** doesn't look at our altered value in **lpszQueryString** at all.

## A Browser-independent CallFunction()

Previously, we've discussed how different browsers may have trouble using the **?command?parameters** format for the **QUERY_STRING**. Now, I will introduce an alternative to the **CallFunction()** given above that solves this problem. Instead of calling:

**http://myhost.com/scripts/myisapi.dll?read?name=Michael**

the client would call:

**http://myhost.com/scripts/myisapi.dll/read?name=Michael**

where a **/** is used to separate the command from the script name. While this looks like you're specifying an additional directory, don't worry, the web server is smart enough to figure out that the **.dll** indicates the filename to be executed and the **/** after that is specifying additional information, not an additional path. The web server even has a special name for this type of extra data–it's called the **PATH_INFO**, and it's stored inside the ECB structure under the name **lpszPathInfo**. In the following code, we simply use the **PATH_INFO** as the command. Since all browsers support sending over the **PATH_INFO**, there's no trouble using this implementation, and it's the one I use for all my ISAPI extensions.

```
int CWroxHttp::CallFunction(CHttpServerContext* pCtxt, LPTSTR pszQuery, LPTSTR
pszCommand)
{
    TCHAR   szTempQueryString[1024];       // Create our dummy "QUERY_STRING"
    LPTSTR   pszTempQuery;
    INT    nCount=0;
    LPSTR    lpszPlaceHolder;
```

```
    INT    nRetVal;

    lpszPlaceHolder = pCtxt->m_pECB->lpszQueryString;   // Save the current state
    pszTempQuery = szTempQueryString;                    // We need the pointer for
CallFunction
    *pszTempQuery = '\0';                    // If the client didn't specify
                          // /command? in the URL, use the default
    if (pszCommand!=NULL)
         pCtxt->m_pECB->lpszQueryString=pszQuery;
    if (*(pCtxt->m_pECB->lpszPathInfo)!='\0')
    {
        strcpy(pszTempQuery,pCtxt->m_pECB->lpszPathInfo+1);
        strcat(pszTempQuery,"?");
    }
    // Make MFC think that client specified only the command, no parameters.
    // All the information we need is pointed to by lpszQueryString
    try {
        nRetVal = CHttpServer::CallFunction(pCtxt, pszTempQuery,  NULL);
        pCtxt->m_pECB->lpszQueryString = lpszPlaceHolder;
    }
    catch (...) {
        // In case an error occured, we need to put this back so the server
        // can free up the memory.
        pCtxt->m_pECB->lpszQueryString = lpszPlaceHolder;
        throw;
    }
    return nRetVal;
}
```

As a note to the reader, the use of the above code is optional. The two functions are entirely interchangeable. However, if you do change them, be sure to call the extensions with a **/** in place of the first **?**.

## Constructor and Destructor

The constructor and destructor both do nothing; this section of code goes before **CallFunction()** in **WroxHttp.cpp**:

```
// WroxHttp.cpp: implementation file
//

#include "stdafx.h"
#include "WroxHttp.h"


//////////////////////////////////////////////////////////////////////
// CWroxHttp

CWroxHttp::CWroxHttp()
{
}


CWroxHttp::~CWroxHttp()
{
}
```

Now that we have the classes to handle variable length forms and cookies, we can start on our extension.

# The Cookie Extension

With all that code to fix up the MFC classes, you'll be surprised at how little code we now have to write to finish our cookie example.

To start with, create a new ISAPI project and call it WroxCookie if you want to follow along with the source. Next, change the declaration of **CWroxCookieExtension** so that it is derived from **CWroxHttp** rather than **CHttpServer**. Also, make sure the proper header files are included by adding

```
#include "WroxHttp.h"
```

above the class declaration in **WroxCookie.h**. At this time, you should either copy the source files for our custom classes into your **WroxCookie** directory, or into a different directory, and include this new directory in the list of directories that the compiler will look in by using Tools | Options Directories. Be sure to include the **.cpp** files in your project as well.

We'll be using two functions to handle the reading and writing of cookies: **ReadCookie()** and **SaveCookie()**. **ReadCookie()** will be the default function, so you can eliminate the **Default()** declaration. We're going to be using **CHttpForm**, so both functions take only the mandatory **CHttpServerContext** parameter.

For our database applications, we'll be using some familiar techniques from the last chapter. In this case, however, we need to generate our own unique key before we insert new rows into the table. If you're using SQL Server or Oracle, you could write stored procedures to take care of this for you; this is the preferred method. However, in this case, we'll select the maximum key during our constructor, and then simply increment it one for each new request. Of course, this assumes that other applications aren't inserting into this table. While this is a valid assumption in this case, you should make sure your own extensions have a valid method for generating unique keys.

The complete **WroxCookie.h** file is given here:

```
// WROXCOOKIE.H - Header file for your Internet Server
//      WroxCookie Extension

#include "resource.h"
#include "WroxHttp.h"
#include "DataPool.h"


class CWroxCookieExtension: public CWroxHttp
{
public:
   CWroxCookieExtension();
   ~CWroxCookieExtension();

   // Overrides
   // ClassWizard generated virtual function overrides
      // NOTE - the ClassWizard will add and remove member functions here.
      //    DO NOT EDIT what you see in these blocks of generated code!
   //{{AFX_VIRTUAL(CWroxCookieExtension)
public:
   virtual BOOL GetExtensionVersion(HSE_VERSION_INFO* pVer);
   //}}AFX_VIRTUAL
```

```
   // TODO: Add handlers for your commands here.
   // For example:

   void ReadCookie(CHttpServerContext* pCtxt);
   void SaveCookie(CHttpServerContext* pCtxt);

   DECLARE_PARSE_MAP()

   //{{AFX_MSG(CWroxCookieExtension)
   //}}AFX_MSG
   LONG    m_CookieIndex;
private:
   CDataPool     *pDataControl;
   CRITICAL_SECTION    csDataLock;
};
```

As you can see, we've also added an include for the **DataPool.h** file, so you'll need to copy the **.h** and **.cpp** files from the Chapter 4 code. The constructor and destructor are given as:

```
CWroxCookieExtension::CWroxCookieExtension()
{
   CDatabase* pDb;
   INT    nConnectionIndex;

   pDataControl = new CDataPool("DSN=WroxData;",30,"WroxCookie",2);

   nConnectionIndex=pDataControl->GetConnection(&pDb);

   CMaxCookie rsMaxCookie(pDb);

   rsMaxCookie.Open(CRecordset::snapshot,"select max(main) from cookie");

   if (rsMaxCookie.IsBOF())
      m_CookieIndex=1;
   else
      m_CookieIndex=rsMaxCookie.m_main;

   rsMaxCookie.Close();
   pDataControl->FreeConnection(nConnectionIndex);
   InitializeCriticalSection(&csDataLock);
}

CWroxCookieExtension::~CWroxCookieExtension()
{
   delete pDataControl;
   DeleteCriticalSection(&csDataLock);
}
```

The database calls in this extension are almost identical to those in the previous one. To create the **CMaxCookie** class, which is derived from **CRecordset**, you should use the Class Wizard as in the previous chapter. First, copy the Visual FoxPro **Cookie.dbf** file (you can get it from the web site) into the same directory as the previous chapter (this way you can use the same ODBC data source). Create the class, but don't bind all data rows. Instead, once the class is created from the ClassWizard, select the **CMaxCookie** class and the Member Variables tab. Select the column main, then Add Variable, and add an

**m_main** value which is **long**. Be sure to add the **#include "MaxCookie.h"** to the top of **WroxCookie.cpp**. The header and implementation files for the **CRecordset** classes in this chapter are on the web site in case you need to reference them, but they will not be listed here.

# Starting the Cookie

We'll start this extension with a call to the **ReadCookie** mechanism. All initial calls should be directed to this function by calling the URL **http://yourhost.com/scripts/WroxCookie.dll?ReadCookie?**. The first thing that **ReadCookie()** does is to check to see if the client sent over a valid cookie. If not, **ReadCookie()** does something similar to our first example in that it redirects the client's request to a file **/Custom.html**. Like the example in Chapter 3, this is accomplished by means of a call to the **ServerSupportFunction()** in the ECB structures. Unlike the example in Chapter 3, this isn't done using the **HSE_REQ_SEND_URL_REDIRECT_RESP** parameter (though it could be). In this case, we call the **HSE_REQ_SEND_URL** instead.

The **HSE_REQ_SEND_URL** is rather a misnomer in that the parameter can't be a full URL. The parameter it takes must be a file on your local server and must begin with a **/** (i.e. no relative paths are allowed). In the example in Chapter 3, the **HSE_REQ_SEND_URL_REDIRECT_RESP** took a full URL and sent it over to the client in the header of a **302 Object moved** response. The client's browser did the actual redirection. In the case of **HSE_REQ_SEND_URL**, the web server actually reads the file from the disk and sends it to the client. The way this is done is shown in the first couple of lines here:

```
void CWroxCookieExtension::ReadCookie(CHttpServerContext* pCtxt)
{
    CHttpCookie    CookieCheck(pCtxt);
    CString stringCookieValue;
    CHAR szCookieHTML[]="/custom.html";
    INT    nConnectionIndex;
    CDatabase*    pDb;

    // Check to see if they already have the cookie
    if (!CookieCheck.GetCookie("wroxcookie",&stringCookieValue))
    {
        // If not, send them to the page to fill out the form.
        pCtxt->ServerSupportFunction(HSE_REQ_SEND_URL, szCookieHTML, (LPDWORD)
sizeof(szCookieHTML), NULL);
        return;
    }

    nConnectionIndex = pDataControl->GetConnection(&pDb);
    try
    {
        CCookieSet    rsUrls(pDb);
        CString    stringSql;

        stringSql = "select * from cookie where main=" + stringCookieValue;
        rsUrls.Open(CRecordset::snapshot, stringSql);

        StartContent(pCtxt);
        WriteTitle(pCtxt);

        *pCtxt << _T("<center><h1>Custom Homepage</h1></center>");
        if (rsUrls.IsBOF())
        {
            *pCtxt << _T("You have no URLs listed.");
            return;
```

```
        }

        while (!rsUrls.IsEOF())
        {
            *pCtxt << _T("<a href=\"") << rsUrls.m_url << _T("\">")
                << rsUrls.m_name << _T("</a><br>");
            rsUrls.MoveNext();
        }
        rsUrls.Close();
    }
    catch(CDBException* pEx)
    {
        pDataControl->FreeConnection(nConnectionIndex);
        pDataControl->DisplayError(pCtxt,pEx);
        return;
    }
    catch (...)
    {
        pDataControl->FreeConnection(nConnectionIndex);
        *pCtxt << _T("UnHandled Error");
        return;
    }
    pDataControl->FreeConnection(nConnectionIndex);
    EndContent(pCtxt);
}
```

If the client does have a cookie, the values are in **stringCookieValue** and we use this to select from our database. In order to create the **CCookieSet** class, use the ClassWizard to bind all columns in the **Cookie.dbf** table. The files come with the source code from the web site in case you need to reference them. Don't forget to put your **#include "CookieSet.h"** in the **WroxCookie.cpp** file. In case you lost track of what **#include**s should be in the file, a complete list is presented here along with the parse maps:

```
// WROXCOOKIE.CPP - Implementation file for your Internet Server
//     WroxCookie Extension

#include "stdafx.h"
#include "HttpCookie.h"
#include "WroxCookie.h"
#include "MaxCookie.h"
#include "CookieSet.h"
#include "HttpForm.h"


/////////////////////////////////////////////////////////////////////
// The one and only CWinApp object
// NOTE: You may remove this object if you alter your project to no
// longer use MFC in a DLL.

CWinApp theApp;

/////////////////////////////////////////////////////////////////////
// command-parsing map

BEGIN_PARSE_MAP(CWroxCookieExtension, CHttpServer)
    // TODO: insert your ON_PARSE_COMMAND() and
    // ON_PARSE_COMMAND_PARAMS() here to hook up your commands.
```

```
    // For example:
    ON_PARSE_COMMAND(SaveCookie, CWroxCookieExtension, ITS_EMPTY)
    ON_PARSE_COMMAND(ReadCookie, CWroxCookieExtension, ITS_EMPTY)
    DEFAULT_PARSE_COMMAND(ReadCookie, CWroxCookieExtension)
END_PARSE_MAP(CWroxCookieExtension)


//////////////////////////////////////////////////////////////////////
// The one and only CWroxCookieExtension object

CWroxCookieExtension theExtension;
```

The parse maps are identical to those we've seen in previous chapters. Even the
**DEFAULT_PARSE_COMMAND** still works. The difference is that all the parameters must be **ITS_EMPTY**. As
noted in the discussion of **CWroxHttp**, we pass the parameters inside the **CHttpServerContext-
>m_pECB->lpszQueryString**.

If the client was sent to our **Custom.html** page, when he or she submits the form, the **SaveCookie()**
function is called. **SaveCookie()** must do two things: it must write the cookie to the client, and it must
save the data to our database. Inserting that data into the database is the same as the previous chapter.
Our calls to the **CreateCookie()** and **AddHeader()** functions are what's interesting here. The call to
**CreateCookie()** creates a valid cookie with the name of **WroxCookie** and a value of the data in
**stringTemp**. The cookie will expire in 30 days. Since **SaveCookie()** doesn't check to see whether the
client already has a **WroxCookie** cookie, this new value will overwrite anything that the client happens to
have already.

Since we aren't passing any additional parameters, the cookie will default to the path that called it (on the
domain that it's on.)

In order to send the cookie back to the client, you must call the **AddHeader()** function as seen below.
This simply adds our cookie header to the headers being sent over to the client. It's important to note that,
as all headers must come before any content, we must call the **AddHeader()** function before we make
any calls to **WriteClient()**, or input anything into the **HTMLstream** via the **<<** operator or calls to
**StartContent()**.

```
    void CWroxCookieExtension::SaveCookie(CHttpServerContext* pCtxt)
    {
        CHttpForm    Form(pCtxt);
        CHttpCookie    Cookie(pCtxt);
        CDatabase*    pDb;
        INT    nNextCookie;
        INT    nConnectionIndex;
        BOOL bHasLinks = FALSE;


        CString stringSql,stringCookie,stringTemp,stringTemp2;

        int    nFormCount=1;

        nConnectionIndex=pDataControl->GetConnection(&pDb);

        try
        {
            // Loop as long as there are non-blank entries
            while (Form.FormFields("name",&stringTemp,nFormCount) && stringTemp!="")
```

```
            {
                if (!bHasLinks)
                {
                    EnterCriticalSection(&csDataLock);
                    nNextCookie=++m_CookieIndex;
                    LeaveCriticalSection(&csDataLock);
                }
                Form.FormFields("url",&stringTemp2,nFormCount);
                stringSql.Format("insert into cookie (main,name,url) values "
                            "(%d,'%-.30s','%-.50s')",nNextCookie, stringTemp, stringTemp2);

                pDb->ExecuteSQL(stringSql);
                bHasLinks=TRUE;
                nFormCount++;
            }
    }
    catch(CDBException* pEx)
    {
        pDataControl->FreeConnection(nConnectionIndex);
        pDataControl->DisplayError(pCtxt,pEx);
        return;
    }
    catch (...)
    {
        pDataControl->FreeConnection(nConnectionIndex);
        *pCtxt << _T("UnHandled Error");
        return;
    }

    pDataControl->FreeConnection(nConnectionIndex);

        // Check to see if any fields were sent over
    if (!bHasLinks)
    {
        *pCtxt << _T("You didn't enter any links!");
        return;
    }

    stringTemp.Format("%d",nNextCookie);
    CHttpCookie     MyFirstCookie(pCtxt);

    // Get a string that holds a properly formated Set-Cookie: header
     stringCookie=MyFirstCookie.CreateCookie("wroxcookie",stringTemp,30);

    // Write the header to the client.  Note this MUST be called before
    // anything is written to the HTMLStream.
    AddHeader(pCtxt,stringCookie);

    // This writes data into the HTMLStream
    StartContent(pCtxt);
    WriteTitle(pCtxt);

    *pCtxt << _T("Your custom home page has been created.<br>\r\n");
    *pCtxt << _T("Click <a href=\"/scripts/WroxCookie.dll?ReadCookie?\">Here</a> to see
it.");

    EndContent(pCtxt);
}
```

Finally, to add database support to the extension, you need to add **#include <afxdb.h>** to your **stdafx.h** file.

## Building and Testing CWroxCookieExtension

By now, you should have no trouble building and debugging ISAPI extensions. Be sure the **Custom.html** file is in your **Wwwroot** directory and load the URL **http://127.0.0.1/scripts/WroxCookie.dll**. (Assuming you're debugging on the same machine that's running the web server.) Once you create your cookie, you can click on the link to read it.

If you haven't done a lot of CGI programming, you might try stepping through some of the **CHttpForm** and **CHttpCookie** functions to see what they actually do for you.

Of all the applications in the book, this one is the least complete. There's no way to edit the page once it has been entered, and the page always expires after 30 days, even if the user revisits it every day. Solutions to these problems don't cover any new material and are left to the reader as exercises.

## Summary

HTTP servers don't store state information about the clients connected to them. This means that it is (almost) impossible for the server to send back information to the client, depending on what that client has done in the past. To alleviate this problem, cookies where introduced.

Cookies are a mechanism that allows the server to remember a client. A cookie is generated by the server to identify the client uniquely, and is passed to the client in response to a URL. When the client receives a cookie, it will send this information back to the server with every URL request as part of its header information.

In this chapter, we've shown how you can generate cookies, and use them to store information into a database so that the server can send HTML documents that are unique to that client.

In the process of doing this, we have extended the functionality of the MFC classes to cope with situations that are not currently handled by them. In particular, we have created three classes:

- ▲ **CWroxHttp**, based on **CHttpServer** is used mainly to allow the use of **CHttpForm**. It strips the query string from the URL, then uses the parse map in **CHttpServer** to select the function to call based on the command passed.

- ▲ **CHttpForm**, derived from **CHttpBase**. This class allows the use of forms where the parameter list is not fixed, or when the form contains a multiple select list box.

- ▲ **CHttpCookie**, derived from **CHttpBase**. This class allows the use of cookies by providing functionality to send a cookie to the client, and read one from the request header if present.

# E-mailing Form Data

A common CGI program is one that takes the input of an HTML form and sends it to someone via e-mail. Usually, this program is written in PERL, and it most often runs on a UNIX system so that it can pipe the data to the **sendmail** command. Under NT, we don't have this option, and so the program that we shall develop will need to be a little more elaborate.

For this example, we need to perform the following tasks:

- Create a connection to an SMTP (Simple Mail Transfer Protocol) server.
- Send the appropriate commands to inform the SMTP server that we wish to send an e-mail message.
- Send the message itself.
- Lastly, we must sign off.

While this chapter is not supposed to teach you everything there is to know about SMTP, we'll need to cover enough of it to get us through the extension. What this chapter is supposed to teach you is how to do sockets programming inside an ISAPI extension. While doing this, however, we will also cover how to create additional threads and introduce another thread synchronization object: the event.

## Sockets Programming

Sockets originated in BSD UNIX in the early 1980s as a mechanism for two computers to communicate over a TCP/IP network. Today, they are used for almost every type of communication on the Internet. Every time you check your e-mail, or request a document from the Web, you are using sockets. A socket is nothing more than an interface that can both send and receive data over a TCP/IP network.

There are three properties which identify a socket: the IP address of the destination computer, the port number it is using, and whether the socket is using a TCP (Transmission Control Protocol) stream or UDP (User Datagram Protocol) datagram. Although you should be familiar with IP addresses, you may not have heard of ports, or the differences between TCP and UDP. A complete coverage of these issues is beyond the scope of this book, but any treatment of Internet programming must, at the very least, take a brief look at these core Internet concepts.

## Ports

A port is an assigned 'slot' that a program is either sending or receiving data on. A host can also be 'listening' on a port for other computers to contact it. A port is not a physical port, like your serial or parallel ports, but rather a header to the TCP or UDP packet which is used to identify where the packet should be delivered. Just as an IP address tells routers which computer to send packets to, ports tell your computer which application to send data to. To see how ports are used, imagine the following situation:

You are downloading a large file via FTP from Microsoft's site, and you want to check your e-mail. The FTP is providing a continuous stream of TCP/IP packets to your computer. The call to your mail server will also return some TCP/IP packets to you. How will your computer figure out whether the packets are supposed to go to your e-mail program or to your FTP program? The answer is this: your computer will look at the TCP header to find the destination port number. Let's say that the FTP program is using port number 24879, and the mail program is using 12782. All the TCP/IP packets with 24879 will go to the FTP program, and those with 12782 will go to your e-mail program.

An application can 'listen' on a certain port for incoming data. Your MSIIS server does this for all the services you have running. It listens on port 80 for incoming HTTP requests, port 21 for FTP requests, and port 70 for gopher requests. The server knows these port numbers through an established list of default socket addresses which servers listen on and clients send requests on. For example, HTTP servers know to listen on port 80, while SMTP servers know to listen on port 25. When your web browser wants to contact a web server, it knows the server will be listening on port 80, and therefore sends the packet to that port. When the server receives a request, it creates a new socket on a different port and starts communication with the client over this new socket. The server is then immediately ready to handle the next request, no matter how long the actual communication takes place for on the new socket. If the server didn't do this, it would only be able to handle one request at a time, which would definitely slow things down on the Internet.

## TCP vs. UDP

As we noted above, when you create a socket, you must specify the protocol which the socket will use. You can choose between TCP and UDP, but TCP is by far the most common, being used in FTP, HTTP, SMTP, and most other popular Internet protocols. TCP is the most popular choice because it provides a 'connection' between the two computers. Of course, this is not an actual physical connection but a virtual one, in the sense that the data packets themselves contain information which allows the two computers to each transmit and receive data (full duplex), verify that data sent was received by the other computer, and control the rate at which data is sent (flow control).

UDP, on the other hand, is referred to as a 'connectionless' protocol. The reason for this is that the source simply sends out a UDP packet and 'hopes' that the other computer gets it; it never checks. The most common use for this is when one server is broadcasting to many clients. For a real world example, imagine a time server that broadcasts the exact time, every minute, to synchronize the clocks of thousands of clients. If each one of these clients had to respond, and the server had to re-send the data to those that failed, then this would create a lot of unnecessary network traffic. Instead, the server simply sends the packets out. If a computer happens to miss a packet one minute, another one will be coming along in another 60 seconds anyway.

As you can probably surmise from the above discussion of the two protocols, we will only be using TCP for our examples. However, rather than concentrate on the exact mechanics of TCP/IP network protocols, let's take a look at how Windows uses them.

## Windows Sockets

If you are familiar with sockets programming in Windows, then you are probably used to the **asynchronous mode**, in which you call a function to perform a sockets operation and the function immediately returns. When the request is finished, your application receives a Windows message and you call another function to read the data.

This type of Windows socket is called a **non-blocking socket**, because the socket call does not block; it returns immediately. This paradigm is fine in an event-driven, Windows environment, where your application is constantly waiting for incoming Windows messages. However, in ISAPI, we don't want to have threads hanging around waiting for messages. Instead, we will use the MFC class **CSocket** to implement a **blocking socket**–one that waits for the socket call to finish before the function returns.

The only problem with this method is that if something is wrong with the connection, it could be a long time before the call finishes. In this case, we want to interrupt the call after so many seconds have elapsed and return an error message to the user.

Unfortunately, there is no time-out mechanism on a blocking sockets call. Instead, we must create another thread that will wait the desired number of seconds and then cancel the blocking sockets call for us. We will encapsulate this functionality into the **CISAPISocket**, which we shall derive from **CSocket**. Now, **CSocket** is itself derived from **CAsyncSocket**. Since **CSocket** does not override many of the **CAsyncSocket** functions, we will see some **CAsyncSocket** function calls as well.

Keep in mind that even though the functions are part of the **CAsyncSocket** class, the **CSocket** class sees to it that these calls are not made asynchronously. First, let us examine **CSocket** and **CAsyncSocket**, to see how they are used in sockets programming.

# CSocket

When the **CSocket** class is instantiated, it takes no parameters. This is because it doesn't actually establish a connection to anywhere. It simply allocates the resources for future calls to the socket. The single-sided socket is created with a call to the **Create()** method. This creates the socket on your machine; it doesn't connect it to another host. The **Create()** function is prototyped here:

```
BOOL Create(UINT nSocketPort = 0,
            int nSocketType = SOCK_STREAM,
            LPCTSTR lpszSocketAddress = NULL);
```

The socket port is the port on your machine that you wish to use. Unless you have a compelling reason (such as wanting the socket to listen on port 80 for incoming HTTP requests), you should let the **CSocket** class pick this port for you. It will pick a socket greater than 1024 that is currently free. The socket type can be either stream or datagram. As discussed above, our application will use the TCP stream, and so we can use the default. The socket address is the address on your machine that you wish to bind to this socket. If you have only one IP address assigned to your machine, you can pass the default of **NULL** and it will use that. If you have more than one IP address configured for your machine, you should specify an address. In this example, it doesn't matter which one you specify.

As with most **CSocket** methods, the **Create()** function returns a **BOOL** value to indicate success or failure. If the method does return a failure, you will need to call the **GetLastError()** function to see why the call failed.

## *Connecting to Another Computer*

Once the socket is created, the connection to the other computer can be made. (Note: it doesn't actually have to be on another computer; you can have two sockets communicating on the same computer, as a method of inter-process communications.) The function to connect to another socket is prototyped as follows:

```
BOOL CAsyncSocket::Connect(LPCTSTR lpszHostAddress,
                           UINT nHostPort);
```

The host address should be a string in the form **"204.124.25.129"** to constitute a valid IP address. The host port is the port to which you wish to connect. In this example, we will use port 25, since that is the default SMTP port.

> There is another **CASyncSocket::Connect()** function which is prototyped. Its use isn't relevant here, and we're going to leave it out of the discussion.

## Passing Information

Once the socket is created and connected, you should be able to read and write from it. The commands are prototyped here:

```
virtual int CASyncSocket::Send(const void* lpBuf,
                                   int nBufLen,
                                   int nFlags = 0);
virtual int CASyncSocket::Receive(void* lpBuf,
                                      int nBufLen,
                                      int nFlags = 0);
```

The **lpBuf** variable is a buffer that is either holding the data to be sent, or waiting to hold the data being received. The **nBufLen** is the size of the buffer. The **nFlags** variable is used only in advanced sockets programming, and will not be discussed here; the default of 0 will suffice.

The **Send()** and **Receive()** functions return three possible value types: **0**, **SOCKET_ERROR**, or the number of bytes sent or received. If an error is indicated by either a value of **0** or **SOCKET_ERROR**, you will need to call **GetLastError()** to determine the reason.

## Canceling Calls

Another method of **CSocket** that we are interested in is **CancelBlockingCall()**. This function takes no parameters, and cancels any blocking calls currently being made by the socket. The blocking call that is canceled will return **SOCKET_ERROR** and **GetLastError()** will show an error of **WSAEINTR**.

While there are a couple of other methods in **CSocket**, and quite a few more in **CASyncSocket**, they aren't used in this simple example. If you are going to program ISAPI extensions that make more extensive use of sockets, you should consult a book which covers more advanced issues of sockets programming.

# The FormMail Extension

The FormMail extension should be able to take any HTML form and send its contents to one or more users, via a standard SMTP mail server. For this example to work, you will need a working SMTP server. You probably use one already to send your e-mail, so simply find out its IP address and you will be ready to start.

The extension should take an HTML form such as:

```
<html><head>
<title>Professional ISAPI Programming - Chapter 6</title>
</head>
<body>
```

```
<form action="http://127.0.0.1/scripts/FormMail.dll" method="GET">
<input type=hidden name="mail-to" value="your_name@your_domain.com">
<input type=hidden name="mail-to" value="another_name@your_domain.com">
<input type=hidden name="mail-subject" value="Web Response">
Your Email Address:<br>
<input type=text name="mail-from">
<br>
Name:<br>
<input type=text name="Name">
<br>
Address:<br>
<input type=text name="Address">
<br>
Phone:<br>
<input type=text name="Phone">
<br>
How do you rate this book?<br>
<table>
<tr><td>Superb:<td><input type=radio name="Rating" value="Superb">
<tr><td>Excellent:<td><input type=radio name="Rating" value="Excellent">
<tr><td>Outstanding:<td><input type=radio name="Rating" value="Outstanding">
</table><p>
Comments:<br>
<textarea name="Comment" cols=60 rows=10></textarea>
<p>
<input type=submit>
</html>
```

When the client clicks the Submit button, the extension will e-mail the result to anyone specified in the hidden **mail-to** items. When received, the e-mail message should look like this:

```
From:joe@anything.com
Subject:Web Response

Name:Joe
Address:1234 Any Street
Phone:800-555-5555
Rating:Outstanding
Comments:  I particularly liked the chapter on the form to email extension.
```

# Starting with AppWizard

As with the cookie extension, create a new ISAPI extension and change the class so that it is derived from **CWroxHttp**, rather than **CHttpServer**. As this extension will only handle one function, we will leave the default parse map in place. The **FormMailExtension.h** file should look like this:

```
// FORMMAIL.H - Header file for your Internet Server
//     FormMail Extension

#include "resource.h"
#include <WroxHttp.h>


class CFormMailExtension: public CWroxHttp
{
public:
```

```
        CFormMailExtension();
        ~CFormMailExtension();

// Overrides
    // ClassWizard generated virtual function overrides
        // NOTE - the ClassWizard will add and remove member functions here.
        //    DO NOT EDIT what you see in these blocks of generated code!
    //{{AFX_VIRTUAL(CFormMailExtension)
    public:
    virtual BOOL GetExtensionVersion(HSE_VERSION_INFO* pVer);
    //}}AFX_VIRTUAL

    // TODO: Add handlers for your commands here.
    // For example:

    void Default(CHttpServerContext* pCtxt);

    DECLARE_PARSE_MAP()

    //{{AFX_MSG(CFormMailExtension)
    //}}AFX_MSG
};
```

The implementation file **CFormMailExtension.cpp** is as follows:

```
// FORMMAIL.CPP - Implementation file for your Internet Server
//      FormMail Extension

#include "stdafx.h"
#include "ISAPISocket.h"
#include "HttpForm.h"
#include "FormMail.h"

///////////////////////////////////////////////////////////////////////
// The one and only CWinApp object
// NOTE: You may remove this object if you alter your project to no
// longer use MFC in a DLL.

CWinApp theApp;

///////////////////////////////////////////////////////////////////////
// command-parsing map

BEGIN_PARSE_MAP(CFormMailExtension, CHttpServer)
    // TODO: insert your ON_PARSE_COMMAND() and
    // ON_PARSE_COMMAND_PARAMS() here to hook up your commands.
    // For example:

    ON_PARSE_COMMAND(Default, CFormMailExtension, ITS_EMPTY)
    DEFAULT_PARSE_COMMAND(Default, CFormMailExtension)
END_PARSE_MAP(CFormMailExtension)


///////////////////////////////////////////////////////////////////////
// The one and only CFormMailExtension object

CFormMailExtension theExtension;
```

```
/////////////////////////////////////////////////////////////////////
// CFormMailExtension implementation

CFormMailExtension::CFormMailExtension()
{
    LoadLibrary("FormMail.dll");
}

CFormMailExtension::~CFormMailExtension()
{
}

BOOL CFormMailExtension::GetExtensionVersion(HSE_VERSION_INFO* pVer)
{
    // Call default implementation for initialization
    CHttpServer::GetExtensionVersion(pVer);

    // Load description string
    TCHAR sz[HSE_MAX_EXT_DLL_NAME_LEN+1];
    ISAPIVERIFY(::LoadString(AfxGetResourceHandle(),
        IDS_SERVER, sz, HSE_MAX_EXT_DLL_NAME_LEN));
    _tcscpy(pVer->lpszExtensionDesc, sz);
    return TRUE;
}
```

## Unloading DLLs and Lost Threads

In the **CFormMailExtension()** constructor, you should have noticed a call to **LoadLibrary("FormMail.dll")**. At first, it may seem odd to have a DLL load itself, but let's look at the following scenario to see why this is necessary.

Associated with each thread is a **Thread Context structure**. It is used to save CPU state information about a thread before it is preempted by NT. For example, if one thread is running and has an important value saved in the AX register, but is pre-empted by another thread, the chances are that the other thread will alter the value in AX. When the first thread gets the CPU again, the value will be different and the program will probably crash.

To prevent this, NT automatically saves all the CPU registers to the Thread Context structure before it switches the thread out. (This is one of the many reasons why you don't want to inundate your system with threads that are waiting on the CPU: a lot of time will be spent just swapping register values.) The particular register that we are interested in here is the IP register. IP (when talking registers) stands for Instruction Pointer. It tells the CPU the memory address of the next instruction that the CPU will execute. The IP is a 32-bit value that points to a memory address somewhere inside the process's address space.

Now, let us say that **FormMail.dll** gets loaded into the memory starting at address 10000000. (By default, this is where it really does get loaded.) The **TimeOutThread()** function will be loaded at 10001180. When the **TimeOutThread()** thread starts, its initial IP will be 10001180; as it begins to execute, this will increment. Now, when the primary thread finishes, it exits, and the web server may try to unload your DLL. (It will always unload the DLL if you have the **CacheExtensions** registry entry set to 0.) In the event that the web server unloads your DLL, the chances are that, if you only have a single processor, the **TimeOutThread()** function thread never got a chance to finish executing. The web server will unload the library and NT will wipe clean the memory starting at 10000000 that the library used to occupy. In a couple more microseconds, when the web server is done with the unload, NT will pre-empt the web server to allow the **TimeOutThread()** function thread to run.

The first thing NT will do is restore all the registers from the **TimeOutThread()**'s Thread Context. Again, we are interested in the IP register. It will probably restore a value of 100011a4, which pointed to the next instruction that it wanted to execute. However, NT has unloaded all the code from that portion of memory. Instead of finding the next instruction, 100011a4 will contain empty data. When NT tries to execute this non-existent code, it will raise an exception and crash your web server.

In most cases, you will not have **CacheExtensions** turned off, as it adversely affects performance. However, we still want to make sure that your DLL will clean itself up when being unloaded. The simple solution is to call **LoadLibrary()** as we did in our constructor, which maps a DLL into a process's address space. If the DLL is already mapped, it simply increments the usage count. Calls to unload the library decrement the usage count. Only when the usage count goes to 0 does NT actually unmap the code from the process's address space. By calling **LoadLibrary()** on itself, this extension makes sure that the increment count never goes to 0 and thus the code will never be unloaded. Of course, NT will unload the whole thing when it cleans up the process's address space at the time the web server itself is shutdown, and cleanup will be smooth.

## CISAPISocket

Before we look at the **Default()** function for this extension, let's look at the **CISAPISocket** class that we need to create. The **ISAPISocket.h** header file looks like this:

```
// ISAPISocket.h

#ifndef _ISAPISOCKET_H
#define _ISAPISOCKET_H

#include <afxsock.h>

#define MAX_RECEIVE    1024

class CISAPISocket: public CSocket
{
public:
    CISAPISocket();
    ~CISAPISocket();
    INT Receive(CString *pstringReceive);
    INT Send(LPCSTR   lpszSend);
    HANDLE   hEventBlocking;
};

#endif
```

In the above code, you can see that we are using another **HANDLE** variable. In this case, it will be for an event rather than a semaphore. The **Receive()** and **Send()** functions are only included to make our programming a little easier. Neither of them adds any functionality to the **CSocket** class.

### Events

Events, like semaphores and critical sections, are thread synchronization objects. The event is very similar to a critical section, except that it allows certain options to be set which give you much more control over what state the event is in. As with all synchronization objects, the event can exist in one of two states: signaled and non-signaled.

An event is created with a call to the **CreateEvent()** function, prototyped here:

```
HANDLE CreateEvent(LPSECURITY_ATTRIBUTES lpEventAttributes,
                   BOOL bManualReset,
                   BOOL bInitialState,
                   LPCTSTR lpName);
```

The **lpEventAttributes** is the same security attributes structure that was used in **CreateSemaphore()**. Since this only applies to child processes, and we are not creating any child processes here, we will pass it **NULL** when we come to creating our event.

The **bManualReset** determines whether or not the event is set to the non-signaled state after a single thread has been released from either a **WaitForSingleObject()** or **WaitForMultipleObjects()** call. If the value passed is **TRUE**, the event is left signaled. If it is **FALSE**, the NT operating system will automatically reset the event to non-signaled for you.

To see how the **bManualReset** affects events, imagine the following situation. You have a thread which is modifying data, and several other threads that are waiting to read the data. While the data is being modified, you can keep other threads from accessing it with an event. All threads must call a **WaitForSingleObject()** and wait for the event to become signaled. Before the modifying thread changes any data, it will manually make the event non-signaled, so that all other threads must wait for it to finish its changes before they can access the data. Once the thread has finished modifying the data, it signals the event. When this occurs, the flood gates are opened, and all waiting threads are allowed to read the data. The event will not be non-signaled again until another thread wants to modify the data and manually marks it as such. Therefore, the call to **WaitForSingleObject()** doesn't change the status of the event in anyway. (We will see an example which uses a similar technique in a later chapter.

If the manual reset is set to **FALSE**, NT will allow only one thread to continue before it automatically resets the event to a non-signaled state. In this case, it is acting identically to a critical section, except that it can be shared across processes, and has a time-out limit. The reader should note that, as with the critical section, you have no choice over which thread will be the one that gets the signaled event. NT decides this for you.

The **bInitialState** parameter sets the event in the signaled state if **TRUE**, non-signaled if **FALSE**.

Like semaphores, events can be created with names, so that the same event can be used across processes to synchronize threads. The event can also be created with a **NULL** name if there is no need to share it with anyone. If you do create a **NULL** name for a thread, the only way to reference it is by its handle. So even if you want to share the same event inside the same process, you may need to give it a name, since one function might not have access to the handle. You should also note that synchronization object names are case-sensitive.

The event is accessed using the familiar **WaitForSingleObject()** or **WaitForMultipleObjects()** functions.

The event is freed by a call to the **CloseHandle()** function. Just as a reminder, it's important to call **CloseHandle()** when you are done with the event, as NT will only delete the object when the process terminates (i.e. the web server is shut down).

### CISAPISocket Implementation

The **WaitForSingleObject()** call comes in the globally defined function **TimeOutThread()**. The thread will wait for a maximum of 10 seconds in the call. If the wait times out, the thread cancels any blocking sockets call; otherwise it just returns.

```
// ISAPISocket.cpp

#include "stdafx.h"
#include "ISAPISocket.h"

UINT TimeOutThread(LPVOID pParam)
{
   DWORD    dwWaitStatus;
   CISAPISocket *pThreadSocket;

   pThreadSocket = (CISAPISocket*)pParam;
   dwWaitStatus = WaitForSingleObject(
                               pThreadSocket->hEventBlocking,10000);
   // Only cancel it if the wait timed out
   if (dwWaitStatus==WAIT_TIMEOUT)
      pThreadSocket->CancelBlockingCall();
   return 0;
}
```

The constructor creates the event in the non-signaled state, and sets the manual reset to **FALSE**. (In this example, the manual reset doesn't matter, since only one thread will be waiting on this event, and it only waits once.) We use a **NULL** name because we will pass the handle to the event to any thread that needs it.

```
CISAPISocket::CISAPISocket()
{
   //Create the event in the NON-SIGNALED state
   hEventBlocking = CreateEvent(NULL,FALSE,FALSE, NULL);
   //Create the thread and pass it a reference to this CISAPISocket class
   AfxBeginThread(TimeOutThread, this);
}
```

The destructor simply frees up the event:

```
CISAPISocket::~CISAPISocket()
{
   // SIGNAL the event so our created thread will finish
   SetEvent(hEventBlocking);
   CloseHandle(hEventBlocking);
}
```

As we mentioned earlier, the **Send()** and **Receive()** functions don't add that much functionality. For the **Send()** function, we simply pass on the request to the base class. For **Receive()**, we do a little more work so that we don't have to worry about passing the length of the buffer to the base class.

```
INT CISAPISocket::Send(LPCSTR lpszSend)
{
   return CSocket::Send(lpszSend, strlen(lpszSend));
}

INT CISAPISocket::Receive(CString *pstringReceive)
{
   INT nRetVal;
   TCHAR    lpReceiveBuf[MAX_RECEIVE];

   nRetVal = CSocket::Receive(lpReceiveBuf, MAX_RECEIVE-1);
```

```
    if (nRetVal == 0 || nRetVal == SOCKET_ERROR)
        *pstringReceive="";
    else
    {
        lpReceiveBuf[nRetVal]='\0';
        *pstringReceive = lpReceiveBuf;
    }

    return nRetVal;
}
```

### Two Threads

The astute reader has probably guessed by now that the call to **AfxBeginThread()** in the constructor creates a new thread.

```
CISAPISocket::CISAPISocket()
{
    //Create the event in the NON-SIGNALED state
    hEventBlocking = CreateEvent(NULL,FALSE,FALSE, NULL);
    //Create the thread and pass it a reference to this CISAPISocket class
    AfxBeginThread(TimeOutThread, this);
}
```

We will cover the actual mechanics of creating a thread shortly, but first, let's look at why the second thread is needed.

All of our calls to the **CISAPISocket** class are blocking sockets calls. That is, they don't return until the function is finished. If the SMTP server is down or you lose your network connection to it, the calls could take forever to finish. As there is no time-out mechanism in **CSocket**, we implement it by using two threads.

First, we will look at the flow of the program if everything works right, and then we will see what happens if a problem occurs while communicating with our SMTP server.

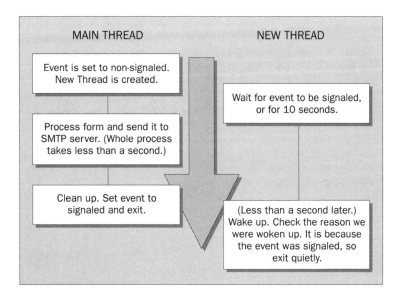

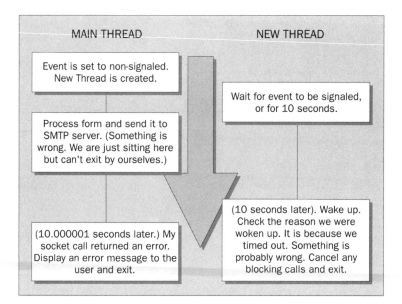

Now, let's see how the execution looks when something goes wrong.

### Creating a New Thread

Creating a new thread is actually much easier than most people think. All it requires is a function that will start the thread, and one parameter to pass to it. Of course, there are some other optional items that can be used, and so we shall prototype the function to create a worker thread here:

```
CWinThread* AfxBeginThread(AFX_THREADPROC pfnThreadProc,
                           LPVOID pParam,
                           int nPriority = THREAD_PRIORITY_NORMAL,
                           UINT nStackSize = 0,
                           DWORD dwCreateFlags = 0,
                           LPSECURITY_ATTRIBUTES lpSecurityAttrs = NULL);
```

The first parameter is a pointer to the function that will become the thread's path of execution. You don't have to do anything to get this address except pass the function's name. The compiler will take care of the rest for you. Of course, the function can't be a member of any class, as the code would be deleted when the class is deleted, and the new thread might still be running.

The second parameter is a pointer to the actual parameter which will be passed to the function. As this parameter can be a pointer to any type, it must be declared **LPVOID** in the new thread function. If you need to pass more than one variable, you should package them in a structure and pass a pointer to that structure. In our example, we are passing a pointer to the whole **CISAPISocket** class. When you create new threads, be sure to note that the data pointed to may be altered or deleted by the parent thread. You should therefore make sure that any variables are copied into local variables by the new thread before they are changed, or go out of scope, in the parent thread.

When you create a thread, you can set its priority level. You can also set its priority level while it's running, using the **SetThreadPriority()** function. Priority levels are used to determine which threads are given CPU time first. In this example, we accept the default.

Each thread that is created receives its own stack. You can specify the size of the stack, in bytes, with the **nStackSize** parameter. The default of **0** gives it the same stack size as the creating thread.

The **dwCreateFlags** parameter allows you to create threads that are suspended. If you create a suspended thread, it won't begin executing until the **ResumeThread()** function is called. This greatly helps the thread synchronization problem. Our example, however, won't use this feature; we simply use the default, which starts the thread executing as soon as it is created.

Finally, you can specify any security attributes that you wish the new thread to have. The default is to have the same attributes as the creating thread.

Getting back to our constructor, you can see that we have used the defaults for most parameters in the call to **AfxBeginThread()**. We pass along the thread function we want executed (**TimeOutThread()** in this case) creating the thread (**this**). Passing **this** is important, since it gives the thread access to all the members of the class, in particular the event handle and the **CancelBlockingCalls()**. To gain access to these members, the thread casts the pointer from a **void** pointer to a **CISAPISocket\***.

## SMTP

Before we get into using our new class in the **Default()** function, let's make sure we understand what happens when we talk to the SMTP server. This process involves the commands and responses required by SMTP. Even though SMTP stands for Simple Mail Transfer Protocol, it's not the same kind of protocol as TCP. Many programmers new to Internet programming become unnecessarily confused because they think that protocols such as SMTP are going to be incredibly complex. In fact, SMTP is nothing more than a series of commands that you send or receive in order to transfer e-mail over the Internet.

Let's demystify SMTP. I will conduct an SMTP session with my SMTP server and send an e-mail message. I will use nothing but telnet to connect to port 25. In the report which follows, **ME>** indicates what I type, and **SMTP>** indicates what the server sends back to me.

*The names have been changed to protect the innocent!*

```
ME> telnet mail.myserver.com 25

SMTP> 220 mail.myserver.com ESMTP Sendmail 8.7.3/8.7.3; Sun, 25 Aug 1996 21:02:11 -
0700 (PDT)

ME> HELO mail.myserver.com

SMTP> 250 mail.myserver.com Hello dev.yourserver.com [127.0.0.2], pleased to meet you

ME> MAIL FROM:<mtracy@myserver.com>

SMTP> 250 <mtracy@myserver.com>... Sender ok

ME> RCPT TO:<webmaster@myserver.com>

SMTP> 250 Recipient ok

ME> DATA

SMTP> 354 Enter mail, end with "." on a line by itself

ME> I like your site. Especially the ISAPI extensions.
ME> .
```

```
SMTP> 250 VAA16675 Message accepted for delivery

ME> QUIT

SMTP> mail.myserver.com closing connection
```

As you can see, there isn't much to sending a piece of e-mail! While not every SMTP server will be exactly the same as the one listed above, there are certain specifications that the protocol must follow:

- ▲ The conversation should start with a **HELO smtpdomain.com** statement.

- ▲ Who the mail is from should be in the form **MAIL FROM:username**.

- ▲ Who the mail is going to should be in the form **RCPT TO:username**. You can send the same piece of mail to more than one person by repeating the **RCPT TO:** command for each user name.

- ▲ The message should start with the **DATA** command.

- ▲ The message should finish with a single period on a line by itself.

- ▲ You should disconnect with the **QUIT** command.

Not every site will respond in the same way. For example, my SMTP server responds to the **HELO** command with:

```
250 mail.myserver.com Hello dev.yourserver.com [127.0.0.2], pleased to meet you
```

Another SMTP server might simply say: **250 dev.yourserver.com**. In order to check whether or not we have received the response we expected, we need to check the response code. Fortunately, the response code always comes first.

The following is a list of some of the possible response codes:

| Code | Meaning |
| --- | --- |
| 211 | System status, or system help reply. |
| 214 | Help message. |
| 220 | Service ready. |
| 221 | Service closing transmission channel. |
| 250 | Requested mail action OK, completed. |
| 251 | User not local; will forward to <forward-path>. |
| 354 | Start mail input; end with <CRLF>.<CRLF>. |
| 421 | Service not available; closing transmission channel. |
| 450 | Requested mail action not taken: mailbox unavailable. |
| 451 | Requested action aborted: local error in processing. |
| 452 | Requested action not taken: insufficient system storage. |

*Table Continued on Following Page*

| Code | Meaning |
|------|---------|
| 500 | Syntax error, command unrecognized. |
| 502 | Command not implemented. |
| 503 | Bad sequence of commands. |
| 504 | Command parameter not implemented. |
| 550 | Requested action not taken: mailbox unavailable. |
| 551 | User not local; please try <forward-path>. |
| 552 | Requested mail action aborted: exceeded storage allocation. |
| 553 | Requested action not taken: mailbox name not allowed. |
| 554 | Transaction failed. |

While there are quite few codes listed above, fortunately enough, we needn't check every one of them, because the numbers tell us something about the type of response. The first digit alone gives us the result of the response, indicating one of the following situations:

| First Digit | Meaning |
|-------------|---------|
| 1 | Positive reply, but the server needs confirmation that the user wants to proceed before it will take any action. |
| 2 | Positive reply, and this portion of the transaction is complete. |
| 3 | Positive reply, but the transaction is not complete yet. (The user needs to send more data.) |
| 4 | A non-fatal error occurred. The transaction can be requested again. |
| 5 | The transaction critically failed. |

The second digit indicates the reason for the response code given in the first digit, and can reflect the following types of event:

| Second Digit | Meaning |
|--------------|---------|
| 0 | Syntax error. |
| 1 | Information: either enough was supplied in the case of success, or not enough in the case of failure. |
| 2 | The network connections either failed or succeeded. |
| 5 | The mail system either failed or succeeded. |

The final digit supplies additional information on the type of response, and varies depending on that response. It's relatively unimportant, and so we won't list all the possible values here.

It should be clear that, in most cases, we really need only look at the first one or two digits to determine the result. Therefore, when we write the code that interacts with the SMTP server, our error checking can be greatly simplified by checking just the first two digits to determine success or failure, and the reason for it.

One final note: the e-mail header items, such as **Subject:** and **To:**, are not part of SMTP. They are optional items which make e-mail more readable and easier to reply to. They are picked up by the recipient's e-mail reading program, but they aren't used by SMTP in the delivery of mail.

## *Bringing it All Together*

Now that we have covered sockets programming and how to create threads, we can finally look at the extension which will use all of this knowledge. First, we create all the local variables that we need, including the all-important **CISAPISocket**.

```
///////////////////////////////////////////////////////////////////////////
// CFormMailExtension command handlers

void CFormMailExtension::Default(CHttpServerContext* pCtxt)
{
    StartContent(pCtxt);
    WriteTitle(pCtxt);
    CString stringFormItem, stringMailTo, stringMailBody;
    CString stringName, stringValue;
    CString stringSend, stringReceive;

    CHttpForm    Form(pCtxt);

    BOOL bRetVal;
    INT   nRetVal;

    // Create the ISAPISocket
    CISAPISocket    SMTPSocket;

    bRetVal = SMTPSocket.Create();
```

The next stage is to open a connection to our SMTP server. Obviously, if you're going to use this code, you should replace the IP address string in the **Connect()** with the IP address of your SMTP server. If it's on the same machine as the web server, then you can use **"127.0.0.1"** which is the loopback address.

```
    //Connect to your SMTP server
    //25 is the SMTP port #
    bRetVal = SMTPSocket.Connect("127.0.0.1",25);

    if (!bRetVal)
    {
        *pCtxt << _T("Can't Open Connection to SMTP server.");
        EndContent(pCtxt);
        return;
    }
```

We should get some kind of welcome message back from the SMTP server if the connection was successful, and so we perform a **Receive()** and make sure there are no errors.

```
// Check that we got a welcome message
nRetVal = SMTPSocket.Receive(&stringReceive);

if(nRetVal == 0 || nRetVal == SOCKET_ERROR)
{
    *pCtxt << _T("Error Connecting to SMTP Server");
    EndContent(pCtxt);
    return;
}
```

Now we can start the SMTP conversation with the server. First off, we greet the server. You will notice that at each stage we check to make sure we get a valid response from the server before continuing.

```
// Send over the HELO message - Note: HELO is not a typo
stringSend ="HELO unix1.listinglink.com\n";
nRetVal = SMTPSocket.Send(stringSend);

nRetVal = SMTPSocket.Receive(&stringReceive);

// Make sure we get the right response back
if (nRetVal ==0 || nRetVal == SOCKET_ERROR)
{
    *pCtxt << _T("Error during HELO\n");
    EndContent(pCtxt);
    return;
}

if (strncmp(stringReceive,"25",2)!=0)
{
    *pCtxt << _T("Unexpected response during HELO");
    EndContent(pCtxt);
    return;
}
```

Next, we tell the server who is sending the mail.

```
if (!Form.FormFields("mail-from",&stringFormItem))
{
    *pCtxt << _T("No From Address specified");
    EndContent(pCtxt);
    return;
}

// Start sending the info
stringSend="MAIL FROM:<" +stringFormItem+ ">\n";

nRetVal = SMTPSocket.Send(stringSend);

nRetVal = SMTPSocket.Receive(&stringReceive);

if (nRetVal ==0 || nRetVal == SOCKET_ERROR)
{
    *pCtxt << _T("Error during MAIL FROM\n");
    EndContent(pCtxt);
    return;
}
```

```
    if (strncmp(stringReceive,"25",2)!=0)
    {
        *pCtxt << _T("Unexpected response during MAIL FROM");
        EndContent(pCtxt);
        return;
    }
```

We then give the server a list of all the intended recipients of this e-mail. We'll also generate the string for the **To:** line of the header.

```
    // Loop through all the mail-to entries to send to more than one person.
    for (int i=1; Form.FormFields("mail-to",&stringFormItem,i);i++)
    {
        if (i>1)
            stringMailTo+=", ";
        stringMailTo+=stringFormItem;
        stringSend = "RCPT TO:<" +stringFormItem +">\n";

        nRetVal = SMTPSocket.Send(stringSend);

        nRetVal = SMTPSocket.Receive(&stringReceive);
        if (nRetVal ==0 || nRetVal == SOCKET_ERROR)
        {
            *pCtxt << _T("Error during RCPT TO:\n");
            EndContent(pCtxt);
            return;
        }

        if (strncmp(stringReceive,"25",2)!=0)
        {
            *pCtxt << _T("At least one user-specified recipient is not valid.
Aborting\n");
            EndContent(pCtxt);
            return;
        }
    }
```

Make sure the server is ready to receive the actual message. This is in two parts: the header and the body.

```
    // Start the data block
    stringSend="DATA\n";
    nRetVal = SMTPSocket.Send(stringSend);

    nRetVal = SMTPSocket.Receive(&stringReceive);

    if (nRetVal ==0 || nRetVal == SOCKET_ERROR)
    {
        *pCtxt << _T("Error during DATA\n");
        EndContent(pCtxt);
        return;
    }

    if (strncmp(stringReceive,"354",3)!=0)
    {
        *pCtxt << _T("Unexpected response during DATA");
        EndContent(pCtxt);
        return;
    }
```

We send the header first. A header only provides information to the end recipient's reader program; none of the header information is used for routing e-mail. The header is separated from the body with a double carriage return.

```
// Send the Mail Headers
// This information is not used in delivery of the mail
Form.FormFields("mail-subject",&stringFormItem);
stringSend = "Subject:" +stringFormItem + "\n";
stringSend+="To: "+stringMailTo;
stringSend+="\r\n\r\n";

nRetVal = SMTPSocket.Send(stringSend);
```

Now we send the body. Here, the **FormFieldsByNumber()** function is used to step through all the items on the form. Thus, you can have any number of HTML form inputs and call then almost anything you wish. Of course, we need to ignore fields with a **mail-** prefix, because these are used by the extension to get sender and recipient information. Also note that **FormFieldsByNumber()** returns **TRUE** until it runs out of fields.

```
// Loop through all the items on the form.
for(i=1;Form.FormFieldsByNumber(&stringName,&stringValue,i);i++)
{
    if (strncmp(stringName,"mail-",5)==0)
       continue;
    stringSend=stringName+": "+stringValue+"\n";
    // Capture the mail body so we can print it out to the client later
    stringMailBody += stringSend + "<br>";
    nRetVal = SMTPSocket.Send(stringSend);
}
```

The message is terminated by sending a period on a single line.

```
// Send the termination of body sequence.
stringSend="\r\n.\r\n";
nRetVal = SMTPSocket.Send(stringSend);
```

A final check to make sure the server got the message OK.

```
// Make sure it received the body properly
nRetVal = SMTPSocket.Receive(&stringReceive);

if (nRetVal ==0 || nRetVal == SOCKET_ERROR)
{
    *pCtxt << _T("Error during mail body\n");
    EndContent(pCtxt);
    return;
}

if (strncmp(stringReceive,"25",2)!=0)
{
    *pCtxt << _T("Unexpected response during body");
    EndContent(pCtxt);
    return;
}
```

Before closing everything down, we politely end the SMTP connection. The class destructor will take care of everything else.

```
    // All done
    stringSend="QUIT\n";
    nRetVal = SMTPSocket.Send(stringSend);

    *pCtxt << _T("The following message has been sent:<p>");
    *pCtxt << stringMailBody;

    EndContent(pCtxt);
}
```

## Building and Testing the Extension

It should be possible to build and test the application as normal. Try setting break points, both in the **Default()** function and in the **TimeOutThread()**, so that you can see the flow of execution actually taking place. You should note that even though this extension creates additional threads of its own, it's entirely thread-safe. You can therefore have as many users (within reason) sending as many forms to e-mail as you wish without any problems.

# Summary

SMTP, FTP, and HTTP are all protocols that use TCP to communicate over an IP network. These protocols use a type of script language that is virtually English and able to communicate requests and responses. In this chapter, we concentrated on SMTP and made an ISAPI extension which takes an HTML form and sends it to a user via e-mail.

Since we didn't have access to an off-the-shelf mail program, as UNIX users do, we needed to write our own interface to an SMTP server. By opening up our own sockets, we were able to communicate directly with an SMTP server, and issue the appropriate commands such as **RCPT TO** and **MAIL FROM**.

Inside an ISAPI extension, there are no message pumps waiting for Windows messages, so we had to use a blocking socket. A blocking socket waits for a complete response before it returns from the function call– it therefore blocks execution of your code until it has finished. A non-blocking socket call returns immediately and communicates with your program via Windows messages. Since we didn't want to wait an inordinate amount of time on a downed network connection, we needed to create an 'alarm-clock' thread that would stop our blocking socket call after a fixed number of seconds. To synchronize this new thread with the thread making the blocking call, we introduced the event as a thread synchronization object.

# 7

# ISAPI Filters

If you are a CGI programmer who's still wondering what ISAPI has to offer over CGI, you should find this second part of the book quite interesting. ISAPI filters form a layer that sits between a client's initial request and the web server's response to the client. They have no equivalent CGI representation; the closest thing to ISAPI filters are the Apache web server's modules.

Apache is the most widely-used web server software for the UNIX operating system. UNIX doesn't support DLLs, so instead Apache uses modules: custom extensions that can be linked to the web server when it is recompiled. The complete source code for Apache is freely available, which makes this an acceptable method for extending the functionality of the web server. However, Microsoft and other providers of Windows web servers will probably not make their source code public any time soon, and so, when we want to extend the functionality of the web server, we must use DLLs.

The ISAPI specification dictates exactly when the web server will call these extension DLLs, what data will be provided to the DLL, and what data can be returned. Since an ISAPI filter has access to data both before the web server starts processing a client request, and before the finished product is written back to the client, the filter can exercise a great deal of control over an HTTP request. ISAPI filters are, therefore, the best tool available for customizing the functionality of your web server.

Like ISAPI extensions, ISAPI filters run in the process space of the web server and therefore must be thread-safe. Unlike ISAPI extensions, which are only called when they are specified in the URL. ISAPI filters are called for every HTTP request. Some filters may even be called several times for a single request. This means that for every HTML page, every GIF, every JPEG, every AVI file, every CGI or ISAPI script, your filter will be called at least once.

Also, there's no way you can make filters respond only to requests intended for particular hosts. In other words, if you have several virtual domains running off one web server, your filter will be called for every request to any one of the domains. If you use a filter on a site that gets a million hits a day, it will be called just as often as a filter for twenty sites that each get fifty thousand hits a day. Because of the number of times a filter is called, it's much more important that the code be optimized. This need for speed will lead us away from implementing filters using MFC, as we shall see later in the chapter.

## The Life Cycle of an HTTP Request

In order to see how an ISAPI filter works, we will look at the events that make up a complete HTTP request and response. As we go over the life cycle of an HTTP request, we will highlight the various points at which our ISAPI filters can make a difference.

The request starts when a user clicks on a link to your site, or simply types in the URL. The client's browser opens up a connection to your web server and sends over a list of client headers that tell the server what it is looking for. The simplest request possible is **GET /**, which tells the web server to give us the default document under the root directory. You can try this yourself: at your MS-DOS prompt, type

```
> telnet www.microsoft.com 80
```

(where 80 is the default port on which the system listens for HTTP requests). When your telnet window opens up, type

```
> GET /
```

As soon as you press the *Enter* key, your screen should fill up with Microsoft's response. If you look at the text, you will see that it is indeed Microsoft's default home page.

In reality, headers aren't as simple as the one above. Most clients send additional information over to the server. Some of this information isn't used by the web server directly, but can be used by our ISAPI extensions and filters. A sample of some of the additional headers that can be sent over by the client are: **Authorization**, **From**, **If-Modified-Since**, **Refer**, **User-Agent**, **Content-Encoding**, and **Accept**. As HTTP evolves, many more headers will be added to those already available. For a complete list of what's available now, and a glimpse of what is planned for the future, you should consult the Internet Engineering Task Force's drafts for HTTP.

> See **ftp://ftp.ietf.org/internet-drafts/draft-ietf-http-v11-spec-07.txt** *for a list of about 40 different possible headers and their uses.*

In this book, we'll be covering the **Authorization**, **Refer**, **User-Agent**, and **Accept** headers, as these are the most common. Although we'll cover each in more detail in their respective chapters, it's important to note that these headers are nothing special–they are nothing more than plain text sent over by the client. The only thing that separates them from the body of the document is a double pair of carriage returns and linefeeds. You should also note that in the first part of the book we covered writing headers back to the client as well as reading them. While ISAPI filters can certainly be used for writing headers, we will primarily be interested in reading the ones that the client is sending over and taking the appropriate action once we've done so.

When the client sends over the request, the first thing that the server does is read it in. We will refer to this event as **OnReadRawData()**, as that is how MFC refers to this stage of the request. Once the raw data has been read in, the web server tries to make sense out of it by processing the headers; this stage will be referred to as **OnPreprocHeaders()**. During this stage, the server parses through the client's request and assigns values to the appropriate variables. In our simple **GET /** example, the following ISAPI variables would be parsed out: **REMOTE_ADDR**, **REMOTE_HOST**, **REQUEST_METHOD**, **SERVER_NAME**, **SERVER_PORT**, **SERVER_PROTOCOL**, and **SERVER_SOFTWARE**. Of course, the only one that actually came from the client is **REQUEST_METHOD**, in this case, **GET**.

One thing that's missing from these CGI/ISAPI variables is the actual URL that we requested. For a CGI script, this would be kept in the **SCRIPT_NAME** variable. However, as this request isn't for a script, the **SCRIPT_NAME** variable isn't set. We'll see in the next chapter how to retrieve this value and use it.

Once the headers have been processed, the server takes the URL we requested and maps it to a physical file on the disk. For example, on my machine, **/** is really **c:\inetsrv\wwwroot\default.htm**. This mapping stage is given the MFC name **OnURLMap()**.

After the mapping is complete, the web server checks to make sure the user has permission to read the file they are trying to access. In our simple example, no authentication is provided by the client, so the web server will use the permissions assigned to the default user, **IUSR_YOURCOMPUTERNAME**. If the user has read permission for the file, or execute permission for the script, then the server will continue to process the request. The process of user authentication is much more complicated on the Microsoft IIS than it is on a typical NCSA-compatible server, and because of this, the whole of the last chapter on filters will be devoted to covering how it works and how you can make it work for you. For now, though, we'll simply refer to this phase as **OnAuthentication()**.

If the user has been authenticated, the web server will send the user the data. This stage is appropriately called **OnSendRawData()**. If the request was for a file, the file is sent over. Nothing surprising about that. If, however, the request was for a script, the data sent will be the *output* of the script, rather than the script itself. If you were to construct a filter that simply reported when each one of these events was occurring, you would see that **OnSendRawData()** is called twice for each request. The first time, it's called to write the headers like **Content-type: text/html** back to the client. The second time, it's called to actually write the body of the request.

Once the data has been written back to the client, the server makes a record of the transaction using the logging mechanism specified in the server's configuration. Before this occurs, the server calls the **OnLog()** event in the filter. We'll look at this **OnLog()** method in more detail when we construct our custom logging filter in Chapter 9.

Lastly, the web server will close the connection after a call to **OnEndOfNetSession()**, although it isn't always quite so simple. If the browser supports **Keep-Alive** connections, the web server may have to send over more than one request before the connection is closed. A **Keep-Alive** connection is a TCP connection in which multiple files are sent over a single connection. Alhough it may seem like common sense to send over more than one file on a connection, that isn't what the web was originally designed to do. Back in the 'old days', when a browser wanted to download a homepage with, let's say, five GIF images on it, it would have had to open a connection, receive the data, and close the connection for each of the six files (1 homepage + 5 GIFs). Over a slow connection, this could be time consuming. If the client indicates that it supports **Keep-Alive,** the server knows not to close the connection down but will instead send all the files over on the single connection before closing it.

Thus, you may have more than one call to the other methods, for each call you have to **OnEndOfNetSession()**. For example, if we had a custom authentication filter, its **OnAuthentication()** routine would be called 6 times for our fictitious homepage. However, **OnEndOfNetSession** would only be called once if the client supported **Keep-Alive**.

In addition to the above, MSIIS 2.0 has added a notification in the event that a user isn't allowed access to a specific request. We'll call this notification **OnAccessDenied()**. Unlike all the other notifications, it isn't called for every request but only for those which would normally result in a **401 Access Denied** error.

# The Filter DLL

Like ISAPI extensions, ISAPI filters have two required exported functions that need to be declared. These are **GetFilterVersion()** and **HttpFilterProc()**. Both are similar in functionality to their extension counterparts. The **GetFilterVersion()** function supplies information about the filter to the server, and **HttpFilterProc()** is the function that is called to do all the work.

# GetFilterVersion

Unlike **GetExtensionVersion()**, **GetFilterVersion()** performs a very important task: it tells the server which types of notifications the filter would like to receive. For example, imagine that when we write our filter for custom logging, we're interested only in the **OnLog()** notification. It would be a waste of processor time to bother this filter with the **OnUrlMap()** or **OnAuthentication()** notifications. You can also specify whether you want your filter to be notified for requests that occur over a secure connection, over a non-secure connection, or both.

Lastly, the filter can tell the server what priority level it should be notified at, with reference to other filters. Let's say, for example, that you have two filters: one encrypting data before it's written back to the client, and the other changing all outbound text to upper case (as the sample filter in the ISAPI SDK does). If the encryption filter is called first, the data will be encrypted *before* being converted into upper case. This will quite probably make it impossible for the client to decrypt the data, which is hardly the desired effect. The encryption notification should, therefore, request the lowest possible priority, so that the data will be encrypted *after* it has been converted to upper case. If two filters have exactly the same priority, the order in which they are called is determined by their order in the **HKEY_LOCAL_MACHINE\System\CurrentControlSet\Services\W3SVC\Parameters\Filter DLLs** registry entry, which we'll cover in the next chapter.

The way in which the filter sets its priority, and requests the proper notifications, is by using a pointer to the **HTTP_FILTER_VERSION** structure, which is passed to **GetFilterVersion()** as its only parameter:

```
typedef struct _HTTP_FILTER_VERSION
{
    DWORD       dwServerFilterVersion;
    DWORD       dwFilterVersion;
    CHAR        lpszFilterDesc[SF_MAX_FILTER_DESC_LEN+1];
    DWORD       dwFlags;
} HTTP_FILTER_VERSION, *PHTTP_FILTER_VERSION;
```

| Member | Context |
|--------|---------|
| dwServerFilterVersion | Version information from the server. |
| DwFilterVersion | Version information from the client. |
| LpszFilterDesc | A short description of the filter. |
| DwFlags | Bitwise combination of the priority levels and notification types listed below. |

The following constants can be used to make up the **dwFlags**. We'll see more about how and when they're used as we work through the examples in the rest of the book.

| Constant | Context |
|---|---|
| SF_NOTIFY_ORDER_DEFAULT | Gives the filter a default priority. Not surprisingly, if you don't specify a priority, this is the default. |
| SF_NOTIFY_ORDER_LOW | A low priority. |
| SF_NOTIFY_ORDER_MEDIUM | A medium priority. |
| SF_NOTIFY_ORDER_HIGH | A high priority. |
| SF_NOTIFY_SECURE_PORT | Requests notification for secure connections. A secure connection is one in which both the server and the client are encrypting all data sent across the Internet. For this, you will need to register an encryption key for your server and have it properly installed. |
| SF_NOTIFY_NONSECURE_PORT | Requests notifications for non-secure ports. If neither or both of these last two is selected, the filter will be notified for both secure and non-secure connections. |
| SF_NOTIFY_READ_RAW_DATA | Requests that the filter be notified when the server is reading raw data. |
| SF_NOTIFY_PREPROC_HEADERS | Requests that the filter be notified when the server is preprocessing the headers. |
| SF_NOTIFY_URL_MAP | Requests that the filter be notified when the server is mapping the URL to a physical file. |
| SF_NOTIFY_AUTHENTICATION | Requests that the filter be notified when the server is authenticating a user. |
| SF_NOTIFY_SEBD_RAW_DATA | Requests that the filter be notified when the server is sending raw data. |
| SF_NOTIFY_LOG | Requests that the filter be notified when the server is logging the data. |
| SF_NOTIFY_END_OF_NET_SESSION | Requests that the filter be notified when the server is terminating the connection. |
| SF_NOTIFY_ACCESS_DENIED | Requests that the filter be notified when the server has denied access to a client (Version 2.0) |

# HttpFilterProc

HttpFilterProc() is the function that forms the filter itself. The server will call it for any notifications the filter requested in GetFilterVersion() as described above. The prototype of HttpFilterProc() is as follows:

```
DWORD WINAPI HttpFilterProc(
    PHTTP_FILTER_CONTEXT pfc,
    DWORD notificationType,
    LPVOID pvNotification
    );
```

The **pfc** is a pointer to the **filter context variable**, which we'll describe shortly. Like the Extension Control Block for extensions, it handles general functions that filters might need and is available for all notifications to use.

Since a filter can request more than one notification type, it needs to know which one it is being called for. It finds out through the second parameter, **notificationType**, which holds this information.

The **pvNotification** variable depends on the type of notification the filter is receiving. Depending on the value of **notificationType**, **pvNotification** will point to one of the following data structures: **HTTP_FILTER_RAW_DATA**, **HTTP_FILTER_PREPROC_HEADERS**, **HTTP_FILTER_URL_MAP**, **HTTP_FILTER_AUTHENT**, **HTTP_FILTER_LOG**. When the function is called, you will need to look at **notificationType** and then typecast **pvNotification** to the appropriate type.

Each of these data types will be covered in detail shortly. The important thing to realize is that different notifications have different data available for them to view and/or alter. Obviously, it wouldn't do us any good to change the user's name and password in the **OnLog()** method, as the usefulness of this information expires once the client has been authenticated. At each filter notification stage, we're given access to any relevant data that we might need. If you need data that isn't available to the specific notification that you're working in, you'll need to collect the data in the filter notification where the data *is* available, and pass it to the notification, where it's needed for a technique which we'll demonstrate later. First, let's examine the structures that all filter notifications have access to, and then look at notification-specific data structures.

## Filter Variables

At every stage of the filter, we have access to generic filter information. This generic information is contained in the **HTTP_FILTER_CONTEXT** structure, defined here:

```
typedef struct _HTTP_FILTER_CONTEXT
{
    DWORD     cbSize;                              //IN
    DWORD     Revision;                            //IN
    PVOID     ServerContext;                       //IN
    DWORD     ulReserved;                          //IN
    BOOL      fIsSecurePort;                       //IN
    PVOID     pFilterContext;                      //IN/OUT

    BOOL      (WINAPI* GetServerVariable) (
        struct    _HTTP_FILTER_CONTEXT* pfc,
        LPSTR     lpszVariableName,
        LPVOID    lpvBuffer,
        LPDWORD   lpdwSize
    );

    BOOL      (WINAPI* AddResponseHeaders) (
        struct    _HTTP_FILTER_CONTEXT* pfc,
        LPSTR     lpszHeaders,
        DWORD     dwReserved
    );

    BOOL      (WINAPI* WriteClient) (
        struct    _HTTP_FILTER_CONTEXT* pfc,
        LPVOID    Buffer,
        LPDWORD   lpdwBytes,
        DWORD     dwReserved
    );
```

```
    VOID*    (WINAPI* AllocMem) (
       struct     _HTTP_FILTER_CONTEXT* pfc,
       DWORD      cbSize,
       DWORD      dwReserved
    );

    BOOL     (WINAPI* ServerSupportFunction) (
       struct     _HTTP_FILTER_CONTEXT* pfc,
       enum       SF_REQ_TYPE sfReq,
       PVOID      pData,
       DWORD      ul1,
       DWORD      ul2
    );
} HTTP_FILTER_CONTEXT, *PHTTP_FILTER_CONTEXT;
```

As you can see, the **HTTP_FILTER_CONTEXT** structure is very similar to the **EXTENSION_CONTROL_BLOCK** structure used in ISAPI extensions. In this case, the data members are used as follows:

| Member | Context |
| --- | --- |
| **cbSize** | The size of the **HTTP_FILTER_CONTEXT** structure. |
| **Revision** | The revision level. |
| **ServerContext** | A unique identifier used by the server to recognize this filter. You should never alter this value. |
| **UlReserved** | Reserved. |
| **FIsSecurePort** | Whether or not the request was made over a secure port. |
| **PFilterContext** | Pointer to additional information that this filter needs to store. This is by far the most useful data member of this structure. |

In addition to the data members, we have access to several functions. Many of these are identical or very similar to member functions of the **EXTENSION_CONTROL_BLOCK** structure:

| Function | Context |
| --- | --- |
| **GetServerVariable()** | Same as **EXTENSION_CONTROL_BLOCK** function. |
| **AddResponseHeaders()** | Adds headers to the default header list before they are written back to the client. This is very similar to **ServerSupportFunction()** in the **EXTENSION_CONTROL_BLOCK** structure, as well as the one described below. |
| **WriteClient()** | Same as **EXTENSION_CONTROL_BLOCK** function. |
| **AllocMem()** | This function is used to allocate memory to be used in the **pFilterContext** described above. Any memory allocated with this function is automatically freed when the filter is done. |
| **ServerSupportFunction()** | Similar to the **EXTENSION_CONTROL_BLOCK** function, but it only supports the functions listed below. |

The **ServerSupportFunction()** of the **HTTP_FILTER_CONTEXT** only supports the following **SF_REQ_TYPE**s:

| ServerSupportFunction() Call | Context |
|---|---|
| **SF_REQ_SEND_RESPONSE_HEADER** | Same as **EXTENSION_CONTROL_BLOCK** |
| **SF_REQ_ADD_HEADERS_ON_DENIAL** | Used to add headers to the response sent back to the client if the request is turned down due to authentication. |
| **SF_REQ_SET_NEXT_READ_SIZE** | If the filter is reading raw data from the client, this is used to set the number of bytes to get during the next read. |

All of the above member variables and functions of **HTTP_FILTER_CONTEXT** are available to every filter notification. And while the list is quite long, it by no means covers every piece of data that a programmer might want. Now let's look at the various other data structures that will be available to the filter depending on the type of notification the filter is receiving.

### OnReadRawData()

When the **OnReadRawData()** notification is called, in addition to the pointer to the **HTTP_FILTER_CONTEXT** variable, the function is also passed a void pointer that needs to be cast into the **HTTP_FILTER_RAW_DATA** structure, given here:

```
typedef struct _HTTP_FILTER_RAW_DATA
{
    PVOID pvInData;
    DWORD cbInData;
    DWORD cbInBuffer;
    DWORD dwReserved;
} HTTP_FILTER_RAW_DATA, *PHTTP_FILTER_RAW_DATA;
```

| Member | Context |
|---|---|
| **pvInData** | Pointer to the buffer containing the raw data. You can both read and edit this buffer. |
| **CbInData** | The size of the data in the buffer. |
| **CbInBuffer** | The size of the buffer. If you need to put more data into the **pvInData** buffer than it currently holds (you are writing a compression/decompression filter, for example) you will need to allocate more memory and point **pvInData** to it. |
| **DwReserved** | Reserved for future use. |

### OnPreprocHeaders()

The following is the prototype for **HTTP_FILTER_PREPROC_HEADERS**:

```
typedef struct _HTTP_FILTER_PREPROC_HEADERS
{
    BOOL    (WINAPI* GetHeader) (
        STRUCT    _HTTP_FILTER_CONTEXT* pfc,
        LPSTR     lpszName,
```

```
        LPVOID      lpvBuffer,
        LPDWORD     lpdwSize
    );

    BOOL      (WINAPI* SetHeader) (
        STRUCT      _HTTP_FILTER_CONTEXT* pfc,
        LPSTR       lpszName,
        LPSTR       lpszValue
    );

    BOOL      (WINAPI* AddHeader) (
        STRUCT      _HTTP_FILTER_CONTEXT* pfc,
        LPSTR       lpszName,
        LPSTR       lpszValue
    );
    DWORD     dwReserved;
} HTTP_FILTER_PREPROC_HEADERS,  *PHTTP_FILTER_PREPROC_HEADERS;
```

| Function | Context |
|---|---|
| **GetHeader()** | Retrieves a header sent over by the client. It can also get the URL, method, and version of the request. |
| **SetHeader()** | Sets a header sent over from the client, i.e. change or delete an existing header. |
| **AddHeader()** | Adds a header to those sent over by the client. You should note that this is different from **AddResponseHeaders()** listed above, which adds to the headers that are being written back to the client. **AddHeader()** only changes the headers that the server will use. It makes the server 'think' that the client actually sent the header over. The client will never be sent headers added with the **AddHeader()** function. |

### OnUrlMap()

The following is the prototype for the structure:

```
typedef struct _HTTP_FILTER_URL_MAP
{
    const CHAR*      pszURL;
    CHAR *           pszPhysicalPath;
    DWORD            cbPathBuff;
} HTTP_FILTER_URL_MAP,  *PHTTP_FILTER_URL_MAP;
```

| Member | Context |
|---|---|
| **pszURL** | The URL requested relative to the server, e.g. **/home.html** rather than the full **http://yourdomain.com/home.html**). |
| **pszPhysicalPath** | The actual location on the server's hard drive. |
| **DbPathBuff** | The size of **pszPhysicalPath**. |

### OnAuthentication()

The following is the prototype for **HTTP_FILTER_AUTHENT**:

```
typedef struct _HTTP_FILTER_AUTHENT
{
    CHAR *     pszUser;
    DWORD      cbUserBuff;
    CHAR *     pszPassword;
    DWORD      cbPasswordBuff;
} HTTP_FILTER_AUTHENT, *PHTTP_FILTER_AUTHENT;
```

| Member | Context |
|--------|---------|
| **pszUser** | Pointer to the username used in authentication. |
| **CbUserBuff** | The size of the buffer. This will be at least **SF_MAX_USERNAME** (255 last time I checked). |
| **PszPassword** | Pointer to the password used in authentication. |
| **CbPasswordBuff** | The size of the password buffer. This will be at least **SF_MAX_PASSWORD**. |

### OnSendRawData()

The same structure is passed to the **OnSendRawData()** notification as to the **OnReadRawData()** notification.

### OnLog()

Here's the prototype for the **HTTP_FILTER_LOG** structure:

```
typedef struct _HTTP_FILTER_LOG
{
    const CHAR *     pszClientHostName;
    const CHAR *     pszClientUserName;
    const CHAR *     pszServerName;
    const CHAR *     pszOperation;
    const CHAR *     pszTarget;
    const CHAR *     pszParameters;
    DWORD            dwHttpStatus;
    DWORD            dwWin32Status;
} HTTP_FILTER_LOG, *PHTTP_FILTER_LOG;
```

| Member | Context |
|--------|---------|
| **pszClientHostName** | The client's IP address. |
| **PszClientUserName** | A user name if authentication was used. |
| **PszServerName** | The IP address of the server. |
| **PszOperation** | The type of request. Usually **GET** or **POST**. |
| **PszTarget** | The document or script requested. |

*Table Continued on Following Page*

| Member | Context |
|---|---|
| PszParameters | Any parameters passed to the script. |
| DwHttpStatus | The return code. 200 is OK, 404 Not Found, 500 Server Error, etc. |
| dwWin32Status | The Win32 error code (hopefully 0 - OK). |

### OnEndOfNetSession()

No information other than the **HTTP_FILTER_CONTEXT** is passed to the **OnEndOfNetSession()** notification. There's nothing you can do here but clean up anything that needs it.

### OnAccessDenied() (IIS 2.0)

This notification receives a **HTTP_FILTER_ACCESS_DENIED** structure, as follows:

```
struct _HTTP_FILTER_ACCESS_DENIED
{
const CHAR * pszURL;
const CHAR * pszPhysicalPath;
DWORD        dwReason;
} HTTP_FILTER_ACCESS_DENIED, *PHTTP_FILTER_ACCESS_DENIED
```

| Member | Context |
|---|---|
| pszUrl | The URL to which the client was denied access. |
| PszPhysicalPath | The physical path to the denied request. |
| DwReason | A bitfield indicating a combination of **SF_DENIED_LOGON**, **SF_DENIED_RESOURCE**, **SF_DENIED_FILTER**, **SF_DENIED_APPLICATION**, **SF_DENIED_CONFIG**. |

## Return Values

When the **HttpFilterProc()** is finished with a notification, it can return one of the following values:

| Value | Context |
|---|---|
| SF_STATUS_REQ_FINISHED | This filter has completely handled the client's request. The server should disconnect the client. Usually returned from the **OnEndOfNetSession()** notification handler. |
| SF_STATUS_REQ_FINISHED_KEEP_CONN | This filter has handled the client's request, but the server should keep the connection open. The server doesn't have to keep the connection open if it has too many other open connections or the client doesn't support **Keep-Alive** connections. |
| SF_STATUS_REQ_NEXT_NOTIFICATION | This filter is done. The server should call the next filter. This is the standard return value. |

*Table Continued on Following Page*

| Value | Context |
|---|---|
| SF_STATUS_REQ_HANDLED_NOTIFICATION | This filter handled the notification. No other filters will be called for this notification type. However, if other filters requested other notification types, they will still be called for those types. |
| SF_STATUS_REQ_ERROR | An error has occurred. The server will pass this along to the client. |
| SF_STATUS_REQ_READ_NEXT | Used only during **OnReadRawData()**. It tells the server to continue to call it when the rest of the data is available. |

# MFC Implementation

The two classes used by MFC in ISAPI filters are **CHttpFilter** and **CHttpFilterContext**. **CHttpFilter** handles calling the various events mentioned above, while **CHttpFilterContext** handles the actual interaction between the web server and your filter.

**CHttpFilter** has the following member functions:

| Function | Context |
|---|---|
| CHttpFilter() | The constructor. |
| GetFilterVersion() | Supplies the server with version information. |
| OnReadRawData() | Override to handle the **OnReadRawData()** event. This would be used for filters that decrypt or decompress data the client is sending over before the web server handles it. |
| OnPreprocHeaders() | Override to handle the **OnPreprocHeaders()** event. This can be used to manipulate any headers the client sends before the server gets them. |
| OnUrlMap() | Override to handle the **OnUrlMap()** event. We will use this to redirect requests dynamically. |
| OnAuthentication() | Override to handle the **OnAuthentication()** event. As you might have guessed, we will use this in our custom authentication scheme. |
| OnSendRawData() | Override to handle the **OnSendRawData()** event. |
| OnLog() | Override to handle the **OnLog()** event. Used in custom logging. |
| OnEndOfNetSession() | Override to handle the **OnEndOfNetSession()** event. Can be used as a clean up. |
| HttpFilterProc() | The actual function that is called for every filter request. This function simply figures out which event is being handled and directs it to the appropriate function. |

The **CHttpFilterContext** class has the following members:

| Member | Context |
|--------|---------|
| **m_pFC** | A pointer to a **HTTP_FILTER_CONTEXT** structure. |
| **CHttpFilterContext()** | The constructor. |
| **GetServerVariable()** | A wrapper for the **GetServerVariable()** member of **HTTP_FILTER_CONTEXT**. |
| **AddResponseHeaders()** | Same as above. |
| **WriteClient()** | Same as above. |
| **AllocMem()** | Same as above. |
| **ServerSupportFunction()** | Same as above. |

# Why Use MFC?

The reason for using MFC is that it simplifies our programming, makes the code easier to manage, and has only a slight performance penalty. When we were writing our extensions, we generally used MFC as much as possible to keep our programs simple and to be able to develop them quickly without having to 'reinvent the wheel' for each extension. Of course, the extensions run more slowly than if we optimized each function for our specific task, but in general the costs were worth the benefits.

However, when programming filters, we must remember that the code is called much more frequently. Filters need to be optimized if you expect any reasonable volume of traffic on your site. Also, as you can see from the descriptions above, MFC provides only a thin wrapper for our regular ISAPI filter functions. It makes no sense to instantiate a class only to continually dereference it. Thus, because MFC doesn't afford us too many benefits and comes with a cost, we'll only develop one filter using MFC before dropping the MFC classes and programming in more of a C-style to try to keep up the performance of our filters.

# A Simple Filter

Now that we've covered the basics of ISAPI filters, let's construct a simple filter that is the filter equivalent of the SimpleDump example we wrote when discussing extensions. This filter will request every possible notification and output to the debug window what it is doing. While it doesn't output *every* available piece of information, it should give you a good idea of the life cycle of an ISAPI filter. As with SimpleDump, it isn't actually necessary for you to do this example as instructions on how to build and test filters are saved until the next chapter. In addition, the **DebugMsg()** macro that's used here to output information to the debug window will also be discussed in the next chapter, where we make a filter that actually does something. Here's the code:

```
/////////////////////////////////////////////////
//   SimpleFilter.cp""p#include <windows.h>
#include <httpfilt.h>


//   DebugMsg() is used for debugging
#define DEST buff
#define DebugMsg(x)                \
```

```
    {                             \
      char buff[256];             \
      wsprintf x;                 \
      OutputDebugString(buff); \
    }


BOOL WINAPI GetFilterVersion(HTTP_FILTER_VERSION* pVer)
{
    // The version of the web server this is running on
    DebugMsg((DEST, "Web Server is version is %d.%d\n",
                HIWORD(pVer->dwServerFilterVersion),
                LOWORD(pVer->dwServerFilterVersion)));

    // Our filter version nuumber.
    pVer->dwFilterVersion = MAKELONG(1, 0);    // Version 0.1

    // The description
    strcpy(pVer->lpszFilterDesc, "Simple Filter, 0.1");

    // Requests Everything
    pVer->dwFlags = (SF_NOTIFY_SECURE_PORT         |
                     SF_NOTIFY_NONSECURE_PORT      |
                     SF_NOTIFY_READ_RAW_DATA       |
                     SF_NOTIFY_PREPROC_HEADERS     |
                     SF_NOTIFY_URL_MAP             |
                     SF_NOTIFY_AUTHENTICATION      |
                     SF_NOTIFY_SEND_RAW_DATA       |
                     SF_NOTIFY_LOG                 |
                     SF_NOTIFY_END_OF_NET_SESSION  |
                     SF_NOTIFY_ORDER_DEFAULT);


    return TRUE;
}


DWORD OnReadRawData(HTTP_FILTER_CONTEXT *pfc,
                    HTTP_FILTER_RAW_DATA *pRawDataInfo)
{
    DebugMsg((DEST,"OnReadRawData\r\n"));
    return SF_STATUS_REQ_NEXT_NOTIFICATION;
}


DWORD OnPreprocHeaders(HTTP_FILTER_CONTEXT* pFC,
                       HTTP_FILTER_PREPROC_HEADERS* pHeaderInfo)
{
    DebugMsg((DEST,"OnPreprocHeaders\r\n"));

    CHAR achUrl[512];
    DWORD cbURL=512;

    pHeaderInfo->GetHeader(pFC, "url",achUrl,&cbURL);

    DebugMsg((DEST,"Requested URL is:%s.\r\n",achUrl));
    return SF_STATUS_REQ_NEXT_NOTIFICATION;
}
```

```
DWORD OnUrlMap(HTTP_FILTER_CONTEXT* pFC, HTTP_FILTER_URL_MAP* pUrlMapInfo)
{
   DebugMsg((DEST,"OnUrlMap\r\n"));
   DebugMsg((DEST,"PhysicalPath: %s\r\n",pUrlMapInfo->pszPhysicalPath));
   return SF_STATUS_REQ_NEXT_NOTIFICATION;
}


DWORD  OnAuthentication(HTTP_FILTER_CONTEXT* pFC,
                        HTTP_FILTER_AUTHENT* pAuthInfo)
{
   DebugMsg((DEST,"OnAuthentication\r\n"));
   DebugMsg((DEST,"UserName: %s\r\n",pAuthInfo->pszUser));
   return SF_STATUS_REQ_NEXT_NOTIFICATION;
}


DWORD OnSendRawData(HTTP_FILTER_CONTEXT* pFC,
                    HTTP_FILTER_RAW_DATA* pRawDataInfo)
{
   DebugMsg((DEST,"OnSendRawData\r\n"));
   return SF_STATUS_REQ_NEXT_NOTIFICATION;
}


DWORD OnLog(HTTP_FILTER_CONTEXT* pFC, HTTP_FILTER_LOG* pLogInfo)
{
   DebugMsg((DEST,"OnLog\r\n"));
   DebugMsg((DEST,"Target:%s\r\n",pLogInfo->pszTarget));
   return SF_STATUS_REQ_NEXT_NOTIFICATION;
}


DWORD OnEndOfNetSession(HTTP_FILTER_CONTEXT* pFC)
{
   DebugMsg((DEST,"OnEndOfNetSession\r\n"));
   return SF_STATUS_REQ_NEXT_NOTIFICATION;
}


DWORD WINAPI HttpFilterProc(HTTP_FILTER_CONTEXT* pFC,
                            DWORD NotificationType, VOID* pvData)
{
   DWORD dwRet;

   // Send this notification to the right function
   switch (NotificationType)
   {
   case SF_NOTIFY_READ_RAW_DATA:
      dwRet = OnReadRawData(pFC, (PHTTP_FILTER_RAW_DATA) pvData);
      break;
   case SF_NOTIFY_PREPROC_HEADERS:
      dwRet = OnPreprocHeaders(pFC,
                              (PHTTP_FILTER_PREPROC_HEADERS) pvData);
      break;
   case SF_NOTIFY_URL_MAP:
      dwRet = OnUrlMap(pFC, (PHTTP_FILTER_URL_MAP) pvData);
```

```
            break;
        case SF_NOTIFY_AUTHENTICATION:
            dwRet = OnAuthentication(pFC, (PHTTP_FILTER_AUTHENT) pvData);
            break;
        case SF_NOTIFY_SEND_RAW_DATA:
            dwRet = OnSendRawData(pFC, (PHTTP_FILTER_RAW_DATA) pvData);
            break;
        case SF_NOTIFY_LOG:
            dwRet = OnLog(pFC, (PHTTP_FILTER_LOG) pvData);
            break;
        case SF_NOTIFY_END_OF_NET_SESSION:
            dwRet = OnEndOfNetSession(pFC);
            break;
        default:
            DebugMsg((DEST,
                       "[HttpFilterProc] Unknown notification type, %d\r\n",
                       NotificationType));
            dwRet = SF_STATUS_REQ_NEXT_NOTIFICATION;
            break;
    }
    return dwRet;
}
```

If you do wish to compile this code, you will need to add the following **.def** file:

```
LIBRARY SimpleFilter

DESCRIPTION 'Simple ISAPI Filter'

EXPORTS
    HttpFilterProc
    GetFilterVersion
```

The following is taken from my debug window when I had the above filter running and requested **http://127.0.0.1/test1.html**, where 127.0.0.1 is the familiar loop-back address. You should also note that we used no user authentication.

```
Web Server is version is 2.0
OnReadRawData
OnPreprocHeaders
Requested URL is:/test1.html.
OnUrlMap
PhysicalPath: C:\InetPub\wwwroot\test1.html
OnAuthentication
UserName:
OnSendRawData
OnSendRawData
OnLog
Target:/test1.html
OnEndOfNetSession
```

# Summary

ISAPI filters provide a layer that surrounds a web request. A filter allows ISAPI programmers to extend the functionality of the web server by programming custom handling routines for various types of requests.

Like ISAPI extensions, ISAPI filters are multithreaded DLLs that run in the process space of the web server. Unlike ISAPI extensions, filters can't be called directly. Filters intercept HTTP requests and alter the incoming request, the outgoing response, or both.

# Automatic Document Selection

With all the different browsers in use, a big problem facing HTML developers is making a flashy looking web site that looks good on everyone's computer. While you can always ask the user to Click here for a text version, it's perfectly possible to have the MSIIS automatically detect what type of browser the client is using and to give them the document appropriate to that browser. In this chapter, we will use an ISAPI filter which demonstrates the ability to read and set various HTTP header variables.

## Mapping .htmx to .htm1, 2, 3

The example filter in this chapter will take a request for a document with a **.htmx** extension, discover the type of browser the client is using, and deliver a document formatted for that browser. If the client is using a browser that supports HTML 3 tags (e.g. Netscape), the server will send the document with a **.htm3** extension. If the client only supports HTML 2 tags (e.g. Microsoft Internet Explorer 2.0), the server will send a **.htm2** document. As a last resort, the server will send a **.htm1** document to browsers with limited tag support (e.g. AOL's 2.0 browser).

For example, let's say we receive a request for a document at:

**http://www.foobar.com/myfiles/mydocument.htmx**.

The filter will detect the browser and return one of:

**http://www.foobar.com/myfiles/mydocument.htm1**,
**http://www.foobar.com/myfiles/mydocument.htm2**,
**http://www.foobar.com/myfiles/mydocument.htm3**.

The disadvantage of doing this is that every document you produce needs to be written three times. The advantage is that you can safely use the proper version of HTML without having to worry about how mangled it will look to the several million AOL users.

## Design of the Filter

Obviously, the filter will have to be called after the HTTP headers have been read from the client. The URL that the client is looking for will then be checked to see if the extension is **.htmx**. If it is, the filter will check the client's browser type and write back the appropriate header. This will make the MSIIS 'think' that the client actually requested the **htm1, 2** or **3** document rather than the **.htmx**. Thus, when it maps the URL to a file on your hard drive, it will deliver the proper file.

# Using the Filter Wizard

To create this project, we will start with the familiar ISAPI extension wizard. To follow along with the source code, you will need to use the project name **MFCXFilter**. On the next screen, click on Generate a Filter object. (Also, be sure to click off Generate a Server Extension object.) Use the MFC library as a shared object, and move to the next screen. The second and final step on the wizard is the more important: adding functionality to your filter.

First, you need to select the priority level at which your filter will be called. As discussed in the previous chapter, every request that your server receives, for any type of file, is processed by each filter you have loaded in turn. The first criterion used to determine the order in which these filters are called is the priority level that you set for them. In the case where two filters request the same notification, and have the save priority set, the order in which they will be called is determined by their order in the `HKEY_LOCAL_MACHINE\System\CurrentControlSet\Services\W3SVC\Parameters\` `Filter DLLs` registry setting–which we will cover in the section *Building and Testing the Filter* later in this chapter. In this example, we don't need any special priority, so we will accept the default.

Second, you need to select which types of connections we want our filter to look at. In most cases, you will select both secured and non-secured sessions, and that is just what we shall do in here.

Lastly, you need to select at which stages of the request's life cycle that you want your filter to get involved. As outlined above, the filter will read the headers that the client sends over, and will modify them as appropriate. Therefore, Post-preprocessing of the request headers is the appropriate option. This will call the filter after any raw data has been converted (e.g. it's been through some type of encryption filter), and before the `<file>.htmx` is mapped to the disk (which would give a 404 object not found message, as there is no file by that name). Note that the End of connection notification is selected by default. This allows your filter to perform any necessary clean-up of variables before the next call. In this example, we don't need to do any cleaning up, so we turn off this notification.

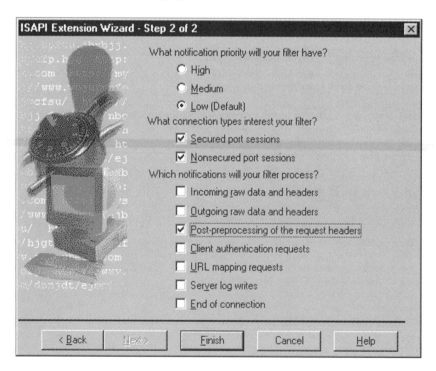

# Looking at the Code

The class definition for **CMFCXFilterFilter** is in the header file **MFCXFilter.h** and is shown below. The ISAPI wizard has included all the overridden functions.

```
// MFCXFILTER.H - Header file for your Internet Server
//     MFCXFilter Filter

#include "resource.h"


class CMFCXFilterFilter: public CHttpFilter
{
public:
   CMFCXFilterFilter();
   ~CMFCXFilterFilter();

// Overrides
   // ClassWizard generated virtual function overrides
   // NOTE - the ClassWizard will add and remove member functions here.
   //    DO NOT EDIT what you see in these blocks of generated code!
   //{{AFX_VIRTUAL(CMFCXFilterFilter)
   public:
   virtual BOOL GetFilterVersion(PHTTP_FILTER_VERSION pVer);
   virtual DWORD OnPreprocHeaders(CHttpFilterContext* pCtxt,
                        PHTTP_FILTER_PREPROC_HEADERS pHeaderInfo);
   //}}AFX_VIRTUAL

   //{{AFX_MSG(CMFCXFilterFilter)
   //}}AFX_MSG
};
```

The implementation is given here, in the file **MFCXFilter.cpp**:

```
// MFCXFILTER.CPP - Implementation file for your Internet Server
//     MFCXFilter Filter

#include "stdafx.h"
#include "MFCXFilter.h"

////////////////////////////////////////////////////////////////////
// The one and only CWinApp object
// NOTE: You may remove this object if you alter your project to no
// longer use MFC in a DLL.

CWinApp theApp;



////////////////////////////////////////////////////////////////////
// The one and only CMFCXFilterFilter object

CMFCXFilterFilter theFilter;



////////////////////////////////////////////////////////////////////
```

```
// CMFCXFilterFilter implementation

CMFCXFilterFilter::CMFCXFilterFilter()
{
}

CMFCXFilterFilter::~CMFCXFilterFilter()
{
}
...
```

The largest piece of code that the wizard writes for us is the **GetFilterVersion()** function, which tells the MSIIS about this filter. In this particular case, it tells the server to call this filter for both secured and non-secured requests, and to call it only in the post-preprocessing of the headers event, as we have specified in the wizard. The last couple of lines in the function give information about the filter: such as a description of the filter, and its version number.

```
...
BOOL CMFCXFilterFilter::GetFilterVersion(PHTTP_FILTER_VERSION pVer)
{
    // Call default implementation for initialization
    CHttpFilter::GetFilterVersion(pVer);

    // Clear the flags set by base class
    pVer->dwFlags &= ~SF_NOTIFY_ORDER_MASK;

    // Set the flags we are interested in
    pVer->dwFlags |= SF_NOTIFY_ORDER_LOW | SF_NOTIFY_SECURE_PORT |
                  SF_NOTIFY_NONSECURE_PORT | SF_NOTIFY_PREPROC_HEADERS;

    // Load description string
    TCHAR sz[SF_MAX_FILTER_DESC_LEN+1];
    ISAPIVERIFY(::LoadString(AfxGetResourceHandle(),
              IDS_FILTER, sz, SF_MAX_FILTER_DESC_LEN));
    _tcscpy(pVer->lpszFilterDesc, sz);
    return TRUE;
}


DWORD CMFCXFilterFilter::OnPreprocHeaders(CHttpFilterContext* pCtxt,
                              PHTTP_FILTER_PREPROC_HEADERS pHeaderInfo)
{
    // TODO: React to this notification accordingly and
    // return the appropriate status code
    return SF_STATUS_REQ_NEXT_NOTIFICATION;
}

// Do not edit the following lines, which are needed by ClassWizard.
#if 0
BEGIN_MESSAGE_MAP(CMFCXFilterFilter, CHttpFilter)
    //{{AFX_MSG_MAP(CMFCXFilterFilter)
    //}}AFX_MSG_MAP
END_MESSAGE_MAP()
#endif   // 0


/////////////////////////////////////////////////////////////////////////
// If your extension will not use MFC, you'll need this code to make
```

```
// sure the extension objects can find the resource handle for the
// module.  If you convert your extension to not be dependent on MFC,
// remove the comments around the following AfxGetResourceHandle()
// and DllMain() functions, as well as the g_hInstance global.

/****

static HINSTANCE g_hInstance;

HINSTANCE AFXISAPI AfxGetResourceHandle()
{
    return g_hInstance;
}

BOOL WINAPI DllMain(HINSTANCE hInst, ULONG ulReason, LPVOID lpReserved)
{
    if (ulReason == DLL_PROCESS_ATTACH)
    {
        g_hInstance = hInst;
    }

    return TRUE;
}

****/
```

The AppWizard also added a large portion of commented-out code, which is explained pretty well by the comment itself. You can safely delete this, since we shall never use it.

## Adding Functionality

The default implementation of **OnPreprocHeaders()** does nothing at this point. We need to insert the following code to achieve our intended functionality:

```
DWORD CMFCXFilterFilter::OnPreprocHeaders(CHttpFilterContext* pCtxt,
                            PHTTP_FILTER_PREPROC_HEADERS pHeaderInfo)
{
    CHAR achUrl[512];
    CHAR achUserAgent[512];
    DWORD dwURL, dwUA;

    dwURL = sizeof(achUrl);
    dwUA = sizeof(achUserAgent);

    //Gets the URL that the user is requesting. Note that url is
    //a "special" header and is retrieved simply by specifying "url"
    if (!pHeaderInfo->GetHeader(pCtxt->m_pFC, "url",achUrl,&dwURL))
    {
        DebugMsg((DEST,
                    "[OnReadPreprocHeaders] GetHeader(url) failed.\r\n"));
        return SF_STATUS_REQ_ERROR;
    }
    // Reset the dwURL to contain the actual length of the URL
    dwURL = strlen(achUrl);
```

```
    //Check to see if we need to do anything, i.e. this url ends in htmx
    if (CheckNeedsMap(achUrl, dwURL))
    {
        // Get user agent (type of browser) from the list of headers.
        if (!pHeaderInfo->GetHeader(pCtxt->m_pFC,"User-Agent:",
                                    achUserAgent, &dwUA))
        {
            DebugMsg((DEST,
                "[OnPreprocHeaders] GetHeader(User-Agent:) failed \r\n"));
            return SF_STATUS_REQ_ERROR;
        }

        if (strstr(achUserAgent,"MSIE 3")!=NULL)
            ReplaceLastChar(achUrl,"3", dwURL);
        else
            if (strncmp(achUserAgent,"Mozilla/3",9) == 0)
                ReplaceLastChar(achUrl,"3", dwURL);
            else
                if (strncmp(achUserAgent,"Mozilla/2",9) == 0)
                    ReplaceLastChar(achUrl,"2", dwURL);
                else
                    ReplaceLastChar(achUrl,"1", dwURL);

        if (!pHeaderInfo->SetHeader(pCtxt->m_pFC, "url",achUrl))
        {
            DebugMsg((DEST,
                    "[OnPreprocHeaders] SetHeader(url) failed \r\n"));
            return SF_STATUS_REQ_ERROR;
        }
    }
    return SF_STATUS_REQ_NEXT_NOTIFICATION;
}
```

The above function first retrieves the value of the URL being requested. It does this with a call to the **GetHeader()** function, which is part of the **HTTP_FILTER_PREPROC_HEADERS** structure. You should note, when calling the **GetHeader()** and later the **SetHeader()** functions, that their first parameter is a pointer to the **HTTP_FILTER_CONTEXT** *structure*. Don't confuse this with the **CHttpFilterContext** *class*. The **HTTP_FILTER_CONTEXT** structure is a data member (in fact, the only data member) of the **CHttpFilterContext** class, and is referenced by using **pCtxt->m_pFC**.

Once the filter has the URL value, it checks to see if this request needs to be mapped (i.e. if it's a **.htmx** file). It does this with a call to the **CheckNeedsMap()** function, listed below:

```
BOOL CMFCXFilterFilter::CheckNeedsMap(CHAR* pchURL, DWORD dwLength)
{
    if (dwLength > 4 && *(pchURL + dwLength - 4) == 'h'
        && *(pchURL + dwLength - 3) == 't'
        && *(pchURL + dwLength - 2) == 'm'
        && *(pchURL + dwLength - 1) == 'x')
        return TRUE;

    return FALSE;
}
```

If the request does need to be mapped, the filter retrieves the **USER-AGENT:** variable from the incoming headers with another call to the **GetHeader()** function. You should note that although we needed a: (colon) following our request to get the header **USER-AGENT:**, we did not need a: to read the header **url**. This is because the URL is not, technically, a header variable, it's actually part of the request line, and therefore doesn't require a colon. The only other variables that have this status are **method** and **version**.

Once we have the **USER-AGENT:** variable, we check to see what type of browser it is. While the checks used here will not cover every browser type, they cover some of the more popular ones and should be sufficient for most uses.

Once the browser type has been determined, the last character of the requested URL is changed to reflect the browser's level. The function that does this is given here:

```
void CMFCXFilterFilter::ReplaceLastChar(CHAR* pchPath, CHAR* pchLetter,
                                        DWORD dwLength)
{
    if(!*pchPath)
        return;

    *(pchPath + dwLength - 1) = *pchLetter;
}
```

Having edited the URL to refer to the desired file, we need to send this result back to the server. This will make the server 'think' that the client actually requested that URL. To do this, we use the **SetHeader()** function, which uses similar syntax to the **GetHeader()** function. This altered header is never sent back to the client; it's used by the server to process just this one request. Thus, the client's browser will still show **http://yourdomain.com/file/myfile.htmx**, even though they are actually reading **http://yourdomain.com/file/myfile.htm2** (or whatever).

With all this done, we return a status of **SF_STATUS_REQ_NEXT_NOTIFICATION**, which tells the server that everything went well and to notify us at the next stage. In this case, our filter didn't ask to be notified at any other stages, and so it's finished.

In case you forgot to prototype your functions in the header, the **MFCXFilter.h** file is give here:

```
// MFCXFILTER.CPP - Implementation file for your Internet Server
//     MFCXFilter Filter


class CMFCXFilterFilter: public CHttpFilter
{
public:
    BOOL CheckNeedsMap(CHAR* pchURL, DWORD dwLength);
    void ReplaceLastChar(CHAR* pchPath, CHAR* pchLetter, DWORD dwLength);

    CMFCXFilterFilter();
    ~CMFCXFilterFilter();

    BOOL GetFilterVersion(PHTTP_FILTER_VERSION pVer);

    DWORD OnPreprocHeaders(CHttpFilterContext* pCtxt,
                           PHTTP_FILTER_PREPROC_HEADERS pHeaderInfo);

};
```

## Debugging

Now there's only one other piece of code that you need to add. To help in debugging your ISAPI filter, place the following macro definition at the top of **MFCXFilter.cpp**. This will allow you to print out debug messages easily, so that you can see what your filter is doing (or not doing).

```
#define DEST buff
#define DebugMsg(x)                    \
{                                      \
    char buff[256];                    \
    wsprintf x;                        \
    OutputDebugString(buff);           \
}
```

You should have noticed that we called this macro a couple of times in the **OnPreprocHeaders()** function. The macro simply prints any information that you give it to the debug window. We didn't have much need for this in the first part of the book, since we could interactively debug our extension to see what was going on. The reason we are using it here is that your filter may need to output some debug information, even though you are actually debugging something else.

Let's say that you have written an encrypting/decrypting filter. You test it out and it seems to work. Now, you start working on an ISAPI extension. When you try to debug the extension, all you get is garbage coming from the web server. You might spend a lot of time looking for the error in your extension, when the problem is really in your filter. If you had put a **DebugMsg((DEST, "Couldn't load decryption key from registry. \r\n"))** call in your filter, the message would have shown up when you were debugging your extension (provided you were using the debug version of the filter, rather than the release...). As you start adding more and more filters to your server, this macro can end up saving you a lot of time.

# Building and Testing the MFCXFilter

Unlike ISAPI extensions, ISAPI filters don't need to be in any special directory. However, you do need to let the web server know which DLLs it should use as filters, by putting a list in the registry. The web server will load all of the filters listed each time it is started; the list is kept in **HKEY_LOCAL_MACHINE\System\CurrentControlSet\Services\W3SVC\Parameters\Filter DLLs**. In order to add our new filter, run Regedit and select the above parameter. Edit the string to add your new filter; the filters are stored in comma delimited order. As noted above, if two filters have the same priority, their order in this list determines the order in which they are called. When you have finished adding this example to the filter list, the string value might look something like this:

```
c:\inetsrv\Server\sspifilt.dll,d:\webdev\MFCXFilter\debug\MFCXFilter.dll
```

While that is all the editing you'll need to do in the registry for a normal filter, in this case you will need to make a few more modifications. In order for the server to recognize **.html**, **.htm2** and **.htm3** as valid HTML files, we need to add some entries in the server **MimeMap**. To do this:

**1** Go **HKEY_LOCAL_MACHINE\System\CurrentControlSet\Services\InetInfo\Parameters\MimeMap**.

**2** Select Edit | Add Value.

**3** Make sure the data type is **REG_SZ**.

**4**  Type in `text\html,htm3,,h` for the value.

**5**  Select OK, and then leave the string value blank - this tells the server that `.htm3` documents are `text/html`. (The other commas and the `h` are used for other services, such as gopher, and you needn't be concerned with them for your web server. Be sure to add similar entries for both `htm2` and `html`.)

You will need to restart all Internet services (web, gopher, and FTP) for this change in the `MimeMap` to take effect.

Now that you have the registry configured, you need to stop and restart the MSIIS services, and the filter will be loaded. In order to test the filter, you will need three files: `file.html`, `file.htm2`, and `file.htm3`. Let's say these are in a directory called `testdir` off your web server's root directory. Each file should look something like this:

`file.htm3`:

```
<html>
<body>
<h1>This is file.htm3</h1>
</body>
</html>
```

If you try `http://yourdomain.com/testdir/file.htmx`, it should give you the appropriate file for your browser. You will need to try it with different browsers to make sure that it's working. You can also add any unrecognized browser types to the code. Simply find out what their **USER-AGENT:** string is and put some code in to map it to an appropriate `htmx` type.

If you need to debug an ISAPI filter, the steps are the same as for an ISAPI extension. Set the executable to the web server and pass it `-e w3svc` as parameters. Be sure to have the filter listed in the registry, set any break points, and you are ready to debug.

# The Filter without MFC

While writing code using MFC and employing an OOP approach may simplify the job of the programmer, it does have some drawbacks. The main one is in speed of execution. While the above program is very small, and you may not see much room for optimization, we will start with this simple example to show how we can discard MFC without creating too much work for ourselves. In the process, we'll eliminate the overhead of referencing a class to get at the functions and variables that we need.

We will start with the source code in C for our `htmx` filter, and then cover the differences. In order to make the project, you should create a new project workspace and call it `HTMXFilter`. Rather than selecting the ISAPI Extension Wizard, you should select Dynamic-Link Library. Create a new text file called `HTMXFilter.cpp` and use the following code. (You should note that most of the code is substantially similar to what you typed in above.)

```
/*++
HTMX Map Filter
--*/
```

```
#include <windows.h>
#include <httpfilt.h>


//  DebugMsg() is used for debugging
#define DEST buff
#define DebugMsg(x)                 \
    {                               \
       char buff[256];              \
       wsprintf x;                  \
       OutputDebugString(buff);     \
    }


BOOL CheckNeedsMap(CHAR* pchURL, DWORD dwLength);
void ReplaceLastChar(CHAR* pchPath,CHAR* pchLetter, DWORD dwLength);


DWORD OnPreprocHeaders(HTTP_FILTER_CONTEXT* pFC,
                       HTTP_FILTER_PREPROC_HEADERS* pHeaderInfo);


BOOL WINAPI GetFilterVersion(HTTP_FILTER_VERSION * pVer)
{
   DebugMsg((DEST,
            "[GetFilterVersion] Server filter version is %d.%d\n",
            HIWORD(pVer->dwServerFilterVersion),
            LOWORD(pVer->dwServerFilterVersion)));
   pVer->dwFilterVersion = MAKELONG(0, 1);   // Version 1.0

   //  Specify the types and order of notification
   pVer->dwFlags = (SF_NOTIFY_SECURE_PORT | SF_NOTIFY_NONSECURE_PORT |
                 SF_NOTIFY_PREPROC_HEADERS | SF_NOTIFY_ORDER_DEFAULT);
   strcpy(pVer->lpszFilterDesc, "HTMX Map, v1.0");
   return TRUE;
}


DWORD WINAPI HttpFilterProc(HTTP_FILTER_CONTEXT* pFC,
                            DWORD NotificationType, VOID* pvData)
{
   DWORD dwRet;

   //  Send this notification to the right function
   switch (NotificationType)
   {
   case SF_NOTIFY_PREPROC_HEADERS:
      dwRet = OnPreprocHeaders(pFC,
                            (PHTTP_FILTER_PREPROC_HEADERS) pvData);
      break;

   default:
      DebugMsg((DEST,
               "[HttpFilterProc] Unknown notification type, %d\n",
               NotificationType));
      dwRet = SF_STATUS_REQ_NEXT_NOTIFICATION;
      break;
```

```
        }
    return dwRet;
}


DWORD OnPreprocHeaders(HTTP_FILTER_CONTEXT* pFC,
                       HTTP_FILTER_PREPROC_HEADERS* pHeaderInfo)

{
    CHAR achUrl[512];
    CHAR achUserAgent[512];
    DWORD dwURL, dwUA;

    dwURL = sizeof(achUrl);
    dwUA = sizeof(achUserAgent);

    // Gets the URL that the user is requesting. Note that url is
    // a "special" header and is retrieved simply by specifying "url"
    if (!pHeaderInfo->GetHeader(pFC, "url",achUrl,&dwURL))
    {
        DebugMsg((DEST,
                  "[OnReadPreprocHeaders] GetHeader(url) failed.\r\n"));
        return SF_STATUS_REQ_ERROR;
    }
    // Get the actual length of the URL
    dwURL = strlen(achUrl);

    // Check if we need to do anything, i.e. this url ends in htmx
    if (CheckNeedsMap(achUrl, dwURL))
    {
        // Get user agent (type of browser) from the list of headers.
        if (!pHeaderInfo->GetHeader(pFC,"User-Agent:",
                                    achUserAgent, &dwUA))
        {
            DebugMsg((DEST,
                "[OnPreprocHeaders] GetHeader(User-Agent:) failed \r\n"));
            return SF_STATUS_REQ_ERROR;
        }

        if (strstr(achUserAgent,"MSIE 3")!=NULL)
            ReplaceLastChar(achUrl,"3", dwURL);
        else
            if (strncmp(achUserAgent,"Mozilla/3",9) == 0)
                ReplaceLastChar(achUrl,"3", dwURL);
            else
                if (strncmp(achUserAgent,"Mozilla/2",9) == 0)
                    ReplaceLastChar(achUrl,"2", dwURL);
                else
                    ReplaceLastChar(achUrl,"1", dwURL);

        if (!pHeaderInfo->SetHeader(pFC, "url",achUrl))
        {
            DebugMsg((DEST,
                      "[OnPreprocHeaders] SetHeader(url) failed \r\n"));
            return SF_STATUS_REQ_ERROR;
        }
    }
    return SF_STATUS_REQ_NEXT_NOTIFICATION;
}
```

**163**

```
void ReplaceLastChar(CHAR* pchPath,CHAR* pchLetter, DWORD dwLength)
{
    if(!*pchPath)
        return;

    *(pchPath + dwLength - 1)=*pchLetter;
}



BOOL CheckNeedsMap(CHAR* pchURL, DWORD dwLength)
{
    if (dwLength > 4 && *(pchURL + dwLength - 4) == 'h'
        && *(pchURL + dwLength - 3) == 't'
        && *(pchURL + dwLength - 2) == 'm'
        && *(pchURL + dwLength - 1) == 'x')
        return TRUE;
    return FALSE;
}
```

From the previous chapter, you know that there are two required functions for a filter DLL: **HttpFilterProc()** and **GetFilterVersion()**. To expose these functions properly, create a new text file called **HTMXFilter.def** and type in the following:

```
LIBRARY HTMXFilter

DESCRIPTION 'Internet Server HTMX Filter'

EXPORTS
    HttpFilterProc
    GetFilterVersion
```

You can now build and test your non-MFC version of the same filter. You should see that the two filters look almost identical. The only thing we had to do was to call the appropriate function from **HttpFilterProc()** and cast the parameter to the appropriate type. Since this is really all that MFC does for us, there is no compelling reason to use it.

### Benchmarking the Filter

The big question: Is it any faster? The answer is yes. In this case, it's about 10% faster than the MFC version. With ISAPI extensions, we can use the Wrox ISAPI Debugger to profile the DLL. (See Appendix A for complete information.) However, with filters, we don't have an easy way to profile code, and so we need to make one of our own. In order to test how fast your ISAPI filter functions are running, you should use the **GetThreadTimes()** function, which gives you start time, stop time, kernel CPU usage and user CPU usage for any thread in the system. The function is prototyped as follows:

```
BOOL GetThreadTimes(HANDLE hThread,
                    LPFILETIME lpCreationTime,
                    LPFILETIME lpExitTime,
                    LPFILETIME lpKernelTime,
                    LPFILETIME lpUserTime);
```

The **hThread** parameter is a handle to the thread object you wish to get information on. In most cases, this will be the current thread that is running. The handle to the current thread is retrieved by calling the Win32 function **GetCurrentThread()**. The other parameters are, respectively, the time that the thread was created, the time it exited, the amount of time the thread spent executing kernel code, and the amount of time it has spent executing user (non-kernel) code. The reason we use **GetThreadTimes()** is that it only returns the amount of time that our thread has been running. This way, even if other programs are running on the computer and slowing things down, it still provides a way to tell exactly how long our particular thread has spent doing work rather than waiting on other threads to do theirs.

The **FILETIME** structure represents a 64-bit measure of time, in 100-nanosecond intervals, and is stored in two **DWORD**s. For ISAPI programming, we have little need to know when the thread was created or exited, since most of the threads will be managed by the web server's pool manager and are totally out of our control. In addition, we don't expect our filters to take days to run. These factors allow us to cheat a little on our code, so that implementing a simple stop watch for your filter is quite easy. In fact, we will implement it as a series of macros. The macros will create the public variables **dwTotalKernelTime** and **dwTotalUserTime** to keep track of how long the sections of your filter spent running. The macro definitions are given here. Note that they are defined so that they are totally inert unless you **#define TIME_ME**.

```
//////////////////////////////////////////////////////////
// Thread timing macro ISAPITimer.h

#ifdef TIME_ME
CRITICAL_SECTION    csTimeMe;

#define START_CLOCK                                             \
   FILETIME ftKernelStart, ftUserStart;                        \
   FILETIME ftKernelStop, ftUserStop;                          \
   FILETIME ftCreation, ftExit;                                \
   GetThreadTimes(GetCurrentThread(), &ftCreation, &ftExit,    \
                  &ftKernelStart, &ftUserStart);


#define STOP_CLOCK                                              \
   GetThreadTimes(GetCurrentThread(), &ftCreation, &ftExit,    \
                  &ftKernelStop, &ftUserStop);                 \
   AddToTime(ftKernelStart, ftKernelStop, ftUserStart, ftUserStop);


#define SETUP_CLOCK                                             \
   InitializeCriticalSection(&csTimeMe);                       \
   dwTotalUserTime=0;                                          \
   dwTotalKernelTime=0;


#define CLEAN_CLOCK                                             \
   DeleteCriticalSection(&csTimeMe);


DWORD dwTotalKernelTime;
DWORD dwTotalUserTime;

void AddToTime(FILETIME ftKernelStart, FILETIME ftKernelStop,
               FILETIME ftUserStart, FILETIME ftUserStop)
{
   EnterCriticalSection(&csTimeMe);

   dwTotalKernelTime += ftKernelStop.dwLowDateTime -
                                      ftKernelStart.dwLowDateTime;
   dwTotalUserTime += ftUserStop.dwLowDateTime -
                                      ftUserStart.dwLowDateTime;
```

```
            LeaveCriticalSection(&csTimeMe);
    }

    #else

    #define START_CLOCK
    #define STOP_CLOCK
    #define SETUP_CLOCK
    #define CLEAN_CLOCK
    #endif
```

To implement this macro in the above example, you'll need to change the code just a little. First, include the header file (be sure that **IsapiTimer.h** is in your include path).

```
/*++
HTMX Map Filter
--*/


#include <windows.h>
#include <httpfilt.h>
```

```
#define TIME_ME
#include "IsapiTimer.h"
```

```
//  DebugMsg() is used for debugging
#define DEST buff
#define DebugMsg(x)                     \
    {                                   \
        char buff[256];                 \
        wsprintf x;                     \
        OutputDebugString(buff);        \
    }
```

Since our macros use a critical section to control access to the data, we need to set up and clean up inside **DllMain()**. Most filters will already have a **DllMain()** function, but in this case, we have to add one:

```
BOOL WINAPI DllMain(HANDLE hModule, DWORD dwReason, LPVOID lpReserved)
{
    switch(dwReason)
    {
    case DLL_PROCESS_ATTACH:
        {
            SETUP_CLOCK;
            break;
        }
    case DLL_THREAD_ATTACH:
        break;
    case DLL_THREAD_DETACH:
        break;
    case DLL_PROCESS_DETACH:
        {
            CLEAN_CLOCK;
            break;
        }
    }
    return TRUE;
}
```

To use the timer, simply include the **START_** and **STOP_CLOCK** macros where you want to begin and end timing.

```
DWORD WINAPI HttpFilterProc(HTTP_FILTER_CONTEXT* pFC,
                            DWORD NotificationType, VOID* pvData)
{
    DWORD dwRet;

    START_CLOCK;
    //  Send this notification to the right function

    switch (NotificationType)
    {
    case SF_NOTIFY_PREPROC_HEADERS:
        dwRet = OnPreprocHeaders(pFC,
                                 (PHTTP_FILTER_PREPROC_HEADERS) pvData);
        break;

    default:
        DebugMsg((DEST,
                  "[HttpFilterProc] Unknown notification type, %d\n",
                  NotificationType));
        dwRet = SF_STATUS_REQ_NEXT_NOTIFICATION;
        break;
    }
    STOP_CLOCK;
    return dwRet;
}
```

In order to really test your application, you should allow the filter to run several times before looking at the timings. To look at the timings, you have to use the debugger. Fortunately, you can simply tell the debugger not to break the program until the code has been executed a fixed number of times. To do this, select Edit | Breakpoints. Select a line that you want to break on and then click on the Conditions button. In the Breakpoint Conditions dialog box you can specify how many times the line will be passed over before the debugger will halt on it, as shown here:

Now, if you don't want to click the Reload button a hundred times just to test your timer out, you can use the following method instead. Create a hypertext document that uses frames to request the document the number of times you want. For example, in this case, we simply want to select **file1.htmx** a hundred times, so we can use the following:

```
<FRAMESET rows=10,10,10,10,10,10,10,10,10,10,10,…(100 times total)…,10>
<FRAME SRC="/file1.htmx">
<FRAME SRC="/file1.htmx">
<FRAME SRC="/file1.htmx">
<FRAME SRC="/file1.htmx">
<FRAME SRC="/file1.htmx">
<FRAME SRC="/file1.htmx">
<FRAME SRC="/file1.htmx">
…
(100 times total)
…
<FRAME SRC="/file1.htmx">
<FRAME SRC="/file1.htmx">
<FRAME SRC="/file1.htmx">
</FRAMESET>
```

Of course, you won't be able to read a word on your browser, but the point here is not to test how pretty your filter looks, but to see how fast it runs. So, while this technique is a far cry from a full profiler, it's simple and quick to use and gives you a reliable timer to use on filters.

# Summary

In this chapter, we demonstrated how you can use filters to read and alter header values that the client sent over. Initially, we used MFC-provided wrapper functions for ISAPI filters. However, there is an overhead associated with using MFC, with little in the way of compensation through ease of use. Since ISAPI filters are called with each request, we need to use all the techniques at our disposal to optimize them. To begin with, we shouldn't use MFC or any other code that is not specifically optimized for the task at hand.

Once we have what we think is a working ISAPI filter, we can use the **IsapiTimer.h** macros that implement the Win32 **GetThreadTimes()** function to time our filter's performance.

# User Authentication

Many web servers have their own methods for controlling access to certain sections of the server. In most cases, this consists of a text file which contains a list of username:password (usually encrypted) combinations. Access to certain directories requires that the user enter a name and password that match with one in the text file for that particular directory. While this method is easy to set up and maintain for a small number of users, if you need to maintain hundreds of users, and allow for different levels of access, it very quickly becomes unmanageable. Another problem with this method is that it requires protected files to be placed in separate directories, which can make it difficult for you to manage the content.

When Microsoft designed their Internet Server, they designed it to be fully integrated with Windows NT security. This design makes it ideal for maintaining an intranet site because it allows seamless security for the web site. The major drawback to having a web security system based around NT accounts is that every user must have a valid NT account. This means that if you want to have a protected section of your site, every person who is given access must be given an account on the NT server. Though this gives rise to some minor security issues (but nothing that can't be fixed by a competent administrator), the biggest problem you'll encounter is simply creating and managing all the user accounts.

Fortunately, the MSIIS gives us the ability to make custom authentication filters which greatly simplify the administrator's life and eases security concerns. In this chapter, we will cover how to construct such a filter.

We'll also focus on making this filter run as quickly as possible; if you are going to be authenticating a lot of users, such high performance is essential. This project will therefore demonstrate some new programming techniques and approaches to optimizing our code for speed.

By focusing on performance, we'll cover advanced thread synchronization techniques, custom memory management, and ODBC API programming. In addition, we will go over how to write important error information to the event log.

## Design of the Filter

Every person that accesses your web site must have a valid NT username and password to get access to any file on your server. If the user doesn't supply a username and password, the web server uses the anonymous username and password that you supplied in the Internet Services Manager. By default, this anonymous user is called **IUSR_computer_name**. If you delete this user, or change the password, people will no longer be able to access your site without having their own Windows NT password.

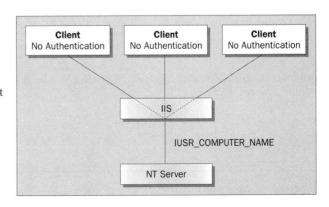

Just as the MSIIS maps all requests that don't have a password onto the anonymous user account, we will construct a filter that maps all requests that supply a username and password onto their corresponding NT username and password.

To illustrate this, let's say that we have the following, rather simple, user authentication requirement. Our site offers a great deal of information. We give it away for free, but do ask users to register with us by filling in a simple form before they are given access to the rest of the site. (The database example in Chapter 4 should be coming to mind.) We want users to be given access as soon as they register.

Since all registered users have access to the same material, we will put them under one account: for example, we could call this account 'webuser' and give it a password of 'webpass'. While you can certainly change these to anything you wish, you must create this account on your system for this example to work. You must also give it all the permissions that are outlined in the 'Building and Testing the Filter' section of this chapter.

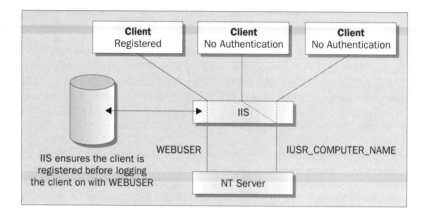

Once the filter is installed, it will take the username and password that the user typed in over the Internet and map it onto the NT username and password associated with it in the database. By doing so, even if we have 500 users registered to use the site, we still need only the one NT username and password.

If you want to have another level of users that have access to even more information on the site, you can do this by creating another NT user and mapping all web usernames and passwords that have access to this section to the new account.

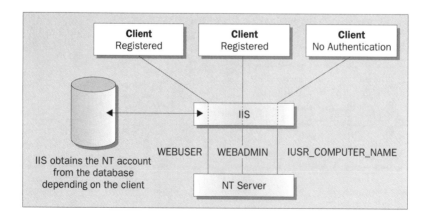

This password mapping file can be any ODBC data source. In this example, we will be using the Visual FoxPro tables used in Chapter 4. The reader should note that in this table, the passwords are stored un-encrypted. It is left as an exercise to the reader to provide such an encrypting mechanism, if you require it. An encrypting technique is not given here, because it would be much easier to protect the passwords by storing them in a DBMS, such as SQL Server or Oracle.

# The Cache

While our user database will be kept in an ODBC data source, it would significantly hinder the performance of our server if we had to query the database every time we needed to authenticate a user. Remember that every request for a document must be authenticated. Even though the browser doesn't ask you for your username and password for every page and image that you view, the server is still authenticating your request. The browser only asks for your username and password once. After that, it automatically provides it for you. Therefore, just because you don't get asked for your username and password, don't assume that our filter isn't mapping it for you.

In order to speed things up, we will cache username and password information for users who recently requested documents. The cache works as follows:

When a user requests a document, the filter first looks to see if he or she is in the cache. It will do a sequential search through the entire cache from beginning to end. If the user is not found, it will query the ODBC data source. Assuming it is found in the ODBC datasource, the entry will be added to the beginning of the cache. If the number of entries in the cache is greater than **MAX_CACHED**, then the last entry in the cache will be deleted.

Since the cache searches sequentially from beginning to end, and a user who just requested a document is very likely to request another one soon, we want to move users who request documents to the front of the list. However, we don't want to waste our time swapping around the first couple of users in the list. To do this, we use a **RESORT_LIMIT** constant. If the user's entry is further back in the list than the **RESORT_LIMIT**, the entry is moved to the front. Otherwise, it's simply left where it is. We have set the **MAX_CACHED** in this example to 50, and the **RESORT_LIMIT** to 10. If you have a large number of users who will simultaneously be requiring authentication, you should increase these limits.

If you are a little fuzzy on how the cache works, we provide a brief example here. Let's say user Joe requests an HTML page. The filter looks in the cache and doesn't find a match. It then loads Joe's information from ODBC and stores it in the cache at position 1. The HTML page has five JPEG images on it that also require authentication. The filter looks in the cache and finds it quickly as it's in the first slot. While Joe is perusing the files, a few more users come to the site; each gets added to the cache. Joe is now moved back to number 8. Joe then requests another document that has a couple of JPEGs in it. This time, the filter finds him after looking in the first seven slots. It doesn't reorder the list, however, because it isn't over the **RESORT_LIMIT**. Now Joe takes a long time to look over this document, and 30 other users come in while he is doing so. When he requests his next document, which has eight JPEG images in it, the cache finds him back in 38. It moves him to slot 1 during the first request for the document. When it tries to find him for each one of the JPEGs, it finds him quickly because he is in slot 1. When Joe goes away, his entry is deleted when 50 (**MAX_CACHED**) other users come to visit.

We will use a double-linked-list to implement the above design. This allows us to easily move an item in the list. The problem we have is that multiple threads will be accessing this list at the same time. If one thread is searching while another is deleting or moving, it can lead to significant problems. One solution to this problem would be to allow only one thread at a time access to the data. This would be fine if we were writing more often than reading.

However, in most cases, users request more than one document or image from your site. Thus, you will have a couple of users at the head of the cache who will constantly need to be validated. Allowing only one in at a time slows things down a little more than we would like. The solution given here will allow any number of threads to read, but will allow only one thread at a time to write data. In addition, this method will also make sure that no threads are reading from the data when another one is writing. Opposite is an outline for the layout of our cache guard.

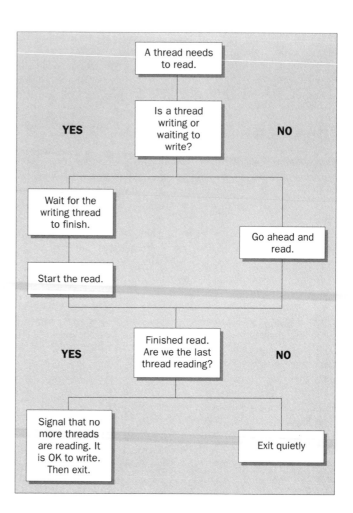

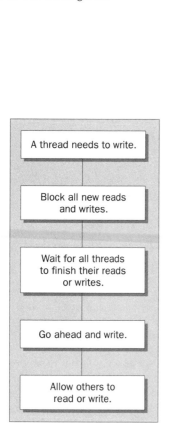

In order to do this, we will need to use an event, a semaphore, and a mutex. While we have used events and semaphores before, we will need to take a minute to go over the uses of the mutex, and how to wait for multiple synchronization objects.

## The Mutex

The mutex (short for mutually exclusive) is a thread synchronization object which operates much like a critical section in that only one thread can have access to it at one time. It does have several additional features. Like a semaphore and an event, it's controlled by a handle–so that code waiting for the mutex to become free can time out. Also similar to semaphores and events, it can be created with a name so that it may be used to synchronize threads of different processes. The function to create a mutex is prototyped here:

```
HANDLE CreateMutex(LPSECURITY_ATTRIBUTES lpMutexAttributes,
                   BOOL bInitialOwner,
                   LPCTSTR lpName);
```

The security attributes and name are used in the same fashion as for the semaphore. (In this example, we won't be using either.) The **bInitialOwner** is used to set the mutex in a signaled (**FALSE**) or non-signaled (**TRUE**) state when it is created. The reasoning for this is that, if a thread 'owns' a mutex, other threads can't use it. Hence, it's in the non-signaled state.

To wait for a mutex, you can use **WaitForSingleObject()** or **WaitForMultipleObjects()**. We will finally cover **WaitForMultipleObjects()** below.

To free up a mutex, use the familiar **CloseHandle()** function.

## WaitForMultipleObjects()

Let's say that you need to wait for an auto-reset event and a mutex (as in this example). You could make two **WaitForSingleObject()** calls, but controlling the time-out mechanism would be awkward. To do this, you should use **WaitForMultipleObjects()**. In addition, **WaitForMultipleObjects()** allows you to specify a list of objects to wait for, but will give you the option of returning when any one or more of the objects becomes signaled. **WaitForMultipleObjects()** is prototyped here:

```
DWORD WaitForMultipleObjects(DWORD nCount,
                             CONST HANDLE *lpHandles,
                             BOOL bWaitAll,
                             DWORD dwMilliseconds);
```

The **nCount** parameter is the number of objects you wish to wait on. The **lpHandles** parameter is an array of handles to thread synchronization objects. The **bWaitAll** specifies that the call should either wait until all objects become signaled before returning (**TRUE**), or return as soon as one or more of the objects in the list becomes signaled (**FALSE**). The **dwMilliseconds** is the same as in **WaitForSingleObject()**. The return values are also the same as **WaitForSingleObject()**, except in the case where **bWaitAll** is set to **FALSE**. If **bWaitAll** is **FALSE**, and at least one of the objects in the array of handles became signaled, the value **(dwReturnValue - WAIT_OBJECT_0)** will give you the index value in the handle array of the object that became signaled. Thus, if in our simple call to wait for an event and a mutex, the event handle were at **lpHandle[0]** and the mutex handle were at **lpHandle[1]**, and the mutex was the only object that was signaled, **(dwReturnValue - WAIT_OBJECT_0)** would equal one. If more than one object became signaled simultaneously, this value would be the lowest index value that became signaled.

If the wait expires because ownership was granted to an abandoned mutex, **(dwReturnValue - WAIT_ABANDONED_0)** will give you the index to the mutex. A mutex is considered abandoned when the thread that owns it terminates without releasing it.

# Cache Guard

In order to maintain control over our cache, we will create a **CACHE_GUARD** structure and some functions to go with it. We could have encapsulated this into a class, but that would create a little bit of overhead. As this is not a large or complex problem, but one in which speed is critical, we will use the more direct approach. The **CacheGuard.h** header file is given here.

```
/// CacheGuard.h


typedef struct CACHE_GUARD {
    HANDLE    hMutexBlockAccess;
    HANDLE    hEventCanWrite;
    HANDLE    hSemaNumReads;
} *PCG;

BOOL InitializeCacheGuard(PCG pCG);
void DeleteCacheGuard(PCG pCG);
void WaitToRead(PCG pCG);
void FinishedRead(PCG pCG);
void WaitToWrite(PCG);
void FinishedWrite(PCG);
```

Since the function names are pretty much self-explanatory, we'll simply present the implementation file **CacheGuard.cpp** here:

```
//// CacheGuard.cpp
#include <windows.h>
#include "CacheGuard.h"
```

When we initialize, we simply create the mutex, the event, and the semaphore. If the initialization fails, we need to clean up what we have already created and return **FALSE**.

```
BOOL InitializeCacheGuard(PCG pCG)
{
    // Create the mutex in the signaled state (OK to Write)
    pCG->hMutexBlockAccess=CreateMutex(NULL,FALSE,NULL);
    if (pCG->hMutexBlockAccess==NULL)
        return FALSE;

    // Create the event in the signaled state (No Current Reads)
    pCG->hEventCanWrite = CreateEvent(NULL, TRUE, TRUE, NULL);
    if (pCG->hEventCanWrite == NULL)
    {
        CloseHandle(pCG->hMutexBlockAccess);
        return FALSE;
    }

    //  Creates some semaphores 0x00000FFF = 65536 (a whole lot)
    pCG->hSemaNumReads = CreateSemaphore(NULL, 0, 0x00000FFF, NULL);
    if (pCG->hSemaNumReads == NULL)
    {
        CloseHandle(pCG->hMutexBlockAccess);
        CloseHandle(pCG->hEventCanWrite);
        return FALSE;
```

```
    }
    return TRUE;
}
```

On the clean up, we simply need to close all the handles. Remember that closing handles is very important with thread synchronization objects, because NT doesn't automatically clean them up for you. If you forget to close the handles before exiting, you'll have to reboot to get rid of them.

```
void DeleteCacheGuard(PCG pCG)
{

    // Clean up
    if (!pCG->hMutexBlockAccess)
        CloseHandle(pCG->hMutexBlockAccess);

    if (!pCG->hEventCanWrite)
        CloseHandle(pCG->hEventCanWrite);

    if (!pCG->hSemaNumReads)
        CloseHandle(pCG->hSemaNumReads);
}
```

Before we can read, we first need to make sure that no-one is writing. We wait on the **hMutexBlockAccess** mutex for this. Once we know that no-one is writing, we need to make sure that no new write can occur until we have finished our read. We increment the **hSemaNumReads** count and set the **hEventCanWrite** event if the previous count was 0. This is because if the previous count was 0, other threads that needed to write could get the **hEventCanWrite** event to begin their write. We need to set the event to non-signaled so that no threads waiting to write can get the **hEventCanWrite** event.

```
void WaitToRead(PCG pCG)
{
    LONG    lOldCount;

    // Block any writes
    WaitForSingleObject(pCG->hMutexBlockAccess, INFINITE);

    // Increment the count of the semaphore
    ReleaseSemaphore(pCG->hSemaNumReads, 1, &lOldCount);

    // If the old count was 0,
    // we need to reset the event so no one can write
    if (lOldCount ==0)
        ResetEvent(pCG->hEventCanWrite);

    // We don't need this any more once the event is set
    ReleaseMutex(pCG->hMutexBlockAccess);
}
```

When we have finished reading, we need to free up the count of the semaphore, which indicates how many threads are currently reading. The problem with semaphores is that you can't read the count without changing it. This gives rise to the rather tricky code in the **FinishedRead()** function. We first call the **WaitForMultipleObjects()** to decrement the read count. We then call **WaitForSingleObject()** with a time-out time of zero. If this thread was the last read, the current count will be zero, and so the **WaitForSingleObject()** call will return **TIME_OUT** immediately. Otherwise, it will decrement the count immediately and return **WAIT_OBJECT_0**. If the wait times out, it means that the count is 0 and that we were the last thread to be reading. In this case, we set the **hEventCanWrite** event to signaled so that other threads can write. If the count was not 0, then when we called **WaitForSingleObject()**, we decremented the count. In order to correct this, we need to release one semaphore, as shown below:

```
void FinishedRead(PCG pCG)
{
    HANDLE    aHandles[2];

    // Stack up our handles into an array.
    aHandles[0] = pCG->hMutexBlockAccess;
    aHandles[1] = pCG->hSemaNumReads;

    // Wait for all the objects to become signaled
    WaitForMultipleObjects(2, aHandles, TRUE, INFINITE);

    // Check to see if we are the last thread in
    if (WaitForSingleObject(pCG->hSemaNumReads,0) == WAIT_TIMEOUT)
        SetEvent(pCG->hEventCanWrite);
    else
        ReleaseSemaphore(pCG->hSemaNumReads, 1, NULL);

    ReleaseMutex(pCG->hMutexBlockAccess);
}
```

When a thread needs to write, it needs to make sure that no-one else can access it and that all reads are finished. The **hMutexBlockAccess** and **hEventCanWrite** ensure this:

```
void WaitToWrite(PCG pCG)
{
    HANDLE    aHandles[2];

    aHandles[0]=pCG->hMutexBlockAccess;
    aHandles[1]=pCG->hEventCanWrite;

    // Make sure no one else is either reading or writing
    WaitForMultipleObjects(2, aHandles, TRUE, INFINITE);
}
```

When we've finished writing, we simply need to free up the mutex, since we didn't reset the **hEventCanWrite**.

```
void FinishedWrite(PCG pCG)
{
    // Allow others to write
    ReleaseMutex(pCG->hMutexBlockAccess);
}
```

There are a couple of things that you should note about the above code. First of all, the semaphore in this case is being used in exactly the opposite way to the semaphore we used in the **CDataPool** class. In **CDataPool**, the semaphore was initialized at its maximum count, and then decremented each time a connection was allocated. When the count was at zero, it meant that no more database connections available. In this case, since we can handle an 'infinite' number of reads, we initialize the semaphore to have a count of 65536, but we start it off at 0. Each time a read begins, a semaphore is released and the count goes up one. When the read is finished, we capture the semaphore to decrement the count. Thus, the number of free semaphores is the number of reads currently in operation. This is an example of releasing the semaphore before we capture it.

You may also be wondering why it's always necessary to wait for **hMutexBlockAccess** in the **WaitToRead()** and **FinishedRead()** functions. To see why the mutex is necessary, let's see what would happen without it if we had two threads, one in **WaitToRead()** and one in **FinishedRead()**, and we didn't wait on **hMutexBlockAccess**. If the thread in **WaitToRead()** is pre-empted just after it executes the **ResetEvent()** command, and execution switches to the **SetEvent()** command in **FinishedRead()**, the event will falsely read that it is OK to write.

You may have thought that you could rewrite **FinishedRead()** so that, rather than waiting on the semaphore to see if it has a zero count, you could simply release the semaphore to get its previous count. If the previous count is 0, set the event. In any case, recapture the semaphore. While this method would work, it's left to the reader to show why the method given is better.

# Cache Manager

Now that we have a mechanism to allow for multiple reads but only single access for a write, we need to set up some functions to manage our cache for us. We need to be able to initialize it, delete it, and maintain it. To do so, we'll use the functions prototyped here in **CacheManager.h**.

```
/// CacheManager.h
#include <windows.h>
#include <httpfilt.h>
#include "CacheGuard.h"

#ifndef _CACHE_MANAGER_H
#define _CACHE_MANAGER_H

#define     MAX_CACHED      50
#define     RESORT_LIMIT    10

#define CM_VALID_USER       100
#define CM_INVALID_PASS     110
#define     CM_NOT_FOUND    120


typedef struct CACHE_LIST {
    LIST_ENTRY    ListEntry;

    CHAR     achWebUser[SF_MAX_USERNAME];
    CHAR     achWebPass[SF_MAX_PASSWORD];
    CHAR     achNTUser[SF_MAX_USERNAME];
    CHAR     achNTPass[SF_MAX_PASSWORD];
} USER_CACHE, *PUSER_CACHE;


void  InitializeCache();
void DeleteCache();

INT CacheLookUpUser(CHAR *pszWebUser, CHAR *pszWebPass,
                    CHAR *pszNTUser, CHAR *pszNTPass);

void CacheAddUser(CHAR *pszWebUser, CHAR *pszWebPass,
                    CHAR *pszNTUser, CHAR *pszNTPass);


#endif
```

If you are familiar with linked lists, you should have little trouble with the Cache Manager. There is one twist that we'll be putting in it, however. Since our filter is running as a DLL inside the process space of the web server, by default we use the web servers heap space. A heap is nothing more than a block of memory, and it's used for memory allocations that are not put on the stack. When you call **new** or **delete**, for example, you are using heap memory. While the web server certainly has plenty of heap space, there are several reasons why we don't want to use it.

First of all, whenever more than one thread tries to manipulate the default heap, one call must wait in line for the previous one to finish. This is called serialization of the threads. While we need to serialize write operations in this filter anyway, we still don't want to have to wait on any other thread that happens to be manipulating the default heap. In addition, all Win32 functions use the default heap, so if any of those are using it, we must wait on them.

Second, our linked list structure is very clean in that all of the objects are the same size. Thus, when we delete one **CACHE_LIST** entry, another one will fit exactly in its place. This keeps NT from wasting time moving around and de-fragmenting memory. If we use the default heap, after we delete a **CACHE_LIST** entry, maybe an **INT** will be placed in the memory space making it just 32 bits too small for another **CACHE_LIST** object. As this goes on, our linked list will be all over the place. When memory is in different pages, it takes longer to access.

Lastly, by creating our own heap, we are guaranteed to clean up after ourselves. If, for any reason, we failed to clean up memory, it will definitely be cleaned up when we destroy the heap we created.

The function to create you own heap is prototyped here:

```
HANDLE HeapCreate(DWORD flOptions,
                  DWORD dwInitialSize,
                  DWORD dwMaximumSize);
```

The **flOptions** can be any combination of **HEAP_GENERATE_EXCEPTIONS** and **HEAP_NO_SERIALIZE**. If you select **HEAP_GENERATE_EXCEPTIONS**, a call to allocate memory that fails will cause an exception to be raised rather than simply returning **NULL**. If you set **HEAP_NO_SERIALIZE**, NT will not serialize manipulation calls to this heap. You should only set this option if you are serializing the calls yourself, as it can lead to memory corruption.

The **dwInitialSize** parameter is used to specify the initial size of the heap in bytes. You should note that NT takes up a little bit of memory for overhead, so that if you need to place 16K of data in the heap, you will need to create a larger heap than 16K, or allow the heap to expand.

The **dwMaximumSize** gives the maximum size in bytes that the heap is allowed to grow to. If you try to allocate more memory than is currently in the heap, the heap will automatically expand up the **dwMaximumSize**. If **dwMaximumSize** is **0**, there is no limit to how big the heap will grow.

Once a heap is created, you can allocate memory on it to create new objects. To do so, call the **HeapAlloc()** function prototyped here:

```
LPVOID HeapAlloc(HANDLE hHeap,
                 DWORD dwFlags,
                 DWORD dwBytes);
```

The **hHeap** parameter is a handle returned by a call to **HeapCreate()**.

The **dwFlags** can be any combination of **HEAP_GENERATE_EXCEPTIONS**, **HEAP_NO_SERIALIZE**, or **HEAP_ZERO_MEMORY**. **HEAP_GENERATE_EXCEPTIONS** and **HEAP_NO_SERIALIZE** are the same as noted above. **HEAP_ZERO_MEMORY** simply sets all memory in the heap to zeros.

The **dwBytes** parameter is the number of bytes you wish to allocate from your heap.

**HeapAlloc()** returns a pointer to the memory which it has allocated for you. In this respect, it is similar to the **new** operator. In fact, we are going to use it as a replacement for the **new** operator here shortly.

When you have finished with the memory you allocated from the heap, you need to free it back up with a call to **HeapFree()**, prototyped here:

```
BOOL HeapFree(HANDLE hHeap,
              DWORD dwFlags,
              LPVOID lpMem);
```

The **hHeap** parameter is again the handle to the heap that you are working with. In this case, **dwFlags** can only be **HEAP_NO_SERIALIZE**. The **lpMem** parameter is the pointer to the memory that you wish to free.

When you have finished with your heap, you need to delete it by calling **DestroyHeap()**, prototyped here:

```
BOOL HeapDestroy(HANDLE hHeap);
```

It takes, as its only parameter, the handle to the heap that you wish to destroy.

While there are many more issues about managing heaps that we can't address here, this gives us enough to work with. Below is the implementation **CacheManager.cpp** file. Note how we use our own heap by overriding the **new** and **delete** operators.

```
/// CacheManager.cpp

#include "CacheManager.h"

LIST_ENTRY    StartOfCache;
INT    nCacheCount;
CACHE_GUARD    CacheGuard;
HANDLE hCacheHeap;

// override the new and delete operators
// to make use of our own stack
void* operator new (size_t sizeToCreate);
void operator delete (void* pToDelete);

void* operator new(size_t sizeToCreate)
{
    // We already serialize writes, so don't have NT
    // duplicate our work
    return  (void*)HeapAlloc(hCacheHeap,HEAP_NO_SERIALIZE,sizeToCreate);
}

void operator delete(void* pToDelete)
{
```

```
        HeapFree(hCacheHeap,HEAP_NO_SERIALIZE,pToDelete);
}

void  InitializeCache()
{
    // Create the heap to the size our cache will use
    // the extra is for overhead that NT uses
    hCacheHeap = HeapCreate(HEAP_NO_SERIALIZE | HEAP_GENERATE_EXCEPTIONS,
                            sizeof(CACHE_GUARD)*MAX_CACHED+1024,0);

    // Set up the CACHE_GUARD
    InitializeCacheGuard(&CacheGuard);

    // Initialize the doube-linked-list
    StartOfCache.Blink = StartOfCache.Flink = &StartOfCache;
}

void DeleteCache()
{
    LIST_ENTRY    *pCurrentLink = StartOfCache.Flink;
    LIST_ENTRY    *pNextLink;
    CACHE_LIST    *pCurrentRecord;
    WaitToWrite(&CacheGuard);
    while (pCurrentLink!= &StartOfCache)
    {
        pNextLink = pCurrentLink->Flink;
        pCurrentRecord = CONTAINING_RECORD(pCurrentLink, CACHE_LIST, ListEntry);
        delete pCurrentRecord;
        pCurrentLink = pNextLink;
    }
    // Free it up when we are done with it
    HeapDestroy(hCacheHeap);
    FinishedWrite(&CacheGuard);
    DeleteCacheGuard(&CacheGuard);
}

INT CacheLookUpUser(CHAR *pszWebUser, CHAR *pszWebPass, CHAR *pszNTUser, CHAR
                    *pszNTPass)
{
    CACHE_LIST    *pCurrentRecord;
    LIST_ENTRY    *pCurrentLink=StartOfCache.Flink;
    INT    nCount=0;

    while (pCurrentLink!= &StartOfCache)
    {
        pCurrentRecord = CONTAINING_RECORD(pCurrentLink, CACHE_LIST, ListEntry);
        if (!strcmp(pszWebUser, pCurrentRecord->achWebUser))
        {
            if (stricmp(pszWebPass, pCurrentRecord->achWebPass))
                return CM_INVALID_PASS;
            strcpy(pszNTUser,pCurrentRecord->achNTUser);
            strcpy(pszNTPass, pCurrentRecord->achNTPass);
            if (nCount > RESORT_LIMIT)
            {
                WaitToWrite(&CacheGuard);
                pCurrentLink->Blink->Flink= pCurrentLink->Flink;
                pCurrentLink->Flink->Blink= pCurrentLink->Blink;
```

```
                    pCurrentLink->Blink = &StartOfCache;
                    pCurrentLink->Flink = StartOfCache.Flink;
                    StartOfCache.Flink->Blink = &(pCurrentRecord->ListEntry);
                    StartOfCache.Flink = &(pCurrentRecord->ListEntry);
                    FinishedWrite(&CacheGuard);
                }
            return CM_VALID_USER;
        }
        pCurrentLink = pCurrentLink->Flink;
        nCount++;
    }

    return CM_NOT_FOUND;
}

void CacheAddUser(CHAR *pszWebUser, CHAR *pszWebPass, CHAR *pszNTUser, CHAR
                    *pszNTPass)
{
    CACHE_LIST    *pCurrentRecord;
    LIST_ENTRY    *pCurrentLink=&StartOfCache;

    pCurrentRecord=new USER_CACHE;

    if (!pCurrentRecord)
        return;

    strcpy(pCurrentRecord->achWebUser, pszWebUser);
    strcpy(pCurrentRecord->achWebPass, pszWebPass);
    strcpy(pCurrentRecord->achNTUser, pszNTUser);
    strcpy(pCurrentRecord->achNTPass, pszNTPass);

    WaitToWrite(&CacheGuard);

    pCurrentRecord->ListEntry.Flink = StartOfCache.Flink;
    pCurrentRecord->ListEntry.Blink = &StartOfCache;
    StartOfCache.Flink->Blink = &(pCurrentRecord->ListEntry);
    StartOfCache.Flink = &(pCurrentRecord->ListEntry);

    if (++nCacheCount> MAX_CACHED)
    {
        pCurrentLink=StartOfCache.Blink;
        pCurrentLink->Blink->Flink = &StartOfCache;
        StartOfCache.Blink = pCurrentLink->Blink;
        delete CONTAINING_RECORD(pCurrentLink, CACHE_LIST, ListEntry);
        nCacheCount--;
    }

    FinishedWrite(&CacheGuard);
}
```

# ODBC API

You probably know by now that we aren't going to use any MFC in this filter. This means that our
database access routines are left entirely up to us. While a complete coverage of ODBC would take a book
by itself, we do need to introduce some of the functions so that we can use them here. We'll cover the
topics necessary to understand how to execute an SQL **select** statement and retrieve the results. Should
you have additional questions, you should consult a book which covers ODBC in depth.

In order for an SQL statement to be executed, three things are necessary: an environment handle, a connection handle, and a statement handle. In order to create a valid ODBC environment handle, you need to call **SQLAllocEnv()** and pass it the address of an **HENV** variable. One **HENV** variable can be shared by all threads, and it's normal to make it a global variable.

Once the **HENV** is allocated, you need to call **SQLAllocConnect()** and pass it your **HENV** variable as well as the address to your **HDBC** database connection variable. At this point, the ODBC driver only allocates memory for the connection. No connection is established, and no authentication material is verified.

In order to establish the connection, you must call **SQLConnect()** and pass it information that it needs to actually make the connection. The function is prototyped here:

```
RETCODE SQLConnect(HDBC hdbc,
                   UCHAR FAR* szDSN,
                   SQORD cbDSN,
                   UCHAR FAR* szUID,
                   SQROD cbUID,
                   UCHAR FAR*  szAuthStr,
                   SDWORD cbAuthStr);
```

The **hdbc** variable is that which **SQLAllocConnect()** initialized for us. The other variables are for the DSN, user ID, and any connection string information that you need. You should also note the corresponding **cb** values for each parameter. Since ODBC is designed to be used by many different languages, and not all of them use **NULL** to terminate strings the way C/C++ does, all ODBC function calls require that you send the size of the string you are sending over. Fortunately, if you are using null-terminated strings (as we are) you can simply pass **SQL_NTS** to tell the ODBC driver that it is a null-terminated string.

After the connection is initialized and opened, you need to allocate an **HSTMT** variable to hold information about the SQL statement that you wish to execute. The **HSTMT** will also be your handle to any data which the ODBC driver returns. To do this, call the **SQLAllocStmt()** function. The function is prototyped here:

```
SQLAllocStmt(HEVN henv,
             HDBC FAR* phdbc);
```

The **henv** is our familiar **HENV** variable that we initialized earlier. (Do you see why it's common to see them as global variables?) We also need to pass the address to our opened database connection.

Having only allocated the SQL statement, you haven't executed it yet. There are two ways to execute an SQL statement in ODBC. The first is to execute the command directly. That is, you send over a complete SQL command, the database parses the statement, makes its execution plan, and finally executes the statement. Another method sends over an incomplete SQL statement. It's incomplete in that it is missing some of the values which the query will need to actually execute. An example would be:

**select \* from authors where book_type=?**

When you send this query to the database server, it still parses it, and it still makes an execute plan, but it doesn't execute it until you pass it the proper parameters and request that it be executed. The reason for this scheme is that you might have one query that will be run over and over again. Rather than have the database server re-parse and re-plan the query each time, it will save the information and simply requery using the new values supplied to it. This makes repetitive queries much faster.

In this case, we will be running the same query many times over with only the username and password changing. We will therefore achieve a better performance by choosing the prepared statement method.

In order to use the same SQL statement over and over again, you must first send a prototype to the database server. Any parameter that you do not yet know should be specified by a **?** as in the above example. The prototype of the SQL statement we will use to look up a user is given here:

**select ntuser, ntpass from user  where upper(username) =? and upper(password) =?**

In order to send this to the ODBC driver, we need to call **SQLPrepare()**, which is given here:

```
SQLPrepare(HSTMT hstmt,
           CHAR FAR* szSql,
           SDWORD cbSql);
```

The **hstmt** parameter is the **HSTMT** for which you want to prepare the statement. The **szSql** is nothing more than the prototype of the SQL statement. The **cbSql** parameter is the length of the **szSql** variable. Since we use null-terminated strings, we can again pass the **SQL_NTS** constant instead.

Once the statement is prepared, we need to let ODBC know where it can find values to fill in the **?** with. To do this, you need to call **SQLBindParameter()** as given here:

```
RETCODE SQLBindParameter(HSTMT hstmt,
                         UWORD ipar,
                         SWORD fParamType,
                         SWORD fCType,
                         SWORD fSqlType,
                         UDWORD cbColDef,
                         SWORD ibScale,
                         PTR rgbValue,
                         SDWORD cbValueMax,
                         SDWORD FAR* pcbValue)
```

The **htsmt** is again the handle to the SQL statement which we allocated and prepared previously. The **ipar** parameter tells what type of parameter is being specified. The following table lists the possible values:

| Parameter Value | Meaning |
| --- | --- |
| **SQL_PARAM_INPUT** | The variable will only be used to input data into the query. For example, **select * from authors where name=?**. |
| **SQL_PARAM_INPUT_OUTPUT** | The variable will be both input information into the query and information received from the result back. This would be used for stored procedures such as **call GetPublisher(?)**. Going into the function, the **?** would denote the author's name. Coming out, it would hold the author's publisher. |
| **SQL_PARAM_OUTPUT** | The parameter will only receive the output of a function. For example, **?=call GetPublisher('Michael Tracy')**. On return, the parameter would hold the value **Wrox**. |

The **fCtype** gives the C/C++ type of variable that the parameter will be bound to. Since we are programming in C/C++, you should have no trouble matching these up. A list of possible values is given here:

| | | |
|---|---|---|
| SQL_C_BINARY | SQL_C_BIT | SQL_C_CHAR |
| SQL_C_DATE | SQL_C_DEFAULT | SQL_C_DOUBLE |
| SQL_C_FLOAT | SQL_C_SLONG | SQL_C_SSHORT |
| SQL_C_STINYINT | SQL_C_TIME | SQL_C_TIMESTAMP |
| SQL_C_ULONG | SQL_C_USHORT | SQL_C_UTINYINT |

If the **SQL_C_DEFAULT** is given, the driver will make the conversion for you based on the type of SQL variable that is being bound. This leads us into the next parameter. The **fSqlType** is the SQL data type which you are attaching to your variable. A list of possible values is given here:

| | | |
|---|---|---|
| SQL_BIGINT | SQL_BINARY | SQL_BIT |
| SQL_CHAR | SQL_DATE | SQL_DECIMAL |
| SQL_DOUBLE | SQL_FLOAT | SQL_INTEGER |
| SQL_LONGVARBINARY | SQL_LONGVARCHAR | SQL_NUMERIC |
| SQL_REAL | SQL_SMALLINT | SQL_TIME |
| SQL_TIMESTAMP | SQL_TINYINT | SQL_VARBINARY |
| SQL_VARCHAR | | |

The **cbColDef** parameter specifies the precision of the SQL variable.

The **rbgValue** parameter is the address space that you wish to bind to the SQL statement. Each time the query is executed, the ODBC driver will look in this address space for the variable to fill in the appropriate **?** in the SQL statement. You should note that since this is an address, you should make sure the variable doesn't go out of scope once you have bound it.

The **cbValueMax** is used to specify the maximum size of the data that can be written into the **rgbValue** space. This is only used for output parameters. For input parameters, as we use in this example, you can simply pass **0**.

Lastly, the **pcbValue** parameter denotes the length of the input parameter. Here, again, it is acceptable to pass **SQL_NTS**.

Once the statement is prepared, and you have bound your parameters, you need to actually execute the statement. With all the work that went into setting up the statement, you will be happy to know that the actual execution couldn't be simpler. It's prototyped here:

```
SQLExecute(HSTMT hstmt);
```

The **hstmt** is the familiar handle to the statement that you wish to execute. Once the parameters are bound, you only need to change their values and re-execute the SQL statement to get a new result.

This brings us to retrieving the data. This first thing we need to do is bring in a row of data returned by the executed SQL statement. To do this we 'fetch' the data, using:

```
RETCODE SQLFetch(HSTMT hstmt);
```

Once the row is fetched from the driver, we need to put the appropriate columns into variables that we can access. To do this, we 'get' the data with **SQLGetData**, prototyped here:

```
RETCODE SQLGetData(HSTMT hstmt,
                   UWORD icol,
                   SWORD fCType,
                   PTR rgbValue,
                   SDWORD cbValueMax,
                   SDWORD FAR * pcbValue);
```

The **hstmt** is the handle to our allocated **HSTMT** that we have just executed. The **icol** parameter is the column number that you wish to retrieve (column numbers start at 1). The **fCType** parameter is the type of data that you are retrieving, as discussed above for **SQLBindParameter()**. The **rgbValue** parameter is a pointer to the variable that will hold the returned value. The **cbValueMax** is the maximum size that the **rgbValue** variable can hold. The **pcbValue** is a pointer to the size of **rgbValue** when the function is called. On return, it's the maximum number of bytes that were available for the requested column. You will need to call **SQLGetData()** for each column value that you wish to receive.

Once you have executed your prepared statement, you should call **SQLFreeStmt()**, given here:

```
RETCODE SQLFreeStmt(HTSMT hstmt,
                    UWORD fOption);
```

You should be familiar with the **hstmt** variable by this point. The **fOption** parameter tells the driver to what extent it should free up the statement. The following are possible values:

| Parameter Values | Meaning |
|---|---|
| **SQL_CLOSE** | Close any results returned by the query, but keep the prepared statement ready to be executed again. |
| **SQL_DROP** | Free up everything that is allocated for this statement. |
| **SQL_UNBIND** | Unbind any columns that were bound to this statement (we did not cover binding columns). |
| **SQL_RESET_PARAMS** | Unbind any parameters that were bound using the **SQLBindParameter()** statement. |

Once you are completely finished with your connection, you should call

```
RETCODE SQLDisconnect(HDBC hdbc);
```

to close the connection, and

```
RETCODE SQLFreeConnect(HDBC hdbc);
```

to free up any memory associated with the connection, and finally

```
RETCODE SQLFreeEnv(HENV henv);
```

to free up the ODBC environment variable.

> You must free all connections with **SQLFreeConnect()** before you can free up the **HENV**.

# The Filter

Now that we have the basics down, we can look at how we use them in our filter. First, we make sure that we have all the necessary **#include**s, global variables, and function declarations. We also define a macro for checking the return value of our calls to ODBC, because the return value can have one of two success codes: **SQL_SUCCESS** and **SQL_SUCCESS_WITH_INFO**.

```
#include <windows.h>
#include <sql.h>
#include <sqlext.h>
#include <stdio.h>
#include <httpfilt.h>
#include "CacheManager.h"


#define ODBC_SUCCESS(rc) \
    (((rc)==SQL_SUCCESS)||((rc)==SQL_SUCCESS_WITH_INFO))


HENV      henv;
HDBC      hdbc;
HSTMT     hstmt;
CRITICAL_SECTION   csUserData;

CHAR      g_szWebUser[SF_MAX_USERNAME];
CHAR      g_szWebPass[SF_MAX_PASSWORD];


DWORD OnAuth(HTTP_FILTER_CONTEXT *pfc, PHTTP_FILTER_AUTHENT pAuth);
BOOL ODBCOpen();
BOOL DBLookUpUser(CHAR *pszWebUser, CHAR *pszWebPass,
                CHAR *pszNTUser, CHAR *pszNTPass);
RETCODE   ExecuteSql(CHAR* pszWebUser, CHAR* pszWebPass);
void Trim(CHAR *pszToTrim);
VOID ReportWFEvent(PTSTR string1,PTSTR string2,PTSTR string3,
                PTSTR string4,WORD eventType, WORD eventID);
```

Next, we need the **DllMain()** entry point. We only have to deal with two notifications:

▲ **DLL_PROCESS_ATTACH**, when we initialize all our global variables, opening the ODBC connection that we'll be using and starting our cache.

▲ **DLL_PROCESS_DETACH**, when we tidy up after ourselves.

We don't have to worry about **DllMain()** being called for threads, as we turn off thread notifications with a call to **DisableThreadLibraryCalls()**.

```
BOOL WINAPI DllMain(HINSTANCE hInst, ULONG ulReason,
                LPVOID lpReserved)
{
   BOOL bReturn = TRUE;

   switch (ulReason)
   {
      case DLL_PROCESS_ATTACH:
```

```
                SQLAllocEnv(&henv);
                SQLAllocConnect(henv, &hdbc);
                bReturn = ODBCOpen();
                InitializeCache();
                InitializeCriticalSection(&csUserData);
                DisableThreadLibraryCalls(hInst);
                break;

            case DLL_PROCESS_DETACH:
                SQLDisconnect(hdbc);
                SQLFreeConnect(hdbc);
                SQLFreeEnv(henv);
                DeleteCache();
                DeleteCriticalSection(&csUserData);
                break;

            default:
                break;

        }
    return (bReturn);
}
```

The required **GetFilterVersion()** is pretty much as we have shown before, indicating to the server that we would like to handle authentication notices. The extra call to **ReportWFEvent()** is a call to our own function to enter an event in the server's log files. We'll get to how this is done in good time.

```
BOOL WINAPI GetFilterVersion(HTTP_FILTER_VERSION *pVer)
{

    pVer->dwFilterVersion = MAKELONG(0, 1);    // Version 1.0


    pVer->dwFlags = (SF_NOTIFY_SECURE_PORT        |
                     SF_NOTIFY_NONSECURE_PORT     |
                     SF_NOTIFY_AUTHENTICATION     |
                     SF_NOTIFY_ORDER_DEFAULT);

    strcpy(pVer->lpszFilterDesc, "User Authenication, v1.0");


    ReportWFEvent("[UserAuth]",
                  "[GetFilterVersion] Starting User Authentication",
                  "",
                  "",
                  EVENTLOG_INFORMATION_TYPE,
                  2);

    return TRUE;
}
```

The other required function, **HttpFilterProc()**, checks to make sure we have the right notification, and if so calls **OnAuth()** which does all the hard work.

```
DWORD WINAPI HttpFilterProc(HTTP_FILTER_CONTEXT *pfc, DWORD NotificationType,
                            VOID *pvData)
```

```
{
    DWORD dwRet;

    switch (NotificationType)
    {
        case SF_NOTIFY_AUTHENTICATION:

            dwRet = OnAuth(pfc, (PHTTP_FILTER_AUTHENT) pvData);
            break;

        default:
            dwRet = SF_STATUS_REQ_NEXT_NOTIFICATION;
            break;
    }

    return dwRet;
}
```

The **OnAuth()** function does all the work of ensuring that the username and password supplied by the client are valid. It starts by finding out if there is any information to check, as we don't want to go through all the effort of trying to authenticate an anonymous user.

```
DWORD OnAuth(HTTP_FILTER_CONTEXT *pfc, PHTTP_FILTER_AUTHENT pAuth)
{
    // Ignore the anonymous user
    if (!*pAuth->pszUser)
        return SF_STATUS_REQ_NEXT_NOTIFICATION;
```

Next, after copying the username and password into local variables, we check the cache to see if the user ID is there. If the ID is there but the password is wrong, then the **CacheLookUpUser()** will return **CM_INVALID_PASS** to us, and we exit the function immediately. You may wonder how this will stop the user from having access to the files. As we haven't changed the username and password to a valid NT account, IIS will try to access the files with the details supplied by the client, causing an access violation.

```
    INT    nResult;

    CHAR szWebUser[SF_MAX_USERNAME];
    CHAR szWebPass[SF_MAX_PASSWORD];

    CHAR szNTUser[SF_MAX_USERNAME];
    CHAR szNTPass[SF_MAX_PASSWORD];

    strcpy(szWebUser, pAuth->pszUser);
    strcpy(szWebPass, pAuth->pszPassword);

    _strupr(szWebUser);
    _strupr(szWebPass);

    // Check in the cache first
    nResult = CacheLookUpUser(szWebUser, szWebPass, szNTUser, szNTPass);
    if (nResult==CM_INVALID_PASS)
        return SF_STATUS_REQ_NEXT_NOTIFICATION;
```

If the user details aren't found in the cache (indicated by **CacheLookUpUser()** returning **CM_NOT_FOUND**), we go and have a look in the database. If the call to **DBLookUpUser()** returns true, we add the details to the cache for future use. On the other hand, if the user isn't found, we call the **SetLastError()** API function. The **SetLastError(DWORD dwErrCode)** sets the Win32 error code for the thread in which it was called. When the web server is returned a value of **SF_STATUS_REQ_ERROR**, it has no idea what might have caused the error, and so it calls **GetLastError()** to find out why the error was returned. In this case, the web server will see the **ERROR_ACCESS_DENIED** and will send a response back to the client, indicating that the username and password supplied were incorrect.

```
if(nResult == CM_NOT_FOUND)
{
   // Check the database next
   if(DBLookUpUser(szWebUser, szWebPass, szNTUser, szNTPass))
      CacheAddUser(szWebUser, szWebPass,szNTUser, szNTPass);
   else
   {
      // Send the not allowed message
      SetLastError(ERROR_ACCESS_DENIED);
      return SF_STATUS_REQ_ERROR;
   }
}
```

Lastly, we set the username and password information in the **HTTP_FILTER_AUTHENT** structure the server passed to us, so that the server can access the files with the correct user details.

```
   // Give the mapped user/password back to the server
   strcpy(pAuth->pszUser, szNTUser);
   strcpy(pAuth->pszPassword, szNTPass);

   return SF_STATUS_REQ_NEXT_NOTIFICATION;
}
```

The **ODBCOpen()** function does just that–it opens the connection to the database. We also use it to prepare the SQL statement and parameters needed to query the database. We don't do all of this in the **DllMain()** function, as the connection to the database may be lost–especially if the database is not on the same machine as the web server.

```
// Used both to open and re-open the database
BOOL ODBCOpen()
{
   RETCODE rc;
   SDWORD   cbData;

   // Does nothing if we are not connected yet.
   SQLDisconnect(hdbc);

   // Connect to our datasource.
   rc=SQLConnect(hdbc, (unsigned char *) "wroxdata", SQL_NTS, NULL, 0, NULL, 0);
   if (!ODBC_SUCCESS(rc))
      return FALSE;

   // Allocate and prepare the statement
   rc = SQLAllocStmt(hdbc,&hstmt);
   rc = SQLPrepare(hstmt,(unsigned char*)"select ntuser, ntpass from user "
```

```
                "where upper(username) =? and upper(password)=?", SQL_NTS);
        if (!ODBC_SUCCESS(rc))
            return FALSE;


        cbData=SQL_NTS;
        // Bind the new user and password into the prepared sql statement
        rc = SQLBindParameter(hstmt, 1, SQL_PARAM_INPUT, SQL_C_CHAR,
                        SQL_CHAR, SF_MAX_USERNAME-1, 0, g_szWebUser, 0, &cbData);
        cbData=SQL_NTS;
        rc = SQLBindParameter(hstmt, 2, SQL_PARAM_INPUT, SQL_C_CHAR,
                        SQL_CHAR, SF_MAX_PASSWORD-1, 0, g_szWebPass, 0, &cbData);
        if (!ODBC_SUCCESS(rc))
            return FALSE;


        return TRUE;
    }
```

**DBLookUpUser()** checks the database to see if the user is registered in there. If we fail to execute the SQL statement, we reopen the database connection and try again. If at anytime we fail, then we log an event indicating the error. Since this filter uses only one single ODBC connection, you must serialize access to the connection with a critical section. (Note: if you are using an ODBC driver that supports multiple active statements on a single connection, such as Oracle, you don't need to use the critical section. However, for both Visual FoxPro and SQL Server, you *will* need it.) The advanced reader may be interested in writing an ODBC pool manager similar to the **CDataPool** class we had for MFC ODBC connections. However, in this case, it's probably not necessary, because database access can be kept to a minimum by expanding the cache.

```
    BOOL DBLookUpUser(CHAR *pszWebUser, CHAR *pszWebPass,
            CHAR *pszNTUser, CHAR *pszNTPass)
{
    RETCODE    rc;
    SDWORD     cbData;

    EnterCriticalSection(&csUserData);
    // Make sure we always leave the critical section;
    try
    {
        strcpy(g_szWebUser,pszWebUser);
        strcpy(g_szWebPass,pszWebPass);

        rc = SQLExecute(hstmt);
        if (!ODBC_SUCCESS(rc))
        {
            // Probably lost the connection to the database
            // Try to reopen
            if(!ODBCOpen())
            {
                ReportWFEvent("[UserAuth]", "[DBLookUpUser] Failed to reopen database",
                            "","",EVENTLOG_ERROR_TYPE,3);
                LeaveCriticalSection(&csUserData);
                return FALSE;
            }
            // Try again.
            rc = SQLExecute(hstmt);
            if (!ODBC_SUCCESS(rc))
```

```
            {
                ReportWFEvent("[UserAuth]",
                            "[DBLookUpUser] Critical Error. Can not validate users.",
                            "","",EVENTLOG_ERROR_TYPE,3);
                LeaveCriticalSection(&csUserData);
                return FALSE;
            }
        }

        rc = SQLFetch(hstmt);

        // No match found.
        if (!ODBC_SUCCESS(rc))
        {
            LeaveCriticalSection(&csUserData);
            return FALSE;
        }

        // We found a match, so get the NT name and pass
        SQLGetData(hstmt, 1, SQL_C_CHAR, (void *)pszNTUser, SF_MAX_USERNAME, &cbData);
        SQLGetData(hstmt, 2, SQL_C_CHAR, (void *)pszNTPass, SF_MAX_PASSWORD, &cbData);

        // NT wont match with spaces at the end
        Trim(pszNTUser);
        Trim(pszNTPass);

        // Keep the prepared statement, just close the result set
        SQLFreeStmt(hstmt, SQL_CLOSE);
    }
    catch(...)
    {
        // Always execute this code.
        LeaveCriticalSection(&csUserData);
        return FALSE;
    }
    LeaveCriticalSection(&csUserData);
    return TRUE;
}
```

**Trim()** simply removes any trailing spaces in the returned data from the database.

```
void Trim(CHAR *pszToTrim)
{
    // username and password can not have spaces
    while (*pszToTrim!=' ' && *pszToTrim!='\0')
        pszToTrim++;
    *pszToTrim='\0';
}
```

## Reporting Events

Hopefully, your filters will always work the way you want them to. However, in the case where they don't, it would be nice to know about it. In order to facilitate this, we have introduced event reporting into this last filter. When an event is reported, it will show up in your system event log. You can view this log using the Event Viewer in the Administrative Tools program group.

In order to write events into this log, you first need to register the event source. The command to do this is aptly called **RegisterEventSource()** and is prototyped here:

```
HANDLE RegisterEventSource(LPCTSTR lpUNCServerName,
                           LPCTSTR lpSourceName);
```

The **lpUNCServerName** parameter is a pointer to a null-terminated string which holds the server's name to which you will be sending the events. If you pass **NULL**, it defaults to the local host. The **lpSourceName** is a pointer to a null-terminated string that must be a subkey in the registry file under one of the following entries:

**HKEY_LOCAL_MACHINE/System/CurrentControlSet/Services/EventLog/Application**
**HKEY_LOCAL_MACHINE/System/CurrentControlSet/Services/EventLog/Security**
**HKEY_LOCAL_MACHINE/System/CurrentControlSet/Services/EventLog/System**

In our example, **W3SVC** is under the **System** key.

The function returns a handle to the event source or **NULL** to indicate an error. Once we have the handle, we need to call **ReportEvent()**, prototyped here:

```
BOOL ReportEvent(HANDLE hEventLog,
                 WORD wType,
                 WORD wCategory,
                 DWORD dwEventID,
                 PSID lpUserSid,
                 WORD wNumStrings,
                 DWORD dwDataSize,
                 LPCTSTR *lpStrings,
                 LPVOID lpRawData);
```

The **hEventLog** parameter is the handle to the event source that was returned by **RegisterEventSource()**. The **wType** indicates the type of event we are reporting. The following is a list of possible values:

**EVENTLOG_ERROR_TYPE**
**EVENTLOG_WARNING_TYPE**
**EVENTLOG_INFORMATION_TYPE**
**EVENTLOG_AUDIT_SUCCESS**
**EVENTLOG_AUDIT_FAILURE**

The **dwEventID** parameter is used to match up this event with one in the message file associated with the event source. You can use any event number you wish, as long as it doesn't interfere with any event IDs that are already in use.

The **wCategory** parameter can specify any **WORD** value as a category type. This is rarely used, and so we default it to **0** in our filter.

The **lpUserSid** is a pointer to the user's security ID that should be attached to the report. If no specific user is attached to the event, you can simply send **NULL**, and the event viewer will list the user as N/A.

The **wNumStrings** parameter indicates how many strings are in the array of strings that we will pass in the parameter **lpStrings**.

The **dwDataSize** parameter indicates the size of any raw data that you are reporting. Since we are not sending any binary data during our reporting here, we default this to **NULL**.

The **lpStrings** parameter is the pointer to an array of strings. These strings are the main piece of information that we will be reporting and they can be read with the Event Viewer.

The **lpRawData** parameter points to any raw data that you will be reporting. As we are not sending any, we leave this to the default of **NULL**.

After you report an event, you should call **DeregisterEventSource()** and pass it the handle to the event source that you wish to close.

The **ReportWFEvent()** uses these APIs to log events that occur during the execution of the filter. This is a good way of letting the system's administrator know that there is something wrong which they need to look into. The code is as follows:

```
VOID ReportWFEvent(PTSTR string1,PTSTR string2,PTSTR string3,PTSTR string4,
              WORD eventType, WORD eventID)
{
   HANDLE hEvent;
   PTSTR pszaStrings[4];
   WORD cStrings;

   // Check to see how many strings were passed
   cStrings = 0;
   if ((pszaStrings[0] = string1) && (string1[0])) cStrings++;
   if ((pszaStrings[1] = string2) && (string2[0])) cStrings++;
   if ((pszaStrings[2] = string3) && (string3[0])) cStrings++;
   if ((pszaStrings[3] = string4) && (string4[0])) cStrings++;
   if (cStrings == 0)
      return;

   hEvent = RegisterEventSource(NULL,"W3SVC");
   if (hEvent)
   {
      ReportEvent(hEvent, eventType, NULL, eventID, NULL, cStrings, NULL,
              (const char **)pszaStrings, NULL);
      DeregisterEventSource(hEvent);
   }
}
```

As a final note about the event reporting procedure above, it would be possible to register the event source only once and call only **ReportEvent()** for each call. However, your **ReportWFEvent()** should really only be called once. ODBC errors are rather rare for a simple filter like this, and we didn't think it was worth the additional overhead of keeping the event source registered. If you think about it, you will probably want almost all of your filters to incorporate some type of error event reporting, and maybe even some of your ISAPI extensions. It wouldn't make much sense to have each one of these constantly register its own event source.

# Building and Testing the Filter

In order to test this filter, you'll need the user DBF file that we used back in Chapter 4. You'll need to create an NT user with the username 'webuser' and password 'webpass'. You should select an HTML file that you wish to protect in order to test this filter. Give read permission to your test file only to webuser.

Put the proper reference for this filter in the Registry and make sure the BASIC user authentication is enabled through the Microsoft Internet Services Manager. Restart your web server, and you should be ready to go. When you try to request your test HTML page, the browser should ask you for your name and password. Type in a username and password that you registered using the Chapter 4 extension, and the filter should give you permission to the file.

You should note that the way this filter is designed requires all users to be listed in the database. You may wish to change the implementation so that, if the filter can't find the user in the database, it performs no mapping, and simply passes the username and password along to the server for authentication. This will allow valid NT users access to their files without the need to have their passwords mapped in the database. Even though this is a better implementation, we didn't give it here because I wanted to demonstrate the use of the **SetLastError()** command to report errors back to the web server. It's left as an exercise to the reader to make the implementation.

# Summary

The MSIIS default security implementation uses NT to control access to web information. This design is ideal for intranets, but makes it impossible for a public web site to maintain a large database of users without a custom authentication filter.

The filter presented in this chapter uses a memory cache to store recent users and queries, and an ODBC datasource in the event that the user is not found in the cache. Since this is a multithreaded filter, control of the memory cache must be managed with thread synchronization objects. In this chapter, we introduced the mutex, which is similar to the critical section in that it grants mutually exclusive (hence, mutex) access. We also introduced **WaitForMultipleObjects()**, which is used when more than one thread synchronization object needs to be captured simultaneously.

If you have ever stepped through the MFC implementation of **CDatabase** to see how it handles ODBC access, you will know that MFC ODBC takes up a great deal of time on error checking. It does this so that it can handle just about any type of ODBC situation that the programmer can think up. In this case, however, our needs were quite simple. We just needed to select a users name and password from a database. We greatly cut down on the overhead by implementing the ODBC through API calls rather than MFC.

# Quick-fit Filters

To put the user authentication filter into sharp relief, we present two very simple filters in this final chapter which are nonetheless valuable to the web administrator in terms of the services that they provide. Filters don't have to be complex to be useful; as long as you make sure they do what they're supposed to do quickly and efficiently, you'll keep your customers happy.

## Custom Logging

Many web administrators are interested in finding out as much information as possible about the users visiting their sites. While the standard MSIIS logging feature does provide a great deal of information about what documents the user requested, it tells us very little about that user other than their IP address. Fortunately, ISAPI filters allow us to gather more information. While there are a couple of HTTP variables that might interest you, in this chapter we'll only cover **HTTP_REFERER**, which, if the browser supports it, tells us the page the user was on before they made their HTTP request. This will enable us to determine how users are getting to our site.

## One Problem, Two Solutions

I am going to present two versions of the custom logging filter. The first of these logs information to a separate file in the form: <document requested>, <previous document>. Furthermore, it only logs the information if the **HTTP_REFERER** is a location off our own site. This is because, in most cases, the **HTTP_REFERER** is a page on your own site: the user is simply browsing from page to page on your server. We are not particularly interested in how a user navigates your site, simply in how he or she gets there. (Of course, if you *are* interested, you can simply delete half a line of code and it will log everything for you.) Logging to a separate file makes it easy to analyze the information. You can also turn the filter on and off without affecting any other log files.

The second version that will be presented simply adds the information to the normal log file. The filter will insert the **HTTP_REFERER** information right after the target URL information in your log file. This method keeps all the log information in one file. The drawback is that all of your present log analysis tools will probably no longer work on this new log format. Also, if you want to turn the filter off, it will mean switching back to your old log analysis tools.

I prefer the first method, since I don't generally leave this logging feature on for long periods. I simply turn it on from time to time to get a general idea of where my traffic is coming from. Unless you really need this additional logging information, remember that it does take extra time and disk space to keep it active.

> While the MSIIS does support logging to an ODBC data source, it is highly recommended that you don't do this. Not only is it much slower than writing to disk, but it may not work with the above example if the HTTP_REFERER information is longer than the column width in the logging table.

# Design of the First Method

In the first method, we will build a log buffer which will be written to disk periodically. The data will be stored in global variables, so we will have to use critical sections to ensure that only one thread is altering the data at one time.

To create the filter, create a new DLL project space and add the **.def** file we wrote in the last chapter, to expose the **HttpFilterProc()** and **GetFilterVersion()** functions. For those of you with short memories, it looks like this:

```
LIBRARY CustomLog1

DESCRIPTION 'Internet Server Custom Logging Filter'

EXPORTS
   HttpFilterProc
   GetFilterVersion
```

Type in the following **CustomLog1.cpp** file and add it to the project as well:

```
#include <windows.h>
#include <httpfilt.h>

#define DEST        buff
#define DebugMsg(x) { char buff[256];               \
                      wsprintf x;                    \
                      OutputDebugString(buff); }

#define DISK_BUFFER_SIZE 4096
#define LOG_ENTRY_SIZE    256
#define REFERER_SIZE      128

DWORD dwLogBufferUsed;
CRITICAL_SECTION CriticalSection;
CHAR szLogBuffer[DISK_BUFFER_SIZE];
CHAR *pszLogBuffer = szLogBuffer;

DWORD OnLog (HTTP_FILTER_CONTEXT *pfc, HTTP_FILTER_LOG *pvData);
BOOL WriteLogBuffer();


BOOL WINAPI DllMain(HINSTANCE hInst, ULONG ulReason, LPVOID lpReserved)
{
   BOOL bReturn = TRUE;

   switch (ulReason)
   {
      case DLL_PROCESS_ATTACH:
      InitializeCriticalSection(&CriticalSection);
      DisableThreadLibraryCalls(hInst);
      break;

      case DLL_PROCESS_DETACH:
      WriteLogBuffer();
      DeleteCriticalSection(&CriticalSection);
      break;
```

```
        default:
        break;
    }
    return (bReturn);
}
```

As with all filters, the first function to get called is **DllMain()**. When it is called, we check to find the reason why. If it is because the DLL is being attached (**DLL_PROCESS_ATTACH**) then we want to initialize any important information that will be used by all threads. In this case, it is our critical section. The counterpart of **DLL_PROCESS_ATTACH** is **DLL_PROCESS_DETACH**, which cleans up anything that needs cleaning up. In the above code, it writes to disk any unsaved log information, and then cleans up the critical section.

You may have noticed that we also included a call to **DisableThreadLibraryCalls()** in **DLL_PROCESS_ATTACH.** If you remember from the first part of the book, MSIIS creates new threads for ISAPI extension requests. In addition, some of our extensions create new threads to assist in the handling of the request. This filter DLL doesn't need to be informed each time a new thread is created inside the web-server process. The call to **DisableThreadLibraryCalls()** simply tells the operating system not to send **DLL_THREAD_ATTACH** and **DLL_THREAD_DETACH** notifications to this DLL, which saves a little time and space.

```
BOOL WINAPI GetFilterVersion(HTTP_FILTER_VERSION *pVer)
{
    pVer->dwFilterVersion = MAKELONG(0, 1);    // Version 1.0

    pVer->dwFlags = (SF_NOTIFY_SECURE_PORT        |
                     SF_NOTIFY_NONSECURE_PORT     |
                     SF_NOTIFY_LOG                |
                     SF_NOTIFY_ORDER_DEFAULT);

    strcpy(pVer->lpszFilterDesc, "CustomLog, v1.0");
    return TRUE;
}
```

Once the DLL is loaded, the usual call to **GetFilterVersion()** is made. We set the notifications for this filter to be similar to those in previous examples, except we only want to be notified in the **SF_NOTIFY_LOG** case, which is done in the line beginning **pVer->dwFlags**

```
DWORD WINAPI HttpFilterProc(HTTP_FILTER_CONTEXT *pfc,
                            DWORD NotificationType, VOID *pvData)
{
    DWORD dwRet;

    //
    // Indicate this notification to the appropriate routine
    //

    switch (NotificationType)
    {
        case SF_NOTIFY_LOG:
        dwRet = OnLog(pfc, (PHTTP_FILTER_LOG) pvData);
        break;

        default:
```

```
        DebugMsg((DEST,
                    "[HttpFilterProc] Unknown notification type, %d\n",
                    NotificationType));
        dwRet = SF_STATUS_REQ_NEXT_NOTIFICATION;
        break;
    }
    return dwRet;
}
```

The handler for this type of notification is taken care of by the **switch** statement inside **HttpFilterProc()** above. **HttpFilterProc()** in turn calls the **OnLog()** function, which looks like this:

```
DWORD OnLog(HTTP_FILTER_CONTEXT *pfc, PHTTP_FILTER_LOG pLog)
{
    CHAR szReferer[REFERER_SIZE];
    DWORD dwRefererSize=REFERER_SIZE;

    // Check to see if the client passed a referer
    // and make sure it is NOT in our own domain.
    if (pfc->GetServerVariable(pfc, "HTTP_REFERER", szReferer,
                                &dwRefererSize) &&!strstr(szReferer,"mydomain.com"))
    {
        // Build the log entry
        EnterCriticalSection(&CriticalSection);

        //start with the file requested
        for (int x=0; (pLog->pszTarget)[x] && x<LOG_ENTRY_SIZE-REFERER_SIZE-3; x++)
            *(pszLogBuffer++) = pLog->pszTarget[x];

        // Separate by a comma
        *(pszLogBuffer++)=',';

        //then add the referer
        for (x=0; szReferer[x] && x<REFERER_SIZE; x++)
            *(pszLogBuffer++)=szReferer[x];

        //Finish it off if a newline
        *(pszLogBuffer++)='\n';

        // Check to see if it is time to write to disk
        if ((dwLogBufferUsed=(pszLogBuffer-szLogBuffer))>
                            (DISK_BUFFER_SIZE-LOG_ENTRY_SIZE-REFERER_SIZE-3))
            WriteLogBuffer();

        LeaveCriticalSection(&CriticalSection);
    }
    return SF_STATUS_REQ_NEXT_NOTIFICATION;
}
```

While you should be familiar with the **HTTP_FILTER_CONTEXT** by now, the **HTTP_FILTER_LOG** structure is the one passed specifically during the **SF_NOTIFY_LOG** call. The **HTTP_FILTER_LOG** structure is given again here. For a complete description of the fields, see Chapter 7.

```
typedef struct _HTTP_FILTER_LOG
{
    const CHAR *  pszClientHostName;
    const CHAR *  pszClientUserName;
    const CHAR *  pszServerName;
    const CHAR *  pszOperation;
    const CHAR *  pszTarget;
    const CHAR *  pszParameters;
    DWORD         dwHttpStatus;
    DWORD         dwWin32Status;
} HTTP_FILTER_LOG, *PHTTP_FILTER_LOG;
```

When the **OnLog()** function is called, it uses the **GetServerVariable()** member of the **HTTP_FILTER_CONTEXT** to retrieve the **HTTP_REFERER** variable. If you wanted to retrieve any additional information (such as **HTTP_USER_AGENT**), you could get it with another call to **GetServerVariable()**. This simple exercise is left to the reader.

Now the filter has the **HTTP_REFERER** information, it checks to make sure it isn't coming from **mydomain.com**. (Change this to your actual domain.) If it isn't, it first grabs the critical section, so that it can modify global data safely, and then appends the information to the end of our temporary buffer. It retrieves the target URL from the **HTTP_FILTER_LOG** structure.

```
BOOL WriteLogBuffer()
{
    DWORD dwWritten;
    HANDLE hCustomLog;

    // If the file does not exist, it creates it.
    // If it does, it simply opens it
    hCustomLog = CreateFile("c:\\mylog.txt", GENERIC_WRITE, 0, NULL,
                            OPEN_ALWAYS, FILE_ATTRIBUTE_NORMAL, NULL);

    // Go to the end of the file
    if(SetFilePointer(hCustomLog, 0, NULL, FILE_END)!=0xFFFFFFFF)
    {
        WriteFile (hCustomLog, szLogBuffer,
                   dwLogBufferUsed, &dwWritten, NULL);
    }

    // Reset the LogBuffer
    pszLogBuffer = szLogBuffer;
    *pszLogBuffer = '\0';
    dwLogBufferUsed = 0;
    CloseHandle(hCustomLog);
    return TRUE;
}
```

Once the filter has added the information to our in-memory buffer, it checks to see if it's time to write it to the disk. If so, then it calls the **WriteLogBuffer()** function. Since the **WriteLogBuffer()** function uses file pointers, it should only be called when the thread has the critical section, as we do here.

The **WriteLogBuffer()** function is also called when the DLL is unloaded. This will cause unwritten log information to be saved to disk if the web server is shut down.

# The Log File

The format for the extra log file is <page requested>, <referring page>. A sample of what it might look like, if you were browsing the demonstration site that comes with MSIIS 2.0, is as follows:

```
/samples/sampsite/sampsite.htm,http://127.0.0.1/
/samples/images/SPACE.gif,http://127.0.0.1/samples/sampsite/sampsite.htm
/SAMPLES/images/mh_sampl.gif,http://127.0.0.1/samples/sampsite/sampsite.htm
/samples/sampsite/sampsite.htm,http://127.0.0.1/
/samples/images/SPACE.gif,http://127.0.0.1/samples/sampsite/sampsite.htm
/SAMPLES/images/mh_sampl.gif,http://127.0.0.1/samples/sampsite/sampsite.htm
/samples/sampsite/sampsite.htm,http://127.0.0.1/
/samples/images/SPACE.gif,http://127.0.0.1/samples/sampsite/sampsite.htm
```

As you can see, most of the time the referring page is the site itself. In the above excerpt, the majority of the entries are for GIF images. Since knowledge of the referring document for these images is of little value, I suggest that you leave in place the code which ignores your own IP address as a referer.

# Design of the Second Method

While this second method captures the same information as the first, it does so in a completely different way. Instead of creating a separate file, we will modify one of the pointers in the **HTTP_FILTER_LOG** structure so that we actually change what the web server itself will write to the log. The code to do this is given first:

```c
#include <windows.h>
#include <httpfilt.h>

#define DEST buff
#define DebugMsg(x) { char buff[256];            \
                      wsprintf x;                \
                      OutputDebugString(buff); }

#define REFERER_SIZE 128
#define LOG_BUFFER_SIZE 256

DWORD OnLog (HTTP_FILTER_CONTEXT *pfc, HTTP_FILTER_LOG *pvData);


BOOL WINAPI GetFilterVersion(HTTP_FILTER_VERSION *pVer)
{
   pVer->dwFilterVersion = MAKELONG(0, 1);    // Version 1.0

   pVer->dwFlags = (SF_NOTIFY_SECURE_PORT        |
                    SF_NOTIFY_NONSECURE_PORT     |
                    SF_NOTIFY_LOG                |
                    SF_NOTIFY_ORDER_DEFAULT);

   strcpy(pVer->lpszFilterDesc, "CustomLog, v1.0");
   return TRUE;
}


DWORD WINAPI HttpFilterProc(HTTP_FILTER_CONTEXT *pfc, DWORD NotificationType, VOID
                            *pvData)
```

```
{
   DWORD dwRet;

   //
   //   Indicate this notification to the appropriate routine
   //

   switch (NotificationType)
   {
      case SF_NOTIFY_LOG:
      dwRet = OnLog(pfc, (PHTTP_FILTER_LOG) pvData);
      break;

      default:
      DebugMsg((DEST, "[HttpFilterProc] Unknown notification type, %d\n",
               NotificationType));
      dwRet = SF_STATUS_REQ_NEXT_NOTIFICATION;
      break;
   }
   return dwRet;
}


DWORD OnLog(HTTP_FILTER_CONTEXT *pfc, PHTTP_FILTER_LOG pLog)
{
   CHAR szTempBuffer[LOG_BUFFER_SIZE];
   CHAR szReferer[REFERER_SIZE];
   DWORD cbRefererSize= REFERER_SIZE;
   DWORD cbLogBufferSize;
   PTSTR pszLogBuffer;

   if (pfc->GetServerVariable(pfc, "HTTP_REFERER", szReferer, &cbRefererSize))
   {
      strcpy(szTempBuffer, pLog->pszTarget);
      strcat(szTempBuffer, ", ");
      strcat(szTempBuffer, szReferer);
      cbLogBufferSize=strlen(szTempBuffer)+1;
      pszLogBuffer = (CHAR *)pfc->AllocMem(pfc, cbLogBufferSize, 0);
      strcpy(pszLogBuffer, szTempBuffer);
      pLog->pszTarget = pszLogBuffer;
   }
   return SF_STATUS_REQ_NEXT_NOTIFICATION;
}
```

Most of the code is the same as in the first method. We still want the same types of notification, and we use the same **GetFilterVersion()** function. In this case, however, there is no **DllMain()** function. Since we don't need to do anything on start up or clean up, we can safely omit it. There are also no supporting functions. Everything is taken care of inside the **OnLog()** function, so let's take a look at what it does.

As before, we get the **HTTP_REFERER** using the **GetServerVariable()** call; however, we don't ignore referers inside our own domain. There would be very little to be gained by doing this, and it would make analysis of our logs much more difficult, since log entries with a referer would have one more column than entries without. We then make a temporary string with the format: <URL requested>, <referer>.

Next, we need a place to put this string. We can't simply point **pLog->pszTarget** to it, since it will go out of scope at the end of the function. Furthermore, we can't create a new string, using the **new** operator, because we would never be able to delete it. The solution is to use the **AllocMem()** member function of the **HTTP_FILTER_CONTEXT** structure. This function not only takes care of the memory allocation, but it safely frees up the memory when the request is finished. Since the **AllocMem()** function returns type **PVOID**, we need to cast it to a pointer to our string. The **AllocMem()** function is prototyped here:

```
VOID *(WINAPI * AllocMem) (struct HTTP_FILTER_CONTEXT *pfc,
                           DWORD  cbSize,
                           DWORD  dwReserved);
```

The **pfc** is simply the pointer to our **HTTP_FILTER_CONTEXT**, and **cbSize** is the amount of memory we want to allocate. In our example, this is **strlen(szTempBuffer)+1**, as **strcpy()** will append **\0**. Once the memory is allocated, we can safely change the pointer to the **pLog->pszTarget**.

> This is the only method you should use to change filter structure pointers. Otherwise, the memory previously pointed to will not be freed up properly.

## Building and Testing the Filters

Once you have built the filters and added the appropriate references to them in the registry, be sure that you have logging turned on (preferably to a file). To properly register the filter in the registry, you need to add the absolute path (**c:\myfilter\filter.dll**, or whatever) to the comma-separated list of active filters in the **HKEY_LOCAL_MACHINE\System\CurrentControlSet\Services\W3SVC\ Parameters\Filter DLLs** registry entry. To turn logging on, use the Internet Service Manager to select the WWW service. In the WWW Service Properties dialog box, select the Logging tab. Ensure that logging is enabled and directed to the appropriate path.

If all has gone well, the output from the second filter should look something like this:

```
127.0.0.1, -, 11/18/96, 0:51:07, W3SVC, ZOD, 127.0.0.1, 51, 309, 72, 304, 0, GET, /
samples/images/tools.gif, http://127.0.0.1/samples/default.htm, -,
127.0.0.1, -, 11/18/96, 0:51:07, W3SVC, ZOD, 127.0.0.1, 0, 313, 72, 304, 0, GET, /
samples/images/backgrnd.gif, http://127.0.0.1/samples/default.htm, -,
127.0.0.1, -, 11/18/96, 0:51:07, W3SVC, ZOD, 127.0.0.1, 0, 310, 72, 304, 0, GET, /
samples/images/h_logo.gif, http://127.0.0.1/samples/default.htm, -,
127.0.0.1, -, 11/18/96, 0:51:07, W3SVC, ZOD, 127.0.0.1, 0, 308, 72, 304, 0, GET, /
samples/images/SPACE.gif, http://127.0.0.1/samples/default.htm, -,
127.0.0.1, -, 11/18/96, 0:51:07, W3SVC, ZOD, 127.0.0.1, 0, 308, 72, 304, 0, GET, /
samples/images/docs.gif, http://127.0.0.1/samples/default.htm, -,
127.0.0.1, -, 11/18/96, 0:51:07, W3SVC, ZOD, 127.0.0.1, 0, 309, 72, 304, 0, GET, /
samples/images/SPACE2.gif, http://127.0.0.1/samples/default.htm, -,
```

## GIF to PNG

The real power of ISAPI filters comes from the fact that you can manipulate the raw data going to *and* from the web server. In our final example, we will show you how this is done. We will also show how to pass information collected in one filter notification function to another such function.

## Design of the Filter

The filter will take a URL reference for a document that contains the **/PNG** artificial path name, and replace all hypertext references to **.gif** files with **.png** if the client browser supports the **PNG** graphics format. For example, let's say that he have a document located at **http://mydomain.com/mydir/home.html**. The file reads as follows:

```
<html>
<body>
<img src="/graphics/mylogo.gif">
</body>
</html>
```

If you request the document **http://mydomain.com/PNG/mydir/home.html**, the filter will edit the above file on the fly, and give the client the following output

```
<html>
<body>
<img src="/graphics/mylogo.png">
</body>
</html>
```

if the client browser supports the inline display of **PNG** images. If it doesn't, it will default to giving the client the regular document.

## Implementation

In order to perform the replacement of data before it is written back to the client, we need to request that our filter be called during the **OnSendRawData()** notification. The **HTTP_FILTER_RAW_DATA** structure is defined again here:

```
typedef struct _HTTP_FILTER_RAW_DATA
{
    PVOID       pvInData;                        //IN
    DWORD       cbInData;                        //IN
    DWORD       cbInBuffer;                      //IN
    DWORD       dwReserved;                      //IN
}
```

As you can see, the structure gives us access only to the actual data being written. Using **HTTP_FILTER_RAW_DATA** alone, it is clearly not possible for us to know that the client requested **http://mydomain.com/PNG/mydir/home.html**. In order for our filter to recognize that the URL needs to have an action taken on it, we need to request a notification during the **OnUrlMap()** notification.

During **OnUrlMap()**, we will look at the URL requested to determine whether the filter needs to take any additional action. If the URL contains **/PNG**, we need to let the **OnSendRawData()** notification know about it. We also need to delete **/PNG** from the requested URL, since there is no physical **PNG** directory.

As the program is fairly short, it's given in its entirety here. Be sure to add the **WroxPNG.def** file to the project, so that the proper functions are exported by the DLL.

```c
#include <windows.h>
#include <stdio.h>
#include <httpfilt.h>

//
// DebugMsg() is used for debugging.

#define DEST          buff
#define DebugMsg(x) { char buff[256];                 \
                      wsprintf x;                      \
                      OutputDebugString(buff); }

DWORD OnUrlMap(HTTP_FILTER_CONTEXT* pfc, PHTTP_FILTER_URL_MAP pUrlMap);
DWORD OnSendRawData(HTTP_FILTER_CONTEXT* pfc,
                    PHTTP_FILTER_RAW_DATA pRawData);


BOOL WINAPI GetFilterVersion(HTTP_FILTER_VERSION* pVer)
{
    pVer->dwFilterVersion= MAKELONG(0,1);

    pVer->dwFlags = (SF_NOTIFY_SECURE_PORT          |
                     SF_NOTIFY_NONSECURE_PORT       |
                     SF_NOTIFY_URL_MAP              |
                     SF_NOTIFY_SEND_RAW_DATA        |
                     SF_NOTIFY_ORDER_LOW);

    pVer->dwFilterVersion = HTTP_FILTER_REVISION;

    strcpy(pVer->lpszFilterDesc, "GIF to PNG Filter");
    return TRUE;
}


DWORD WINAPI HttpFilterProc(HTTP_FILTER_CONTEXT* pfc,
                            DWORD NotificationType, VOID* pvData)
{
    DWORD dwRetVal;

    switch (NotificationType)
    {
       case SF_NOTIFY_URL_MAP:
       dwRetVal = OnUrlMap(pfc, (PHTTP_FILTER_URL_MAP) pvData);
       break;

       case SF_NOTIFY_SEND_RAW_DATA:
       dwRetVal= OnSendRawData(pfc, (PHTTP_FILTER_RAW_DATA) pvData);
       break;

       default:
       dwRetVal = SF_STATUS_REQ_NEXT_NOTIFICATION;
       break;
    }
    return dwRetVal;
}
```

```
DWORD OnUrlMap(HTTP_FILTER_CONTEXT* pfc, PHTTP_FILTER_URL_MAP pUrlMap)
{
    LPCSTR pszURL = pUrlMap->pszURL;
    CHAR* pszPhysicalPath = pUrlMap->pszPhysicalPath;

    // Set the filter context
    pfc->pFilterContext = (VOID*) FALSE;

    // Check to see if the URL started with /PNG/
    if (*(pszURL)=='/' && *(pszURL+1) == 'P' && *(pszURL+2) == 'N' &&
                          *(pszURL+3) == 'G' && *(pszURL+4) == '/')
    {
        // Delete the /PNG so that it will map to the write path
        while (*pszPhysicalPath)
        {
            if (*(pszPhysicalPath)=='\\' && *(pszPhysicalPath+1) == 'P' &&
                *(pszPhysicalPath+2) == 'N' && *(pszPhysicalPath+3) == 'G' &&
                *(pszPhysicalPath+4) == '\\')
            {
                while (*(pszPhysicalPath+4))
                {
                    *pszPhysicalPath = *(pszPhysicalPath+4);
                    pszPhysicalPath++;
                }
                *pszPhysicalPath = '\0';
                pfc->pFilterContext = (VOID*) TRUE;
            }
            pszPhysicalPath++;
        }
        // If this is not an htm or html file we won't try to replace anything
        if (NULL==strstr(pszURL,".htm"))
            pfc->pFilterContext = (VOID*) FALSE;
    }
    return SF_STATUS_REQ_NEXT_NOTIFICATION;
}


DWORD OnSendRawData(HTTP_FILTER_CONTEXT* pfc, PHTTP_FILTER_RAW_DATA pRawData)
{
    DWORD cbBuffer=0;
    BOOL bInTag;
    CHAR* pchRaw = (CHAR*) pRawData->pvInData;
    CHAR szHttpAccept[512];
    DWORD cbHttpAccept=sizeof(szHttpAccept);

    // Check to see if the OnUrlMap notification
    // told us that we need to do anything
    if (pfc->pFilterContext!= (VOID*)TRUE)
        return SF_STATUS_REQ_NEXT_NOTIFICATION;

    // Get the mime types that the client will accept
    if (!pfc->GetServerVariable(pfc, "HTTP_ACCEPT", szHttpAccept, &cbHttpAccept))
        return SF_STATUS_REQ_NEXT_NOTIFICATION;

    // See if the client accepts PNG files
    if (strstr(szHttpAccept,"image/png")==NULL)
        return SF_STATUS_REQ_NEXT_NOTIFICATION;
```

```
        DebugMsg((DEST, "[OnSendRawData] Editing Raw output.\r\n"));

        // Loop through all the raw data
        while (cbBuffer+3 < pRawData->cbInData)
        {
            // Make sure we are inside a hypertext tag
            if (pchRaw[cbBuffer]=='<')
            {
                bInTag=TRUE;
                cbBuffer++;
                continue;
            }
            if (pchRaw[cbBuffer]=='>')
            {
                bInTag=FALSE;
                cbBuffer++;
                continue;
            }
            if (bInTag)
            {
                // look for gif
                if ((pchRaw[cbBuffer]=='.') &&
                    (pchRaw[cbBuffer+1]=='g' || pchRaw[cbBuffer+1]=='G') &&
                    (pchRaw[cbBuffer+2]=='i' || pchRaw[cbBuffer+2]=='I') &&
                    (pchRaw[cbBuffer+3]=='f' || pchRaw[cbBuffer+3]=='F'))
                {
                    // replace gif with png
                    pchRaw[cbBuffer+1]='p';
                    pchRaw[cbBuffer+2]='n';
                    pchRaw[cbBuffer+3]='g';
                    cbBuffer+=3;
                }
            }
            cbBuffer++;
        }
        return SF_STATUS_REQ_NEXT_NOTIFICATION;
}
```

# Passing Data Between Notifications

When the **OnUrlMap()** notification is called, it sets the **pFilterContext** member of the **HTTP_FILTER_CONTEXT** structure. The **pFilterContext** variable is defined as a pointer to an unknown type of data, and can therefore take any kind of 32-bit value. If you need to store more than a simple 32-bit value, you should create a structure and place a pointer to it in the **pFilterContext** variable. In our case, we only need to store a **TRUE** or **FALSE** value, and do so by casting it to a void pointer.

If you have several filters in different DLLs, each of them gets its own **pFilterContext** variable. Thus, if you set the **pFilterContext** variable in one filter, it will not interfere with, or overwrite, the **pFilterContext** variable that you set inside another filter.

If you do create a new structure using the **new** or **malloc** functions, you should be sure to delete it when you have finished with it. You might put this clean-up code in the **OnEndOfNetSession()** notification handler, but keep in mind that for browsers that support **Keep-Alive**, there will be multiple requests before the **OnEndOfNetSession()** notification is called. Because of this, **OnEndOfNetSession()** is not a reliable way to free up memory. Instead, you should free it up as soon as you have finished with it.

## Building and Testing the Filter

No surprises here. Compile the code, register the filter in the registry, and that should be that. The best method of testing the filter is probably use the sample HTML code we supplied earlier, and to store two different images with the same name but different formats and extensions (**.gif** and **.png**). Now, when you enter the URL into your (**PNG**-supporting) browser, with and without **/PNG**, you'll have proof that the extension is working as it should.

# Summary

To round off the book, in this chapter we've given you code and explanations for a couple of simple but effective ISAPI filters.

Our first example, the custom logging filter, gave just a little more theory about thread-safety and controlling critical sections, with the help of **DLL_PROCESS_ATTACH** and **DLL_PROCESS_DETACH**. We also needed to know something about the default log file, in order to be able to add our own data to it.

The **GIF**-to-**PNG** filter was a good example of how to make changes to raw data in response to more than one notification, and of how to use the **pFilterContext** member of **HTTP_FILTER_CONTEXT** to pass information between the handlers of each notification type.

With that, we've come to the end of **Professional Visual C++ ISAPI Programming**. If you've read the theory and built all the examples, you should have gained a thorough understanding of what ISAPI programming has to offer and how you can make it work for you.

# The Wrox ISAPI Debugger

In Chapter 3, we presented the Wrox ISAPI Debugger for use on ISAPI extensions. In this appendix, we will look at how the debugger works so that you will have a more in-depth understanding of ISAPI itself. This appendix assumes that you know how to use the AppWizard to create an MFC dialog-based application.

## Inside the Debugger

In order to create the debugger, you will need to use AppWizard to create an MFC dialog-based application. Once AppWizard has created the framework, you should add a new dialog box which looks like the one below. Note that, because of size limitations, it wasn't feasible to fit every possible HTTP variable on to the form. However, all HTTP variables will be passed to the extension, regardless of whether or not they are actually represented on the form. The reader should feel free to add or delete variables from the form so that the variables present are relevant to the type of debugging they're doing.

```
ISAPIDebug                                                            [X]

DLL:      [Edit                    ]   Method: [      ▼]  PathInfo: [Edit        ]

Query:    [Edit                                                              ]

REMOTE_ADDR:   [Edit          ]        AUTH_TYPE:    [Edit        ]
REMOTE_USER:   [Edit          ]        AUTH_PASS:    [Edit        ]
USER_AGENT:    [Edit          ]        HTTP_COOKIE:  [Edit        ]
HTTP_ACCEPT:   [Edit          ]        HTTP_REFERER: [Edit        ]

Response
[Edit                                                                    ▲]
[                                                                          ]
[                                                                          ]
[                                                                          ]
[                                                                          ▼]

        [  Submit  ]      □ DLL Loaded          [  Quit  ]
```

The **DoDataExchange()** function in **ISAPIDebug** will tell you what to name your controls and which variables to map them to. The code is listed here:

```
// ISAPIDebug.cpp: Defines the class behaviors for the application.
//

#include "stdafx.h"
#include "ISAPIDebug.h"
#include "ISAPIDebugDlg.h"

#ifdef _DEBUG
#define new DEBUG_NEW
#undef THIS_FILE
static char THIS_FILE[] = __FILE__;
#endif

/////////////////////////////////////////////////////////////////////////////
// CISAPIDebugApp

BEGIN_MESSAGE_MAP(CISAPIDebugApp, CWinApp)
    //{{AFX_MSG_MAP(CISAPIDebugApp)
        // NOTE - the ClassWizard will add and remove mapping macros here.
        //    DO NOT EDIT what you see in these blocks of generated code!
    //}}AFX_MSG
    ON_COMMAND(ID_HELP, CWinApp::OnHelp)
END_MESSAGE_MAP()

/////////////////////////////////////////////////////////////////////////////
// CISAPIDebugApp construction

CISAPIDebugApp::CISAPIDebugApp()
{
    // TODO: add construction code here,
    // Place all significant initialization in InitInstance
}

/////////////////////////////////////////////////////////////////////////////
// The one and only CISAPIDebugApp object

CISAPIDebugApp theApp;

// Global http class used to call parsing functions.
CHttpBase http;

/////////////////////////////////////////////////////////////////////////////
// CISAPIDebugApp initialization

BOOL CISAPIDebugApp::InitInstance()
{
    // Standard initialization
    // If you are not using these features and wish to reduce the size
    //  of your final executable, you should remove from the following
    //  the specific initialization routines you do not need.

#ifdef _AFXDLL
    Enable3dControls();          // Call this when using MFC in a shared DLL
#else
```

```
    Enable3dControlsStatic();     // Call this when linking to MFC statically
#endif

    CISAPIDebugDlg dlg;
    m_pMainWnd = &dlg;

    dlg.m_stringServerVariables=m_lpCmdLine;

    CString stringValue;
    if(http.GetFromString(m_lpCmdLine,""," ",&stringValue))
    {
        http.UrlDecode(&stringValue);
        dlg.m_dll_path=stringValue;
    }

    if(http.GetFromString(m_lpCmdLine,"AUTH_PASS:"," ",&stringValue))
    {
        http.UrlDecode(&stringValue);
        dlg.m_auth_pass=((LPCSTR)stringValue)+10;
    }

    if(http.GetFromString(m_lpCmdLine,"PATH_INFO:"," ",&stringValue))
    {
        http.UrlDecode(&stringValue);
        dlg.m_pathinfo=((LPCSTR)stringValue)+10;
    }

    if(http.GetFromString(m_lpCmdLine,"HTTP_ACCEPT:"," ",&stringValue))
    {
        http.UrlDecode(&stringValue);
        dlg.m_http_accept=((LPCSTR)stringValue)+12;
    }

    if(http.GetFromString(m_lpCmdLine,"METHOD:"," ",&stringValue))
    {
        http.UrlDecode(&stringValue);
        dlg.m_method=((LPCSTR)stringValue)+7;
    }
    else
        dlg.m_method="GET";

    if(http.GetFromString(m_lpCmdLine,"QUERY_STRING:"," ",&stringValue))
    {
        http.UrlDecode(&stringValue);
        dlg.m_query_string=((LPCSTR)stringValue)+13;
    }

    if(http.GetFromString(m_lpCmdLine,"HTTP_COOKIE:"," ",&stringValue))
    {
        http.UrlDecode(&stringValue);
        dlg.m_http_cookie=((LPCSTR)stringValue)+12;
    }

    if(http.GetFromString(m_lpCmdLine,"HTTP_REFERER:"," ",&stringValue))
    {
        http.UrlDecode(&stringValue);
        dlg.m_http_referer=((LPCSTR)stringValue)+13;
    }
```

```
    if(http.GetFromString(m_lpCmdLine,"REMOTE_ADDR:"," ",&stringValue))
    {
        http.UrlDecode(&stringValue);
        dlg.m_remote_addr=((LPCSTR)stringValue)+12;
    }


    if(http.GetFromString(m_lpCmdLine,"USER_AGENT:"," ",&stringValue))
    {
        http.UrlDecode(&stringValue);
        dlg.m_user_agent=((LPCSTR)stringValue)+11;
    }


    if(http.GetFromString(m_lpCmdLine,"REMOTE_USER:"," ",&stringValue))
    {
        http.UrlDecode(&stringValue);
        dlg.m_remote_user=((LPCSTR)stringValue)+12;
    }


    if(http.GetFromString(m_lpCmdLine,"AUTH_TYPE:"," ",&stringValue))
    {
        http.UrlDecode(&stringValue);
        dlg.m_auth_type=((LPCSTR)stringValue)+10;
    }
```

```
    int nResponse = dlg.DoModal();
    if (nResponse == IDOK)
    {
        // TODO: Place code here to handle when the dialog is
        //   dismissed with OK
    }
    else
        if (nResponse == IDCANCEL)
        {
            // TODO: Place code here to handle when the dialog is
            //   dismissed with Cancel
        }

    // Since the dialog has been closed, return FALSE so that we exit the
    //   application, rather than start the application's message pump.
    return FALSE;
}
```

In the above code, the reader should note that we are using **CHttpBase** to do our URL decoding for us, so be sure to add **HttpBase.cpp** to your project. The reader should also note that the primary job of **CISAPIDebugApp::InitInstance()** is to populate the appropriate fields with data from the command line. The data must be placed on the command line in the form HTTP_VARIABLE_1: <value>; HTTP_VARIABLE_2: <value>. This allows us to pass as many HTTP variables as we want via the command line. Since we can specify what parameters are passed on the command line using the Visual C++ IDE debugger, this is very handy.

Now that we have the HTTP variables that we require, we can add the functionality to our debugger. When the user clicks on Load DLL, the debugger will load the DLL and get pointers to the two exported functions. This processing is handled in the **CISAPIDebugDlg::LoadDLL()** function. Once the DLL is loaded, the user can submit an ISAPI request to it. The first thing that the debugger does when the user submits a request, is to create and initialize an ECB structure that it can pass to the ISAPI extension. The function **CISAPIDebugDlg::OnSubmit()** handles this, and most of it is fairly straightforward. However, the following lines might lead to some confusion:

```
ecb.ServerSupportFunction =::ServerSupportFunction;
ecb.GetServerVariable =::GetServerVariable;
ecb.WriteClient =::WriteClient;
ecb.ReadClient =::ReadClient;
```

In the above lines, pointers are assigned to various members of the ECB structure. Therefore, when the ECB block needs to execute **ServerSupportFunction()**, the pointer to the code to execute will point to the **ServerSupportFunction()** that we will write as part of the debugger. When you examine the code below, you will see that we write our own implementations of **ServerSupportFunction()**, **GetServerVariable()**, **ReadClient()**, and **WriteClient()**. Since we are writing these functions ourselves, the user can implement any type of behavior desired. However, the user should by no means expect the functions to mimic exactly the behavior of the web server.

Another line of particular interest is:

```
ecb.ConnID = (HCONN) this;
```

In this line, the ECB's **ConnID** is actually set to be a pointer to a **CISAPIDebugDlg** class. Remember that the **ConnID** is simply a unique identifier that the web server uses to keep track of ISAPI extensions running simultaneously. In the debugger, we use it to pass a pointer to the class, so that our functions can get access to **CISAPIDebugDlg** member functions. For example, the implementation of the **ServerSupportFunction()** simply calls **CISAPIDebugDlg::ServerSupportFunction()**. To do so, it needs a pointer to a **CISAPIDebugDlg** class, and the **ecb.ConnID** provides just that. The alternative would be to use public variables which, in general, is bad programming practice.

The code for the **ISAPIDebugDlg** class is listed here:

```
// ISAPIDebugDlg.cpp: implementation file
//

#include "stdafx.h"
#include "ISAPIDebug.h"
#include "ISAPIDebugDlg.h"

#ifdef _DEBUG
#define new DEBUG_NEW
#undef THIS_FILE
static char THIS_FILE[] = __FILE__;
#endif

/////////////////////////////////////////////////////////////////////////
// CAboutDlg dialog used for App About

class CAboutDlg: public CDialog
{
public:
    CAboutDlg();

// Dialog Data
    //{{AFX_DATA(CAboutDlg)
    enum { IDD = IDD_ABOUTBOX };
    //}}AFX_DATA

    // ClassWizard generated virtual function overrides
    //{{AFX_VIRTUAL(CAboutDlg)
```

```
protected:
    virtual void DoDataExchange(CDataExchange* pDX);   // DDX/DDV support
//}}AFX_VIRTUAL

// Implementation
protected:
    //{{AFX_MSG(CAboutDlg)
    //}}AFX_MSG
    DECLARE_MESSAGE_MAP()
};

CAboutDlg::CAboutDlg(): CDialog(CAboutDlg::IDD)
{
    //{{AFX_DATA_INIT(CAboutDlg)
    //}}AFX_DATA_INIT
}

void CAboutDlg::DoDataExchange(CDataExchange* pDX)
{
    CDialog::DoDataExchange(pDX);
    //{{AFX_DATA_MAP(CAboutDlg)
    //}}AFX_DATA_MAP
}

BEGIN_MESSAGE_MAP(CAboutDlg, CDialog)
    //{{AFX_MSG_MAP(CAboutDlg)
        // No message handlers
    //}}AFX_MSG_MAP
END_MESSAGE_MAP()

/////////////////////////////////////////////////////////////////////
// CISAPIDebugDlg dialog

CISAPIDebugDlg::CISAPIDebugDlg(CWnd* pParent /*=NULL*/)
    : CDialog(CISAPIDebugDlg::IDD, pParent)
{
    //{{AFX_DATA_INIT(CISAPIDebugDlg)
    m_http_accept = _T("");
    m_user_agent = _T("");
    m_http_cookie = _T("");
    m_auth_pass = _T("");
    m_pathinfo = _T("");
    m_query_string = _T("");
    m_http_referer = _T("");
    m_response = _T("");
    m_method = _T("");
    m_bIsLoaded = FALSE;
    m_dll_path = _T("");
    m_remote_addr = _T("");
    m_remote_user = _T("");
    m_auth_type = _T("");
    //}}AFX_DATA_INIT
    //Note that LoadIcon does not require a subsequent DestroyIcon in Win32
    m_hIcon = AfxGetApp()->LoadIcon(IDR_MAINFRAME);
}

void CISAPIDebugDlg::DoDataExchange(CDataExchange* pDX)
{
```

```
    CDialog::DoDataExchange(pDX);
    //{{AFX_DATA_MAP(CISAPIDebugDlg)
    DDX_Text(pDX, IDC_ACCEPT, m_http_accept);
    DDX_Text(pDX, IDC_AGENT, m_user_agent);
    DDX_Text(pDX, IDC_COOKIE, m_http_cookie);
    DDX_Text(pDX, IDC_PASS, m_auth_pass);
    DDX_Text(pDX, IDC_PATH, m_pathinfo);
    DDX_Text(pDX, IDC_QUERY, m_query_string);
    DDX_Text(pDX, IDC_REFERER, m_http_referer);
    DDX_Text(pDX, IDC_RESPONSE, m_response);
    DDX_CBString(pDX, IDC_METHOD, m_method);
    DDX_Check(pDX, IDC_ISLOADED, m_bIsLoaded);
    DDX_Text(pDX, IDC_DLL, m_dll_path);
    DDX_Text(pDX, IDC_ADDR, m_remote_addr);
    DDX_Text(pDX, IDC_USER, m_remote_user);
    DDX_Text(pDX, IDC_TYPE, m_auth_type);
    //}}AFX_DATA_MAP
}

BEGIN_MESSAGE_MAP(CISAPIDebugDlg, CDialog)
    //{{AFX_MSG_MAP(CISAPIDebugDlg)
    ON_WM_SYSCOMMAND()
    ON_WM_PAINT()
    ON_WM_QUERYDRAGICON()
    ON_BN_CLICKED(IDC_ISLOADED, OnIsloaded)
    ON_BN_CLICKED(IDC_SUBMIT, OnSubmit)
    ON_BN_CLICKED(IDC_CANCEL, OnCancel)
    //}}AFX_MSG_MAP
END_MESSAGE_MAP()

//////////////////////////////////////////////////////////////////////
// CISAPIDebugDlg message handlers

BOOL CISAPIDebugDlg::OnInitDialog()
{
    CDialog::OnInitDialog();

    // Add "About..." menu item to system menu.

    // IDM_ABOUTBOX must be in the system command range.
    ASSERT((IDM_ABOUTBOX & 0xFFF0) == IDM_ABOUTBOX);
    ASSERT(IDM_ABOUTBOX < 0xF000);

    CMenu* pSysMenu = GetSystemMenu(FALSE);
    CString strAboutMenu;
    strAboutMenu.LoadString(IDS_ABOUTBOX);
    if (!strAboutMenu.IsEmpty())
    {
        pSysMenu->AppendMenu(MF_SEPARATOR);
        pSysMenu->AppendMenu(MF_STRING, IDM_ABOUTBOX, strAboutMenu);
    }

    // Set the icon for this dialog.  The framework does this automatically
    //  when the application's main window is not a dialog
    SetIcon(m_hIcon, TRUE);          // Set big icon
    SetIcon(m_hIcon, FALSE);         // Set small icon
```

```
    // TODO: Add extra initialization here

    m_bIsLoaded=FALSE;
    m_hDLL=NULL;

    return TRUE;  // return TRUE  unless you set the focus to a control
}

void CISAPIDebugDlg::OnSysCommand(UINT nID, LPARAM lParam)
{
    if ((nID & 0xFFF0) == IDM_ABOUTBOX)
    {
        CAboutDlg dlgAbout;
        dlgAbout.DoModal();
    }
    else
    {
        CDialog::OnSysCommand(nID, lParam);
    }
}

// If you add a minimize button to your dialog, you will need the code
// below to draw the icon.  For MFC applications using the document/view
// model, this is automatically done for you by the framework.

void CISAPIDebugDlg::OnPaint()
{
    if (IsIconic())
    {
        CPaintDC dc(this); // device context for painting

        SendMessage(WM_ICONERASEBKGND, (WPARAM) dc.GetSafeHdc(), 0);

        // Center icon in client rectangle
        int cxIcon = GetSystemMetrics(SM_CXICON);
        int cyIcon = GetSystemMetrics(SM_CYICON);
        CRect rect;
        GetClientRect(&rect);
        int x = (rect.Width() - cxIcon + 1) / 2;
        int y = (rect.Height() - cyIcon + 1) / 2;

        // Draw the icon
        dc.DrawIcon(x, y, m_hIcon);
    }
    else
    {
        CDialog::OnPaint();
    }
}

// The system calls this to obtain the cursor to display while the user
//  drags the minimized window.
HCURSOR CISAPIDebugDlg::OnQueryDragIcon()
{
    return (HCURSOR) m_hIcon;
}
```

```
BOOL WINAPI ServerSupportFunction (HCONN hConn, DWORD dwHSERequest,
                                   LPVOID lpvBuffer,
                                   LPDWORD lpdwBufferSize,
                                   LPDWORD lpdwDataType)
{
    return ((CISAPIDebugDlg*)hConn)->ServerSupportFunction(dwHSERequest,
                                                           lpvBuffer,
                                                           lpdwBufferSize,
                                                           lpdwDataType);
}

BOOL WINAPI GetServerVariable (HCONN hConn, CHAR* pszServerVariable,
                               VOID* pvValue, DWORD* pcchValue)
{
    return ((CISAPIDebugDlg*)hConn)->GetServerVariable(pszServerVariable,
                                                       pvValue, pcchValue);
}

BOOL WINAPI WriteClient (HCONN hConn, LPVOID lpvBuffer,
                         LPDWORD lpdwBytesToWrite, DWORD dwReserved)
{
return ((CISAPIDebugDlg*)hConn)->WriteClient(lpvBuffer, lpdwBytesToWrite,
                                             dwReserved);
}

BOOL WINAPI ReadClient (HCONN hConn, LPVOID lpvBuffer, LPDWORD lpdwBufferSize)
{
    *(CHAR*)lpvBuffer='\0';
    *lpdwBufferSize=0;
    return FALSE;
}

BOOL CISAPIDebugDlg::LoadDLL()
{
    if (!m_hDLL)
        m_hDLL = LoadLibrary(m_dll_path);
    if (!m_hDLL)
    {
        AfxMessageBox("Dll Failed to Load");
        return FALSE;
    }
    m_pfnExtensionVersion = (pfnHttpExtVer)GetProcAddress(m_hDLL,
                                                          "GetExtensionVersion");
    m_pfnExtensionProc = (pfnHttpExtProc)GetProcAddress(m_hDLL,
                                                        "HttpExtensionProc");
    if (!(m_pfnExtensionProc  && m_pfnExtensionVersion))
    {
        AfxMessageBox("Couldn't get entry points");
        return FALSE;
    }

    // Call the ExtensionVersion function
    HSE_VERSION_INFO hviInfo;
    m_pfnExtensionVersion(&hviInfo);
    return TRUE;
}
```

```cpp
BOOL CISAPIDebugDlg::UnLoadDLL()
{
    if (m_hDLL)
    {
        if(!FreeLibrary(m_hDLL))
        {
            AfxMessageBox("Can't unload library");
            return FALSE;
        }
    }
    m_hDLL = NULL;
    m_pfnExtensionVersion = NULL;
    m_pfnExtensionProc = NULL;
    return TRUE;
}

BOOL CISAPIDebugDlg::GetServerVariable (CHAR* pszServerVariable,
                                        VOID* pvValue, DWORD* pcchValue)
{
    BOOL bRetVal;
    CString stringValue;
    UINT unCount=0;
    INT nOffset;
    INT nLength;
    CHttpBase http;

    if (!pszServerVariable ||!pvValue ||!pcchValue)
        return FALSE;
    if((bRetVal=m_http.GetFromString(m_stringServerVariables,
                                pszServerVariable, " ", &stringValue))!=TRUE)
        return FALSE;
    nOffset=strlen(pszServerVariable)+1;
    nLength = stringValue.GetLength();
    while (unCount< (*pcchValue) && ((INT)unCount+nOffset)<nLength)
    {
        ((char* const)pvValue)[unCount]=stringValue.GetAt(unCount+nOffset);
        unCount++;
    }
    ((char* const)pvValue)[unCount++]='\0';
    *pcchValue=unCount+1;
    return TRUE;
}


BOOL CISAPIDebugDlg::ServerSupportFunction (DWORD dwHSERequest,
                                            LPVOID lpvBuffer,
                                            LPDWORD lpdwBufferSize,
                                            LPDWORD lpdwDataType)
{
    switch(dwHSERequest)
    {
    case HSE_REQ_DONE_WITH_SESSION:
    {
        return TRUE;
    }
    case HSE_REQ_SEND_RESPONSE_HEADER:
    {
        m_response+=(char*)lpvBuffer;
```

```
                return TRUE;
            }
        case HSE_REQ_SEND_URL_REDIRECT_RESP:
            {
                m_response+="302 Object Unknown response \r\n"
                        "The browser would normally redirect to Location: ";
                m_response+=(char*)lpvBuffer;
                m_response+="\r\n";
                return TRUE;
            }
        case HSE_REQ_SEND_URL:
            {
                m_response+="Web server would send the following file: ";
                m_response+=(char*)lpvBuffer;
                m_response+="\r\n";
                return TRUE;
            }
        default:
            {
                m_response+="The extension requested a ServerSupportFunction "
                        "which is not supported by this Debugger.\r\n";
                return FALSE;
            }
        }
    }


BOOL CISAPIDebugDlg::WriteClient (LPVOID lpvBuffer,
                                    LPDWORD lpdwBytesToWrite,
                                    DWORD dwReserved)
{
    if (lpvBuffer)
    {
        m_response+=(const char*)lpvBuffer;
        m_response+="\r\n";
    }
    return TRUE;
}
```

```
void CISAPIDebugDlg::OnIsloaded()
{
    if (!m_bIsLoaded)
    {
        UpdateData(TRUE);
        if(LoadDLL())
        {
            m_bIsLoaded=TRUE;
        }
    }
    else
    {
        UnLoadDLL();
        m_bIsLoaded=FALSE;
    }
    UpdateData(FALSE);
}

void CISAPIDebugDlg::OnSubmit()
{
```

```
      DWORD dwRetVal;
      EXTENSION_CONTROL_BLOCK ecb;

      UpdateData(TRUE);
      m_response="";

      if (m_bIsLoaded)
      {
         CHAR szMethod[10];
         CHAR szQueryString[1024];
         CHAR szEmpty[] = "";
         CHAR szPathInfo[256];
         CHAR szPathTranslated[256];

         strcpy(szMethod,m_method);
         strcpy(szQueryString,m_query_string);
         strcpy(szPathInfo,m_pathinfo);
         strcpy(szPathTranslated,szEmpty);

         if (m_method=="POST")
         {
            ecb.lpbData = (unsigned char*)szQueryString;
            ecb.cbTotalBytes= strlen(szQueryString);
            ecb.cbAvailable = ecb.cbTotalBytes;
            ecb.lpszQueryString = szEmpty;
         }
         else
         {
            ecb.lpszQueryString=szQueryString;
            ecb.cbTotalBytes = 0;
            ecb.cbAvailable = 0;
            ecb.lpbData = NULL;
         }

         ecb.lpszPathTranslated=szPathTranslated;
         ecb.lpszPathInfo=szPathInfo;
         ecb.lpszMethod=szMethod;
         ecb.ConnID=(HCONN) this;
         ecb.ServerSupportFunction =::ServerSupportFunction;
         ecb.GetServerVariable =::GetServerVariable;
         ecb.WriteClient=::WriteClient;
         ecb.ReadClient =::ReadClient;

         dwRetVal = m_pfnExtensionProc(&ecb);
      }
      UpdateData(FALSE);
}

void CISAPIDebugDlg::OnCancel()
{
   UnLoadDLL();
   CDialog::OnCancel();
}
```

To make it work, you'll need to add a few lines to the associated **ISAPIDebugDlg.h** file:

```
// ISAPIDebugDlg.h: header file
//

/////////////////////////////////////////////////////////////////////////////
// CISAPIDebugDlg dialog

typedef BOOL (*pfnHttpExtVer)(HSE_VERSION_INFO*);
typedef DWORD (*pfnHttpExtProc)(EXTENSION_CONTROL_BLOCK*);

class CISAPIDebugDlg: public CDialog
{
// Construction
public:
    HINSTANCE m_hDLL;
    CISAPIDebugDlg(CWnd* pParent = NULL);    // standard constructor
    BOOL LoadDLL();
    BOOL UnLoadDLL();
    BOOL GetServerVariable (CHAR* pszServerVariable, VOID* pvValue, DWORD* pcchValue);
    BOOL ServerSupportFunction (DWORD dwHSERequest, LPVOID lpvBuffer,
                                LPDWORD lpdwBufferSize, LPDWORD lpdwDataType);
    BOOL WriteClient (LPVOID lpvBuffer, LPDWORD lpdwBytesToWrite, DWORD dwReserved);
    CString m_stringServerVariables;

// Dialog Data
    //{{AFX_DATA(CISAPIDebugDlg)
    enum { IDD = IDD_ISAPIDEBUG_DIALOG };
    CString m_dll_path;
    CString m_method;
    CString m_pathinfo;
    CString m_query_string;
    CString m_remote_addr;
    CString m_remote_user;
    CString m_http_accept;
    CString m_auth_type;
    CString m_auth_pass;
    CString m_http_cookie;
    CString m_http_referer;
    CString m_response;
    CString m_user_agent;
    BOOL m_bIsLoaded;
    //}}AFX_DATA

    // ClassWizard generated virtual function overrides
    //{{AFX_VIRTUAL(CISAPIDebugDlg)
    protected:
    virtual void DoDataExchange(CDataExchange* pDX);    // DDX/DDV support
    //}}AFX_VIRTUAL

// Implementation
protected:
    HICON m_hIcon;
    pfnHttpExtVer m_pfnExtensionVersion;
    pfnHttpExtProc m_pfnExtensionProc;

    // Generated message map functions
    //{{AFX_MSG(CISAPIDebugDlg)
    virtual BOOL OnInitDialog();
    afx_msg void OnSysCommand(UINT nID, LPARAM lParam);
```

```
   afx_msg void OnPaint();
   afx_msg HCURSOR OnQueryDragIcon();
   afx_msg void OnSubmit();
   afx_msg void OnIsloaded();
   afx_msg void OnCancel();
   //}}AFX_MSG
   DECLARE_MESSAGE_MAP()
};
```

The **ISAPIDebug.h** header is listed here for completeness, but most of it is generated by the AppWizard. The only thing you need to do add is the **#include** for **HttpBase.h**:

```
// ISAPIDebug.h: main header file for the ISAPIDEBUG application
//

#ifndef __AFXWIN_H__
   #error include 'stdafx.h' before including this file for PCH
#endif
#include "HttpBase.h"
#include "resource.h"       // main symbols

/////////////////////////////////////////////////////////////////////////////
// CISAPIDebugApp:
// See ISAPIDebug.cpp for the implementation of this class
//

class CISAPIDebugApp: public CWinApp
{
public:
   CISAPIDebugApp();

// Overrides
   // ClassWizard generated virtual function overrides
   //{{AFX_VIRTUAL(CISAPIDebugApp)
   public:
      virtual BOOL InitInstance();
   //}}AFX_VIRTUAL

// Implementation

   //{{AFX_MSG(CISAPIDebugApp)
      // NOTE - the ClassWizard will add and remove member functions here.
      //    DO NOT EDIT what you see in these blocks of generated code!
   //}}AFX_MSG
   DECLARE_MESSAGE_MAP()
};


/////////////////////////////////////////////////////////////////////////////
```

That's all you need to create your own Wrox ISAPI debugger. For full instructions on how to use it, go back to the section entitled 'Debugging an ISAPI Extension' in Chapter 3.

# Alphabetical List of Tags

Here we give a full listing of all the tags and their attributes. We have also marked which tags and attributes are part of the HTML 2.0 and HTML 3.2 standards, and which are supported by the two leading browsers: Internet Explorer 3.0 and Netscape Navigator 3.0.

The following key explains the icons used to indicate browser support for the tags.

Key:  **HTML 2.0**   **HTML 3.2**   **Navigator**        **IE**

  | **2.0** |   | **3.2** |   | **N** |   | **IE** |

A complete reference to these tags can be found in Instant HTML also published by Wrox Press.

**<!-- -->** | **2.0** | **3.2** | **N** | **IE** |
Allows authors to add comments to code.

**!DOCTYPE** | **2.0** | **3.2** | **N** | **IE** |
Defines the document type. Required by all HTML documents.

**A** | **2.0** | **3.2** | **N** | **IE** |
Used to insert an anchor, which can be either a local reference point or a hyperlink to another URL.

| Attributes | HTML 2.0 | HTML 3.2 | Navigator 3.0 | IE 3.0 |
|---|---|---|---|---|
| HREF=url | ✓ | ✓ | ✓ | ✓ |
| NAME=name | ✓ | ✓ | ✓ | ✓ |
| TITLE=name | x | ✓ | x | x |
| TARGET=window | x | x | ✓ | ✓ |

**Notes:** The **REL** and **REV** attributes are not well-defined and should not be used.

**ADDRESS** | **2.0** | **3.2** | **N** | **IE** |
Indicates an address. The address is typically displayed in italics.

## APPLET 3.2 N IE

Inserts an applet.

| Attributes | HTML 2.0 | HTML 3.2 | Navigator 3.0 | IE 3.0 |
|---|---|---|---|---|
| ALIGN=left\|right\|top\|texttop\|middle\|<br>absmiddle\|baseline\|bottom\|absbottom | x | ✓ | ✓ | ✓ |
| ALT=alternativetext | x | ✓ | ✓ | ✓ |
| CODE=appletname | x | ✓ | ✓ | ✓ |
| CODEBASE=url | x | ✓ | ✓ | ✓ |
| HEIGHT=n | x | ✓ | ✓ | ✓ |
| HSPACE=n | x | ✓ | x | ✓ |
| NAME=name | x | ✓ | x | ✓ |
| VSPACE=n | x | ✓ | x | ✓ |
| WIDTH=n | x | ✓ | ✓ | ✓ |

## AREA 3.2 N IE

Defines a client-side imagemap area.

| Attributes | HTML 2.0 | HTML 3.2 | Navigator 3.0 | IE 3.0 |
|---|---|---|---|---|
| ALT=alternativetext | x | ✓ | ✓ | x |
| COORDS=coords | x | ✓ | ✓ | ✓ |
| HREF=url | x | ✓ | ✓ | ✓ |
| NOHREF | x | ✓ | ✓ | ✓ |
| SHAPE=RECT\|CIRCLE\|POLY | x | ✓ | ✓ | ✓ |
| TARGET="window"\|_blank\|_parent\|_self\|_top | x | x | ✓ | ✓ |

**Notes:** Internet Explorer also supports the values **RECTANGLE**, **CIRC**, and **POLYGON** for **SHAPE**.

## B 2.0 3.2 N IE

Emboldens text.

## *BASE*   `2.0`  `3.2`  `N`  `IE`

Base URL–defines the original location of the document. It is not normally necessary to include this tag. May be used only in **HEAD** section.

| Attributes | HTML 2.0 | HTML 3.2 | Navigator 3.0 | IE 3.0 |
|---|:---:|:---:|:---:|:---:|
| `HREF=url` | ✓ | ✓ | ✓ | ✓ |
| `TARGET="window"`\|`_blank`\|`_parent`\|`_self`\|`_top` | x | x | ✓ | ✓ |

## *BASEFONT*   `N`  `IE`

Defines font size over a range of text.

| Attributes | HTML 2.0 | HTML 3.2 | Navigator 3.0 | IE 3.0 |
|---|:---:|:---:|:---:|:---:|
| `COLOR` | x | x | x | ✓ |
| `FACE` | x | x | x | ✓ |
| `SIZE=1`\|`2`\|`3`\|`4`\|`5`\|`6`\|`7` | x | x | ✓ | ✓ |

## *BGSOUND*   `IE`

Plays a background sound.

| Attributes | HTML 2.0 | HTML 3.2 | Navigator 3.0 | IE 3.0 |
|---|:---:|:---:|:---:|:---:|
| `LOOP` | x | x | x | ✓ |
| `SRC=url` | x | x | x | ✓ |

## *BIG*   `3.2`  `N`  `IE`

Changes the physical rendering of the font to one size larger.

## *BLINK*   `N`

Defines text that will blink on and off.

## *BLOCKQUOTE*   `2.0`  `3.2`  `N`  `IE`

Formats a quote–typically by indentation.

## *BODY*    `2.0`  `3.2`  `N`  `IE`

Contains the main part of the HTML document.

| Attributes | HTML 2.0 | HTML 3.2 | Navigator 3.0 | IE 3.0 |
|---|:---:|:---:|:---:|:---:|
| `ALINK="#rrggbb"` | x | ✓ | ✓ | x |
| `BACKGROUND=url` | x | ✓ | x | ✓ |
| `BGCOLOR="#rrggbb"` | x | ✓ | ✓ | ✓ |
| `LINK="#rrggbb"` | x | ✓ | ✓ | ✓ |
| `TEXT="#rrggbb"` | x | ✓ | ✓ | ✓ |
| `VLINK="#rrggbb"` | x | ✓ | ✓ | ✓ |
| `BGPROPERTIES=fixed` | x | x | x | ✓ |
| `LEFTMARGIN=n` | x | x | x | ✓ |
| `TOPMARGIN=n` | x | x | x | ✓ |

## *BR*    `2.0`  `3.2`  `N`  `IE`

Line break.

| Attributes | HTML 2.0 | HTML 3.2 | Navigator 3.0 | IE 3.0 |
|---|:---:|:---:|:---:|:---:|
| `CLEAR=left|right|all` | x | ✓ | ✓ | ✓ |

## *CAPTION*    `3.2`  `N`  `IE`

Puts a title above a table.

| Attributes | HTML 2.0 | HTML 3.2 | Navigator 3.0 | IE 3.0 |
|---|:---:|:---:|:---:|:---:|
| `ALIGN=top|bottom|left|right` | x | ✓ | ✓ | ✓ |

**Notes:** Netscape Navigator does not support the **left** and **right** values for the **ALIGN** attribute.

## *CENTER*    `3.2`  `N`  `IE`

Centers text or graphic.

### CITE    `2.0`  `3.2`  `N`  `IE`

Indicates a citation, generally displaying the text in italics.

### CODE    `2.0`  `3.2`  `N`  `IE`

Renders text in a font resembling computer code.

### COL    `3.2`  `IE`

Defines column width and properties for a table.

| Attributes | HTML 2.0 | HTML 3.2 | Navigator 3.0 | IE 3.0 |
|---|---|---|---|---|
| ALIGN=left\|right\|center | x | x | x | ✓ |
| SPAN=n | x | x | x | ✓ |

### COLGROUP    `3.2`  `IE`

Defines properties for a group of columns in a table.

| Attributes | HTML 2.0 | HTML 3.2 | Navigator 3.0 | IE 3.0 |
|---|---|---|---|---|
| ALIGN=left\|right\|center | x | x | x | ✓ |
| SPAN=n | x | x | x | ✓ |

### DD    `2.0`  `3.2`  `N`  `IE`

Definition description. Used in definition lists with **&lt;DT&gt;** to define the term.

### DFN    `3.2`  `N`  `IE`

Indicates the first instance of a term or important word.

### DIR    `2.0`  `3.2`  `N`  `IE`

Defines a directory list by indenting the text.

## DIV    `3.2`

Defines a block division of the `<BODY>`.

| Attributes | HTML 2.0 | HTML 3.2 | Navigator 3.0 | IE 3.0 |
|---|---|---|---|---|
| `ALIGN=left\|right\|center` | x | ✓ | ✓ | ✓ |
| `NOWRAP` | x | x | x | x |
| `CLEAR=left\|right\|all` | x | x | x | x |

## DL    `2.0`  `3.2`  `N`  `IE`

Defines a definition list.

## DT    `2.0`  `3.2`  `N`  `IE`

Defines a definition term. Used with definition lists.

## EM    `2.0`  `3.2`  `N`  `IE`

Emphasized text–usually italic.

## EMBED    `N`  `IE`

Defines an embedded object in an HTML document.

| Attributes | HTML 2.0 | HTML 3.2 | Navigator 3.0 | IE 3.0 |
|---|---|---|---|---|
| `HEIGHT=n` | x | x | ✓ | ✓ |
| `NAME=name` | x | x | ✓ | ✓ |
| `PALETTE=foreground\|background` | x | x | x | ✓ |
| `SRC=url` | x | x | ✓ | ✓ |
| `WIDTH=n` | x | x | ✓ | ✓ |

*FONT*   `3.2`  `N`  `IE`

Changes font properties.

| Attributes | HTML 2.0 | HTML 3.2 | Navigator 3.0 | IE 3.0 |
|---|---|---|---|---|
| `COLOR="#rrggbb"` | x | ✓ | ✓ | ✓ |
| `FACE=typeface` | x | x | ✓ | ✓ |
| `SIZE=1｜2｜3｜4｜5｜6｜7` | x | ✓ | ✓ | ✓ |

*FORM*   `2.0`  `3.2`  `N`  `IE`

Defines part of the document as a user fill-out form.

| Attributes | HTML 2.0 | HTML 3.2 | Navigator 3.0 | IE 3.0 |
|---|---|---|---|---|
| `ACTION=url` | ✓ | ✓ | ✓ | ✓ |
| `ENCTYPE=enc_method` | ✓ | ✓ | ✓ | ✓ |
| `METHOD=get｜post` | ✓ | ✓ | ✓ | ✓ |
| `TARGET="window"｜_blank｜_parent｜_self｜_top` | x | x | ✓ | ✓ |

*FRAME*   `N`  `IE`

Defines a single frame in a frameset.

| Attributes | HTML 2.0 | HTML 3.2 | Navigator 3.0 | IE 3.0 |
|---|---|---|---|---|
| `ALIGN=top｜bottom｜left｜center｜right` | x | x | ✓ | ✓ |
| `FRAMEBORDER=0｜1` | x | x | x | ✓ |
| `MARGINHEIGHT=n` | x | x | ✓ | ✓ |
| `MARGINWIDTH=n` | x | x | ✓ | ✓ |
| `NAME=name` | x | x | ✓ | ✓ |
| `NORESIZE` | x | x | ✓ | ✓ |
| `SCROLLING=yes｜no｜auto` | x | x | ✓ | ✓ |
| `SRC=url` | x | x | ✓ | ✓ |

*FRAMESET*  | N | IE |

Defines the main container for a frame.

| Attributes | HTML 2.0 | HTML 3.2 | Navigator 3.0 | IE 3.0 |
|---|---|---|---|---|
| COLS=colswidth | x | x | ✓ | ✓ |
| FRAMEBORDER=1\|0 | x | x | ✓ | ✓ |
| FRAMESPACING=n | x | x | x | ✓ |
| ROWS=rowsheight | x | x | ✓ | ✓ |

*HEAD*  | 2.0 | 3.2 | N | IE |

Contains information about the document itself. Can include the following tags: **TITLE**, **META**, **BASE**, **ISINDEX**, **LINK**, **SCRIPT**, **STYLE**.

*Hn*  | 3.2 | N | IE |

Defines a heading, can be one of **<H1>**, **<H2>**, **<H3>**, **<H4>**, **<H5>**, **<H6>** where **<H1>** is the largest and **<H6>** is the smallest.

| Attributes | HTML 2.0 | HTML 3.2 | Navigator 3.0 | IE 3.0 |
|---|---|---|---|---|
| ALIGN=left\|right\|center | x | ✓ | ✓ | ✓ |

*HR*  | 2.0 | 3.2 | N | IE |

Defines a horizontal rule.

| Attributes | HTML 2.0 | HTML 3.2 | Navigator 3.0 | IE 3.0 |
|---|---|---|---|---|
| ALIGN=left\|right\|center | x | ✓ | ✓ | ✓ |
| NOSHADE | x | ✓ | ✓ | ✓ |
| SIZE=n | x | ✓ | ✓ | ✓ |
| WIDTH=width | x | ✓ | ✓ | ✓ |
| COLOR="#rrggbb" | x | x | x | ✓ |

### HTML · 2.0 · 3.2 · N · IE

Signals the start and end of an HTML document.

### I · 2.0 · 3.2 · N · IE

Defines italic text.

### IFRAME · IE

Defines a 'floating' frame within a document.

| Attributes | HTML 2.0 | HTML 3.2 | Navigator 3.0 | IE 3.0 |
|---|---|---|---|---|
| ALIGN=top\|middle\|bottom\|left\|right | x | x | x | ✓ |
| FRAMEBORDER=0\|1 | x | x | x | ✓ |
| HEIGHT=n | x | x | x | ✓ |
| MARGINHEIGHT=n | x | x | x | ✓ |
| MARGINWIDTH=n | x | x | x | ✓ |
| NAME=name | x | x | x | ✓ |
| NORESIZE | x | x | x | ✓ |
| SCROLLING=yes\|no\|auto | x | x | x | ✓ |
| SRC=url | x | x | x | ✓ |
| WIDTH | x | x | x | ✓ |

### IMG · 2.0 · 3.2 · N · IE

Defines an inline image.

| Attributes | HTML 2.0 | HTML 3.2 | Navigator 3.0 | IE 3.0 |
|---|---|---|---|---|
| ALIGN=top\|middle\|bottom\|left\|right | ✓ | ✓ | ✓ | ✓ |
| ALT=alternativetext | ✓ | ✓ | ✓ | ✓ |
| BORDER=n | x | ✓ | ✓ | ✓ |
| HEIGHT=n | x | ✓ | ✓ | ✓ |

*Table Continued on Following Page*

**237**

| Attributes | HTML 2.0 | HTML 3.2 | Navigator 3.0 | IE 3.0 |
|---|:---:|:---:|:---:|:---:|
| HSPACE=n | x | ✓ | ✓ | ✓ |
| ISMAP | ✓ | ✓ | ✓ | ✓ |
| SRC=url | ✓ | ✓ | ✓ | ✓ |
| USEMAP=mapname | x | ✓ | ✓ | ✓ |
| VSPACE=n | x | ✓ | ✓ | ✓ |
| WIDTH=n | x | ✓ | ✓ | ✓ |
| CONTROLS | x | x | x | ✓ |
| DYNSRC | x | x | x | ✓ |
| LOOP | x | x | x | ✓ |
| START | x | x | x | ✓ |
| LOWSRC | x | x | ✓ | x |

### INPUT      `2.0` `3.2` `N` `IE`

Defines a user input box.

| Attributes | HTML 2.0 | HTML 3.2 | Navigator 3.0 | IE 3.0 |
|---|:---:|:---:|:---:|:---:|
| ALIGN=top\|middle\|bottom | ✓ | ✓ | ✓ | ✓ |
| CHECKED | ✓ | ✓ | ✓ | ✓ |
| MAXLENGTH=n | ✓ | ✓ | ✓ | ✓ |
| NAME=name | ✓ | ✓ | ✓ | ✓ |
| SIZE=n | ✓ | ✓ | ✓ | ✓ |
| SRC=url | ✓ | ✓ | ✓ | ✓ |
| TYPE=checkbox\|hidden\|image\|password\|radio\| reset\|submit\|text | ✓ | ✓ | ✓ | ✓ |
| VALUE=value | ✓ | ✓ | ✓ | ✓ |

### *ISINDEX*   `3.2`  `N`  `IE`

Defines a text input field for entering a query.

| Attributes | HTML 2.0 | HTML 3.2 | Navigator 3.0 | IE 3.0 |
|---|---|---|---|---|
| `ACTION=url` | x | x | ✓ | ✓ |
| `PROMPT=message` | ✓ | ✓ | ✓ | ✓ |

### *KBD*   `2.0`  `3.2`  `N`  `IE`

Indicates typed text. Useful for instruction manuals, etc.

### *LH*   `3.2`  `N`  `IE`

Defines a list heading in any type of list.

### *LI*   `3.2`  `N`  `IE`

Defines a list item in any type of list other than a definition list.

| Attributes | HTML 2.0 | HTML 3.2 | Navigator 3.0 | IE 3.0 |
|---|---|---|---|---|
| `TYPE=A|a|I|i|1` | ✓ | ✓ | ✓ | ✓ |
| `VALUE=n` | ✓ | ✓ | ✓ | ✓ |

**Note:** Netscape Navigator also supports `TYPE=disc|square|circle` for use with unordered lists.

### *LINK*   `3.2`  `IE`

Defines the current document's relationship with other documents.

| Attributes | HTML 2.0 | HTML 3.2 | Navigator 3.0 | IE 3.0 |
|---|---|---|---|---|
| `REL=` | x | ✓ | ✓ | ✓ |
| `HREF=url` | x | ✓ | ✓ | ✓ |
| `REV=` | x | ✓ | ✓ | ✓ |
| `TITLE=` | x | ✓ | ✓ | ✓ |

## MAP    `3.2` `N` `IE`

Defines the different regions of a client-side imagemap.

| Attributes | HTML 2.0 | HTML 3.2 | Navigator 3.0 | IE 3.0 |
|---|---|---|---|---|
| `NAME=mapname` | x | ✓ | ✓ | ✓ |

## MARQUEE    `IE`

Sets a scrolling marquee.

| Attributes | HTML 2.0 | HTML 3.2 | Navigator 3.0 | IE 3.0 |
|---|---|---|---|---|
| `ALIGN=top\|middle\|bottom` | x | x | x | ✓ |
| `BEHAVIOR=scroll\|slide\|alternate` | x | x | x | ✓ |
| `BGCOLOR="#rrggbb"` | x | x | x | ✓ |
| `DIRECTION=left\|right` | x | x | x | ✓ |
| `HEIGHT=n` | x | x | x | ✓ |
| `HSPACE=n` | x | x | x | ✓ |
| `LOOP=n` | x | x | x | ✓ |
| `SCROLLAMOUNT=n` | x | x | x | ✓ |
| `SCROLLDELAY=n` | x | x | x | ✓ |
| `VSPACE=n` | x | x | x | ✓ |
| `WIDTH=n` | x | x | x | ✓ |

## MENU    `2.0` `3.2`

Defines a menu list.

## META    `2.0` `3.2` `N` `IE`

Describes the content of a document.

| Attributes | HTML 2.0 | HTML 3.2 | Navigator 3.0 | IE 3.0 |
|---|---|---|---|---|
| CONTENT= | ✓ | ✓ | ✓ | ✓ |
| HTTP-EQUIV | x | ✓ | ✓ | ✓ |
| NAME | x | ✓ | ✓ | ✓ |
| URL=document url | x | x | x | ✓ |

### NOBR  N  IE

Prevents a line of text breaking.

### NOFRAMES  N  IE

Allows for backward compatibility with non-frame-compliant browsers.

### OBJECT  IE

Inserts an object.

| Attributes | HTML 2.0 | HTML 3.2 | Navigator 3.0 | IE 3.0 |
|---|---|---|---|---|
| ALIGN=baseline\|center\|left\|middle\|right\| textbottom\|textmiddle\|texttop | x | x | x | ✓ |
| BORDER=n | x | x | x | ✓ |
| CLASSID=url | x | x | x | ✓ |
| CODEBASE | x | x | x | ✓ |
| CODETYPE=codetype | x | x | x | ✓ |
| DATA=url | x | x | x | ✓ |
| DECLARE | x | x | x | ✓ |
| HEIGHT=n | x | x | x | ✓ |
| HSPACE=n | x | x | x | ✓ |
| NAME=url | x | x | x | ✓ |
| SHAPES | x | x | x | ✓ |
| STANDBY=message | x | x | x | ✓ |
| TYPE=type | x | x | x | ✓ |

*Table Continued on Following Page*

| Attributes | HTML 2.0 | HTML 3.2 | Navigator 3.0 | IE 3.0 |
|---|---|---|---|---|
| USEMAP=url | x | x | x | ✓ |
| VSPACE=n | x | x | x | ✓ |
| WIDTH=n | x | x | x | ✓ |

## OL   `2.0` `3.2` `N` `IE`

Defines an ordered list.

| Attributes | HTML 2.0 | HTML 3.2 | Navigator 3.0 | IE 3.0 |
|---|---|---|---|---|
| COMPACT | x | ✓ | ✓ | x |
| START=n | x | ✓ | ✓ | ✓ |
| TYPE=1\|A\|a\|I\|i | x | ✓ | ✓ | ✓ |

## OPTION   `3.2` `IE`

Used within the `<SELECT>` tag to present the user with a number of options.

| Attributes | HTML 2.0 | HTML 3.2 | Navigator 3.0 | IE 3.0 |
|---|---|---|---|---|
| SELECTED | x | ✓ | ✓ | ✓ |
| PLAIN | x | ✓ | ✓ | ✓ |
| VALUE | x | ✓ | ✓ | ✓ |
| DISABLED | x | ✓ | ✓ | ✓ |

## P   `2.0` `3.2` `N` `IE`

Defines a paragraph.

| Attributes | HTML 2.0 | HTML 3.2 | Navigator 3.0 | IE 3.0 |
|---|---|---|---|---|
| ALIGN=left\|right\|center | x | ✓ | ✓ | ✓ |

### *PARAM*   `3.2`   `N`   `IE`

Defines parameters for a Java applet.

| Attributes | HTML 2.0 | HTML 3.2 | Navigator 3.0 | IE 3.0 |
|---|---|---|---|---|
| `NAME=name` | x | ✓ | ✓ | ✓ |
| `VALUE=value` | x | ✓ | ✓ | ✓ |
| `VALUETYPE=Data\|Ref\|Object` | x | x | x | ✓ |
| `TYPE=InternetMediaType` | x | x | x | ✓ |

### *PRE*   `2.0`   `3.2`   `N`   `IE`

Preformatted text. Renders text exactly how it is typed, i.e. carriage returns, styles, etc., *will* be recognized.

| Attributes | HTML 2.0 | HTML 3.2 | Navigator 3.0 | IE 3.0 |
|---|---|---|---|---|
| `WIDTH` | x | ✓ | ✓ | x |

### *S*   `3.2`   `N`   `IE`

Strikethrough. Renders the text as deleted (crossed out).

### *SAMP*   `3.2`   `N`   `IE`

Sample output.

### *SCRIPT*   `3.2`   `N`   `IE`

Inserts a script.

| Attributes | HTML 2.0 | HTML 3.2 | Navigator 3.0 | IE 3.0 |
|---|---|---|---|---|
| `LANGUAGE=VBScript\|JavaScript` | x | ✓ | Note | ✓ |

**Note:** Netscape Navigator 3.0 only supports JavaScript.

*SELECT*    2.0  3.2  N  IE

Defines the default selection in a list.

| Attributes | HTML 2.0 | HTML 3.2 | Navigator 3.0 | IE 3.0 |
|---|---|---|---|---|
| MULTIPLE | x | x | ✓ | ✓ |
| NAME=name | ✓ | ✓ | ✓ | ✓ |
| SIZE=n | x | x | ✓ | ✓ |

*SMALL*    3.2  N  IE

Changes the physical rendering of a font to one size smaller.

*SPAN*    IE

Defines localized style information, e.g. margin width.

| Attributes | HTML 2.0 | HTML 3.2 | Navigator 3.0 | IE 3.0 |
|---|---|---|---|---|
| STYLE=Style | x | x | x | ✓ |

*STRIKE*    3.2  N  IE

Strikethrough. Renders the text as deleted or crossed out.

*STRONG*    2.0  3.2  N  IE

Strong emphasis–usually bold.

*STYLE*    3.2  IE

Reserved for future use with style sheets.

*SUB*    3.2  N  IE

Subscript.

*SUP*    3.2  N  IE

Superscript.

## TABLE   `3.2`  `N`  `IE`

Defines a series of columns and rows to form a table.

| Attributes | HTML 2.0 | HTML 3.2 | Navigator 3.0 | IE 3.0 |
|---|:---:|:---:|:---:|:---:|
| `ALIGN= left\|right\|center` | x | ✓ | ✓ | ✓ |
| `VALIGN` | x | ✓ | x | x |
| `BORDER=n` | x | ✓ | ✓ | ✓ |
| `WIDTH=n` | x | ✓ | ✓ | ✓ |
| `CELLSPACING=n` | x | ✓ | ✓ | ✓ |
| `CELLPADDING=n` | x | ✓ | ✓ | ✓ |
| `FRAME=void\|above\|below\|hsides\|lhs\|`<br>`rhs\|vsides\|box\|border` | x | ✓ | x | ✓ |
| `RULES=none\|groups\|rows\|cols\|all` | x | ✓ | x | ✓ |
| `BACKGROUND=url` | x | x | x | ✓ |
| `BGCOLOR="#rrggbb"` | x | x | ✓ | ✓ |
| `COLS=n` | x | ✓ | x | ✓ |
| `BORDERCOLOR="#rrggbb"` | x | x | x | ✓ |
| `BORDERCOLORDARK="#rrggbb"` | x | x | x | ✓ |
| `BORDERCOLORLIGHT="#rrggbb"` | x | x | x | ✓ |

**Notes: ALIGN, CHAR, CHAROFF**, and **VALIGN** are common to all cell alignments, and may be inherited from enclosing elements.

The **CENTER** value for the **ALIGN** attribute is not supported by Netscape Navigator 3.0 or Internet Explorer 3.0.

## TBODY   `3.2`  `IE`

Defines the table body.

### TD     `3.2` `N` `IE`

Marks the start point for table data.

| Attributes | HTML 2.0 | HTML 3.2 | Navigator 3.0 | IE 3.0 |
|---|---|---|---|---|
| ALIGN=left\|right\|center | x | ✓ | ✓ | ✓ |
| ASIX | x | ✓ | x | x |
| AXES | x | ✓ | x | x |
| COLSPAN=n | x | ✓ | ✓ | ✓ |
| ROWSPAN=n | x | ✓ | ✓ | ✓ |
| NOWRAP | x | ✓ | ✓ | ✓ |
| WIDTH=n | x | Note | ✓ | x |
| BACKGROUND | x | x | x | ✓ |
| BGCOLOR="#rrggbb" | x | x | ✓ | ✓ |
| BORDERCOLOR="#rrggbb" | x | x | x | ✓ |
| BORDERCOLORDARK="#rrggbb" | x | x | x | ✓ |
| BORDERCOLORLIGHT="#rrggbb" | x | x | x | ✓ |
| VALIGN=top\|middle\|bottom\|baseline | x | ✓ | ✓ | ✓ |

The **WIDTH** attribute is not in HTML 3.2, but support is recommended for backward compatibility. Use the **WIDTH** attribute for **COL** instead.

### TEXTFLOW     `3.2`

Replacement for text in applet. May be inserted inside **<APPLET>** tag.

### TEXTAREA     `2.0` `3.2` `N` `IE`

Defines a text area inside a **FORM** element.

| Attributes | HTML 2.0 | HTML 3.2 | Navigator 3.0 | IE 3.0 |
|---|---|---|---|---|
| NAME=name | ✓ | ✓ | ✓ | ✓ |
| ROWS=n | ✓ | ✓ | ✓ | ✓ |

*Table Continued on Following Page*

| Attributes | HTML 2.0 | HTML 3.2 | Navigator 3.0 | IE 3.0 |
|---|---|---|---|---|
| COLS=n | ✓ | ✓ | ✓ | ✓ |
| WRAP=off\|virtual\|physical | x | x | ✓ | x |

## TFOOT   `3.2`  `IE`

Defines a table footer.

## TH   `3.2`  `N`  `IE`

Defines names for columns and rows.

| Attributes | HTML 2.0 | HTML 3.2 | Navigator 3.0 | IE 3.0 |
|---|---|---|---|---|
| ALIGN=left\|center\|right | x | ✓ | ✓ | ✓ |
| AXIS | x | ✓ | x | x |
| AXES | x | ✓ | x | x |
| COLSPAN | x | ✓ | ✓ | ✓ |
| ROWSPAN | x | ✓ | ✓ | ✓ |
| WIDTH=n | x | Note | ✓ | x |
| NOWRAP | x | ✓ | ✓ | ✓ |
| BACKGROUND | x | x | x | ✓ |
| BGCOLOR="#rrggbb" | x | x | ✓ | ✓ |
| BORDERCOLOR="#rrggbb" | x | x | x | ✓ |
| BORDERCOLORDARK="#rrggbb" | x | x | x | ✓ |
| BORDERCOLORLIGHT="#rrggbb" | x | x | x | ✓ |
| VALIGN=n | x | ✓ | ✓ | ✓ |

The **WIDTH** attribute is not in HTML 3.2, but support is recommended for backward compatibility. Use the **WIDTH** attribute for **COL** instead.

## THEAD   `3.2`  `IE`

Defines a table header.

## TITLE   `2.0`  `3.2`  `N`  `IE`

Defines the title of the document. Required by all HTML documents.

*TR*        `3.2`  `N`  `IE`

Defines the start of a table row.

| Attributes | HTML 2.0 | HTML 3.2 | Navigator 3.0 | IE 3.0 |
|---|---|---|---|---|
| `ALIGN=left\|right\|center` | x | ✓ | ✓ | ✓ |
| `CHAR` | x | ✓ | x | x |
| `CHAROFF` | x | ✓ | x | x |
| `BACKGROUND` | x | x | x | ✓ |
| `BGCOLOR="#rrggbb"` | x | x | ✓ | ✓ |
| `BORDERCOLOR="#rrggbb"` | x | x | x | ✓ |
| `BORDERCOLORDARK="#rrggbb"` | x | x | x | ✓ |
| `BORDERCOLORLIGHT="#rrggbb"` | x | x | x | ✓ |
| `VALIGN=top\|middle\|bottom\|baseline` | x | ✓ | ✓ | ✓ |

*TT*        `2.0`  `3.2`  `N`  `IE`

Renders text in fixed width, typewriter style font.

*U*        `3.2`  `N`  `IE`

Underlines text. Not widely supported at present, and not recommended, as could cause confusion with hyperlinks, which also normally appear underlined.

*UL*        `2.0`  `3.2`  `N`  `IE`

Defines an unordered, usually bulleted list.

| Attributes | HTML 2.0 | HTML 3.2 | Navigator 3.0 | IE 3.0 |
|---|---|---|---|---|
| `COMPACT` | x | ✓ | ✓ | x |
| `TYPE=disc\|circle\|square` | x | ✓ | ✓ | x |

## VAR    3.2

Indicates a variable.

## WBR

Defines the word to break and wrap to the next line. Often used with `<NOBR>`

# Crash Course in HTTP

The Hypertext Transfer Protocol (HTTP) is nothing more than a text-based protocol that uses TCP/IP to relay messages back and forth between a client and a server. In this appendix, we will look at exactly what makes up an HTTP request, how a 'typical' ISAPI web server would handle it, and what the response might look like.

While, in reality, an HTTP request may have to travel though a firewall, a proxy server, or some type of gateway, here we will deal only with the simple case where a client is talking directly to a server.

This appendix by no means covers every aspect of HTTP. If you would like more detail, you should consult the RFCs regarding HTTP. A good one to start on is RFC 1945, which can be found at this address:

```
http://www.pilgrim.umass.edu/pub/networking/internet-rfc/rfc1945.txt
```

In addition, a draft specification for HTTP/1.1 can be found at this address:

```
http://www.w3.org/pub/WWW/Protocols/HTTP/Issues/Revs/Rev84Clean.txt
```

## The Request

Since you can't simply broadcast your web site to unsuspecting computer users who just happen to be connected to the Internet, all HTTP communications must start with a request.

> *If you were thinking of developing a web server that would broadcast your web pages to random Internet-connected hosts, you would be wasting your time. Not only would it seriously annoy anyone who happened to get your message, it is simply impossible. As discussed in Chapter 6, all TCP/IP communications must be directed to a socket. Host computers that are only running a browser are not 'listening' for incoming requests, and would therefore be deaf to your broadcast.*

In order to dissect the request in detail, let's develop our own web browser—as we did in Chapter 7. Of course, we didn't make a real web browser, we just used telnet. The point of doing this again here is to let you see that there is nothing special going on 'behind the scenes'.

To start with, we can request a simple HTML document from our local server. By default, HTTP servers know to listen on port 80 for incoming requests. When an HTTP server receives a call on port 80, it opens up another port to handle the actual communication, and port 80 immediately goes back to listening for the next request. Thus, one request doesn't have to finish before another can be started. The command to initiate a connection to your local HTTP server is:

```
telnet 127.0.0.1 80
```

Once connected, you should make the following request:

`GET /somefile.html HTTP/1.0`

> **Two carriage return/linefeed combinations are necessary to submit the request to the server.**

After typing this in to the telnet window, the web server should return some data to you. We will look at this data shortly, but for now, let's stay focused on the request.

The **GET** method is the simplest type of request. As its name implies, it is used to get information from the web server. All HTTP requests must be in the following format:

REQUEST_TYPE     URL         HTTP_VERSION

In the example above, **GET** was the request type, the URL was **/somefile.html**, and we were using **HTTP/1.0**.

In addition to the **GET** method, HTTP/1.0 also supports the **POST** and **HEAD** methods. Up for review for HTTP/1.1 are **OPTIONS**, **PUT**, **DELETE**, and **TRACE**. Since you're reading this book, you're probably most interested in methods that would be used by ISAPI programmers. The two most common methods are **GET** and **POST**, and so we will restrict our discussion to those.

In most cases, you won't be interested in simple **GET** requests for HTML documents–the web server will handle all of these for you. However, you can also use the **GET** method to request an ISAPI extension. For the rest of this appendix, we will look exclusively at how HTTP interacts with your ISAPI extensions. To do this, we will want to use the **SimpleDump.dll** example that was presented in Chapter 2. This simple, non-MFC extension, simply takes the HTTP variables and writes them back to the client. A request to **http://127.0.0.1/scripts/SimpleDump.dll** using Netscape should produce the following:

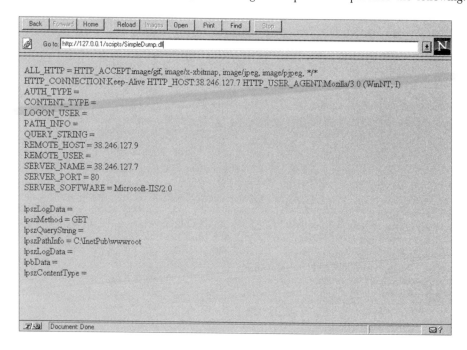

As you can see, the web server took the **GET** method and passed it to our **ECB->lpszMethod** variable.

The most common variable that ISAPI programmers are interested in, when using the **GET** method, is the **QUERY_STRING**. To make a request that will send a **QUERY_STRING** to the web server, simply do the following:

**telnet 127.0.0.1 80**

**GET /scripts/SimpleDump.dll?paramter=value HTTP/1.0**

When you look at the output, you will see that **lpszQueryString** is set to **parameter=value**.

In order to see how other ISAPI variables are set, we should note that all web requests consists of two parts: a headers section and a body section. The only thing that separates the headers from the body is a double pair of carriage return/linefeed combinations (hereafter denoted CRLF.) All HTTP variables are passed over in the headers; the body isn't used at all for the **GET** method (i.e. nothing is allowed after the double CRLF). The body is only used in the **POST** method, which we will discuss shortly.

Setting HTTP variables is probably much simpler than you might imagine. You need only know the proper name, and then set a value for it. For example, let's create our own browser type which we will send to the HTTP server. We will call our browser Bogus Exploritor (a cross between a Navigator and an Explorer). To do this, simply enter the following:

**telnet 127.0.0.1 80**

**GET /scripts/SimpleDump.dll HTTP/1.0**
**User-Agent: Bogus Exploritor v.01**

The response you should get is as follows:

```
HTTP/1.0 200 OK
Server: Microsoft-IIS/2.0
Date: Sat, 16 Nov 1996 06:45:54 GMT
Content-type: text/html

ALL_HTTP = HTTP_USER_AGENT:Bogus Exploritor v.01
<br>AUTH_TYPE =
<br>CONTENT_TYPE =
<br>LOGON_USER =
<br>PATH_INFO =
<br>QUERY_STRING =
<br>REMOTE_HOST = 127.0.0.1
<br>REMOTE_USER =
<br>SERVER_NAME = 127.0.0.1
<br>SERVER_PORT = 80

<p>lpszLogData =
<br>lpszMethod = GET
<br>lpszQueryString =
<br>lpszPathInfo = C:\InetPub\wwwroot
```

As you can see, the web server parsed out our **User-Agent:** header and turned it into **HTTP_USER_AGENT**. We can do the same for cookies:

```
telnet 127.0.0.1 80

GET /scripts/SimpleDump.dll HTTP/1.0
User-Agent: Bogus Exploritor v.01
Cookie: MyCookie= Cookie Value
```

The resulting **ALL_HTTP** should read:

```
ALL_HTTP = HTTP_USER_AGENT:Bogus Exploritor v.01
                        HTTP_COOKIE:MyCookie= Cookie Value
```

Any additional headers that the client wants to send over are also included in the header section. Typical headers that might be included are **If-Modified-Since**, **Pragma**, **Referer**, and **WWW-Authenticate**.

> **A significant limit to the GET method is that the QUERY_STRING variable can only be 1024 bytes long.**

Many ISAPI extensions will require much more input than this. In order to support these longer forms, you must use the **POST** method. The **POST** method differs from **GET** in that it passes information to the web server in the body of the request as well as the header.

The body of the message is simply anything that follows the double CRLF combination in the headers. When using the **GET** method, the server knew when to stop receiving data and when to start processing the request: when it received the CRLF pair. However, when using the **POST** method, the server will continue to receive information after the CRLF pair, and so it needs a way to know when the client has finished sending information. The way by which the server knows when to stop listening for more information, is through stipulating that the client must tell the web server how much data it is going to send. The client does this by sending the **Content-Length** header to the server, which indicates the number of bytes that will follow the CRLF pair. For example, the following is a properly formatted **POST** request:

```
telnet 127.0.0.1 80

POST /scripts/SimpleDump.dll HTTP/1.0
Content-Length: 14

this is a test
```

The **Content-Length** header is parsed by the web server and placed into the **ECB->cbTotalBytes** field. The web server then reads as much data as it can into the **ECB->lpbData** buffer and sets **ECB->cbAvailable** to the amount that it read. Of course, if the client accidentally indicated a content length longer than the actual content length, the web server will sit there and continue to wait for the client to send the rest of the data until a time-out occurs, when the server automatically closes the connection. In the above example, the web server simply puts **this is a test** into **ECB->lpdData** and **14** into both **ECB->cbTotalBytes** and **ECB->cbAvailable**.

# The Response

Now that we have the basics of how the client sends us data, let's look at how we write data back to the client. Fortunately, writing data back to the client is much simpler than reading it.

Like the request, the response is split into two parts: the headers and the body. The headers contain supplementary information that might be used by the client's browser, but will not be displayed to the end user. For example, in

**GET /somefile.html HTTP/1.0**

the headers will read:

```
HTTP/1.0 200 OK
Server: Microsoft-IIS/2.0
Date: Sat, 16 Nov 1996 07:31:21 GMT
Content-Type: text/html
Accept-Ranges: bytes
Last-Modified: Sun, 10 Nov 1996 21:57:06 GMT
Content-Length: 75
```

The first header, as above, always indicates the result of the response. Possible values under HTTP/1.1 are:

| Response Code | Response Message |
|---------------|------------------|
| 200 | OK |
| 202 | Accepted |
| 204 | No Content |
| 301 | Moved Permanently |
| 302 | Moved Temporarily |
| 304 | Not Modified |
| 400 | Bad Request |
| 403 | Forbidden |
| 404 | Not Found |
| 500 | Internal Server Error |
| 501 | Not Implemented |
| 503 | Service Unavailable |

In most cases, the ISAPI programmer doesn't need to worry about this first header, since the **ECB->ServerSupportFunction()** takes care of it for us. Normally, the value is **200 OK**, but, as you may recall from Chapter 3, the **ServerSupportFunction()** can return different values. In Chapter 3, it returned

```
HTTP/1.0 302 Object moved
```

which automatically told the client browser to try to locate the URL at a new address. The address at which it was supposed to find the document was supplied later in the headers, with:

```
Location: http://www.microsoft.com
```

Aside from the status header, there are several other headers that are of interest to clients. (Headers such as **Server** and **Date** are usually ignored by clients, and many servers simply don't send them, since they are by no means required, and do little more than take up bandwidth.) A common header that causes the client to take action is the **Set-Cookie** header, which was covered in Chapter 5. When the client sees a header of the format:

```
Set-Cookie: NAME=VALUE; expires=DATE; path=PATH; domain=DOMAIN_NAME; secure
```

it knows to set the cookie for the indicated path. (Of course, if the client doesn't support cookies, it simply ignores this header.)

A very important header to include in all of your responses is the **Content-Type** header. The **Content-Type** header tells the client what type of document the web server is sending over. For example, the most common type, which is **text/html**, tells the browser that it will need to parse the following body for hypertext tags before it displays it to the user. However, if the type is **text/plain**, the browser will not parse any of the body, and will simply display that data as text, ignoring any hypertext tags. A type of **image/gif** tells the browser that the file should be displayed as a GIF image.

If you noticed the **Content-Length** header, and are wondering if you need to compute this for each request, you will be happy to know that you don't. During a request, the client must stay connected if it hopes to get a response back. Therefore, simply disconnecting from the server to indicate completion would not work, and so the client must specify the content length when sending a body. However, when a response is sent, there is nothing more for the server to do—and so it simply disconnects. When the client sees that the server has disconnected, it assumes that it has all the data that it needs. If you do send a **Content-Length** header, and disconnect before the specified number of bytes has been transferred, most browsers will display some type of 'Transfer Interrupted' message, so that the client will know that not all the data was received.

Of course, the body of the response is the most important thing, since this is what the end user will see. One interesting aspect of the body is that it can be used to stream data to the client. This can be used to send live audio or video across, using HTTP, although you'll appreciate that these topics are all beyond the scope of this book.

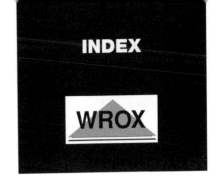

**INDEX**

# WROX

# Wrox Press Developer's Journal

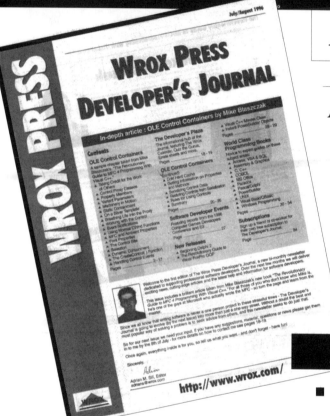

## Free subscription

A 40-page bi-monthly magazine for software developers, The Wrox Press Developer's Journal features in-depth articles, news and help for everyone in the software development industry. Each issue includes extracts from our latest titles and is crammed full of practical insights into coding techniques, tricks and research.

## In forthcoming editions

■ Articles on Unix, SQL Server 6.5, WordBasic, Java, Internet Information Server, Visual Basic and lots, lots more.

■ Hard hitting reports from cutting edge technical conferences from around the world.

■ Full and extensive list of all Wrox publications including a brief description of contents.

## To Subscribe:

Please send in your full name and address to Wrox Press and receive the next edition of the Wrox Press Developer's Journal.

■ Wrox Press, 30 Lincoln Rd, Olton, Birmingham, B27 6PA, UK.
  Contact: Gina Mance, +44 121 706 6826

■ Wrox Press, 2710, W. Touhy, Chicago, IL 60645, USA.
  Contact: Kristen Schmitt, +1 312 465 3559

or e-mail us on devjournal@wrox.com